A Guide to Outcomes Assessment in Education Abroad

Mell C. Bolen, Editor

A publication of
THE FORUM ON EDUCATION ABROAD

The Forum on Education Abroad Board of Directors, 2006–2007

The Forum Council

Sheila Bayne , Chair
Tufts University

Mell Bolen, Vice-Chair
Brethren Colleges Abroad

Lynn Anderson
University of California, San Diego

Bill Anthony
Northwestern University

Kate Darian-Smith
University of Melbourne, Australia

Carol Dickerman
University of Michigan

Dennis R. Gordon
Santa Clara University

Stephen Hall
Bowdoin College

Lance Kenney
Villanova University

Kim Kreutzer
University of Colorado at Boulder

Patricia C. Martin
The University of Pennsylvania

Natalie A. Mello
Worcester Polytechnic Institute

Vija G. Mendelson
Academic Programs International

Michael Steinberg
Institute for the International Education of Students (IES)

Anders Uhrskov
DIS: Denmark's International Study Program

Forum Council Outcomes Committee

Mell Bolen, Chair
Brethren Colleges Abroad

David Comp
University of Chicago

Darla Deardorff
Association of International Education Administrators (AIEA)

Lilli Engle
American University Center of Provence

Patricia C. Martin
The University of Pennsylvania

Elaine Meyer-Lee
Saint Mary's College (Indiana)

Michael Vande Berg
CIEE

This publication has been made possible in partnership with:

Boston University International Programs

Institute for the International Education of Students (IES)

The Scholar Ship

University of California Education Abroad Program (UC-EAP)

And with the support of these sponsors:

Arcadia University

Cultural Experiences Abroad (CEA)

Kalamazoo College

Suffolk University Madrid Campus

University of Pennsylvania Office of International Programs

University of Minnesota Learning Abroad Center

Contents

From the Forum on Education Abroad

The Forum on Education Abroad is pleased to provide to its members and to the field of education abroad a publication that it hopes will foster significant efforts to assess education abroad outcomes. Around the world there are increasing calls for greater accountability and more extensive efforts to document student learning outcomes. There is an important opportunity for the field of education abroad to contribute to these efforts. The Forum hopes that this *Guide* provides a useful resource for institutions and organizations to meet the challenges of initiating and sustaining an outcomes assessment strategy for education abroad.

As editor, Mell Bolen has done tremendous work to oversee the development and production of this volume. She has guided a stellar group of authors in their goal to present a comprehensive *Guide* that covers the myriad topics and issues that relate to outcomes assessment for education abroad. The Forum Council's Outcomes Assessment Committee, of which Mell serves as Chair, has assisted in steering this project from the very beginning. Those committee members are: David Comp, Darla Deardorff, Lilli Engle, Pat Martin, Elaine Meyer-Lee, and Mick Vande Berg.

The Forum provides its members and the education abroad field with distinctive resources that support outcomes assessment. In addition to this *Guide*, these resources include publications and online resources such as the *Glossary of Education Abroad Terms*, the Research in Education Abroad Database (READ), special publications in cooperation with *Frontiers: The Interdisciplinary Journal of Study Abroad* such as the Undergraduate Research Special Issues that present the very best examples of student learning. In addition, the Forum's annual State of the Field Survey takes the pulse of the field of education abroad and provides useful data on key topics and issues. Finally, position papers on outcomes research describe useful approaches to the assessment of outcomes. These resources can be found on the Forum web site.

Providing resources and information is only part of the Forum's mission to promote outcomes assessment. Another significant goal is to offer opportunities for Forum member institutions to participate directly in outcomes research. Recently, the Forum has announced two such opportunities. The first involves using the Beliefs, Events, Values Inventory, a promising new instrument that Forum member institutions are helping to refine as they document changes in their students that study abroad. Offered in cooperation with James Madison University's International Beliefs and Values Institute and Office of International Programs, this research study will involve the testing of hundreds of students over the next two years. The second research study, Study Abroad for Global Engagement (SAGE), is offered to Forum member institutions in cooperation with the University of Minnesota and will survey and interview alumni of education abroad programs to measure the long-term impact of the experience.

The Forum's initiatives in promoting and sponsoring outcomes assessment are only in the beginning stages. Nonetheless, they are critically important for helping to fulfill the Forum's central purpose: to improve education abroad programs for the benefit of the students who participate in them.

Brian Whalen, President and CEO
The Forum on Education Abroad

Introduction

Mell C. Bolen, Editor

This project grew from the ideas of many people in the field of education abroad who realized that outcomes assessment had become vitally important to the field. When a group of committed education abroad professionals created the Forum on Education Abroad, they sponsored a survey of members and potential members to discover the five most important topics that needed more attention from education abroad professionals. Outcomes assessment was one of these topics, and from this, the Forum's Outcomes Assessment Committee was born.

Committee members began to outline projects to improve and encourage outcomes assessment projects in education abroad. An early conversation led to several people looking at literature in the field, and we quickly discovered there was not a single guide for outcomes assessment projects specifically related to education abroad. The committee felt that an important first step to encouraging such efforts would be to create a guide that helped education abroad professionals, very few of whom are assessment experts, understand the basics of assessment and how assessment could be applied in the education abroad field.

Like the Forum members surveyed, the committee had many reasons for trying to encourage understanding of assessment among education abroad professionals. Commitment to improving our work, political pressures, and growth as a field all contributed to the perception that outcomes assessment should be part of our education abroad agenda. Whether we've concluded outcomes assessment is important because of our need to foster productive program improvements, to convince doubters of the validity of our enterprise, or to convince state or federal officials to fund our work, we have become convinced of the need for this type of research. If you are reading this, you probably share some notion that documenting outcomes should have a place in education abroad as well. After all, how can we know whether what we are doing really works without carefully collecting data of many different kinds?

Why to collect such data; what types to think about collecting; and some outlines of research protocols and dissemination plans—these form the subject of this guide. Outcomes assessment of education abroad can cover a vast amount of theoretical and physical territory. To make this manageable for our authors and readers, this work focuses on U.S. students going to another country for educational purposes. However, many of the resources described cover theories and methods that could be applied to multiple international education contexts. Therefore we hope this guide will have some interest for those outside the United States.

Assessment theories and methods comprise their own specialized field of inquiry. In writing this text, we tried to choose information that added an education abroad dimension to this existing body of work without repeating what can be found clearly articulated in general assessment texts. Therefore we do not discuss in great depth general methods of assessment that can be found in many different guides to educational assessment. The resources chapter does cite some of these guides; those interested in more general information will find a starting point here. Where we outline basic research protocols and rubrics, we do so from the perspective of education abroad contexts.

Because this field of research, education abroad outcomes assessment, is still in its infancy, this work can only be a first attempt at outlining topics of inquiry and methods for exploring them. Many of the instruments and methodologies we need have yet to be invented, or they are just being tested in their first large studies. We hope this text will inspire some researchers to take on the projects necessary for a future guide to have a vast array of texts, instruments, methodologies and protocols to cite.

Given the external realities of academe today, we cannot wait too long before real harm results from not developing such an array of tools. We have nearly become a victim of our own success at extending our programs into all aspects of the curriculum and to all students. As education abroad becomes more integral to and integrated into the educational fabric of the United States, the same pressures to define and measure outcomes that exist in academe also apply to international education. These pressures arise from social, economic, and political factors embedded in a globalizing world, and they form the subject of the first chapter of this guide. The demands of a knowledge-based economy for more educated workers, along with the demands of taxpayers that academia concretely demonstrate how we contribute to creating such workers, blend into the political demands of nations to compete in a global economy.

Many people have become convinced that they need the types of skills our programs claim to produce. For a critical mass of people, especially leaders in business, politics, and education, social spheres have expanded to encompass those who think and act differently from themselves. They recognize that the skills needed to comfortably navigate such culturally mixed settings can only come from practice in doing so. They want an educational process that teaches languages, disciplinary knowledge in an international context, and concrete cultural knowledge of others. But they want proof that what we do actually provides this learning.

As a result of these factors and their own desires to improve learning, many external agencies have begun demanding data on the outcomes of educational programs. Disciplinary associations, like AASCB and ABET, are looking at assessment as important to their accreditation of programs. Accreditation associations like the North Central States Association of Colleges and Schools (NCA) have defined outcomes as vital to the accreditation process, and campuses are being asked to design measures of their outcomes. Even the federal government has held various commission meetings and conducted longitudinal studies on the ways higher education prepares students for a global economy. All these external organizations will hold our programs and organizations accountable for the learning goals we set and whether our students attain them.

To reply to these concerns, priorities must be set as to the types of learning most urgently in need of outcomes data. Chapter 2 places these types of learning into a framework useful for mapping out individual learning assessment goals. When deciding what areas to assess, rubrics and frameworks within which to organize the research plan help researchers to understand how their studies may connect to others in the field. As mentioned above, our field does not yet have a vast array of research to draw on. The frameworks provided help us to see what gaps exist. From there we can begin to plan research that can answer underexplored questions. Frameworks also provide clarity of organization, so a research plan can be developed that focuses appropriately on the specific areas of assessment the researchers desire. Without such clarity, studies can become too vague or too diffuse to retain academic rigor.

Defining the specific topic of inquiry constitutes one of the key elements of a strong assessment study for similar reasons of focus and clarity described above. The more precisely the questions are defined, the better able a researcher will be to choose appropriate measurement tools. While chapter 2 provides an organizational rubric, chapter 3 highlights many specific topic areas that education abroad researchers might wish to explore in assessment projects. Some, such as student learning described above, probably readily spring to mind. Others, such as faculty leader learning and institutional cross-cultural development, may spark some new ideas of potential projects.

Chapter 3 explores topics at all three levels of assessment—individual, programmatic, and institutional. In the end, to convince others that our work adds important educational value, we will need to demonstrate how our efforts succeed at all three levels. In defining topics, we not only need to know the topic but also at which level it is most important for us to understand it. Do we need to demonstrate that our institution provides for this type of learning? That our programs do? Or that students do make progress in learning it? Each level requires its own research design.

When confronted with the complexity of the potential topics and the extensive variables that could be studied, it is important to understand how to begin to plan a study that examines the topic we want at the level we want. As chapter 4 emphasizes, the study cannot happen by chance or just because a particular tool looks intriguing. Long before deciding on methods, careful research design requires deciding who will need to participate in order to create a quality study, what the desired inquiry is, what data might already exist that can help answer it, and what resources will be needed to complete the project. Even if you do not intend to do the research yourself but will work with experts to conduct such studies, understanding the basic facets of an assessment plan will help ensure that the results are relevant to what you wish to discover.

Only after refining our basic plan do we turn to specific methodologies. Chapter 5 describes the differences between direct and indirect methods of inquiry. It helps us place education abroad research methods into the larger assessment context by summarizing methods used to assess student learning and those used to assess the learning process itself. In all cases, solid research plans generally use a combination of both methods. Multiple methods provide one of the most trusted strategies to ensure the reliability of the data collected by checking it across multiple measurements.

While international education may not have the extensive range of research studies of some other disciplines, we do have a body of published research that we can comb for research protocols and methods that will help us answer our specific questions. Chapter 6 gives us an annotated summary of the studies relevant to the framework of areas outlined earlier in the guide. It gives basic reference points for further explorations of assessment in general. It helps round out our picture of what topics have been explored and what methods they employed. It may be that a particular research strategy in one of these studies would work well for a question you wish to examine. In such cases, why not use a methodology that has been tested? This allows us to build a body of work that can be compared, and to increase the validity of the findings if they are replicated in a different population. If results are not replicated, that, too, raises interesting perspectives on how populations may differ or methodologies may need further development.

One facet of methodologies—one some people focus on too quickly—is measurement instruments. Instruments form only one category of possible methodologies for assessment, and not every question can be adequately answered by turning to such instruments. Having the topic and inquiry defined allows the researcher to vet instruments with a critical eye. We can decide on using one not because an instrument seems elegantly designed, but because it actually contributes to answering our specific research question. An instrument is only as useful to a study as it is pertinent to the outcomes being measured.

Chapter 7 explains various instruments, providing a basic understanding of what they do and do not measure. This allows for key decisions about whether using and evaluating the results of this particular measurement tool are worth the investment of resources. As the chapter also discusses, developing instruments requires extensive testing for reliability and validity. Such work really should be done by teams of researchers with many years to devote to the development process. In light of this, the chapter highlights those instruments already used in studies and describes whether they have undergone such testing.

Along with the development of measurement tools, researchers need a shared vocabulary, so concepts can be clearly communicated across the field as a whole, across studies, and among researchers. Chapter 8 presents the first large team effort to define central terms of our field in a way that allows for standardization of usage. As explained in greater detail in the chapter, the presentation of the terms in this guide comprises only one subset of the entire glossary project. The guide focuses on terms most relevant to assessment. The full glossary project, still undergoing review by professionals in the field, will be published online in the next year. At that time, more input will be sought from international educators as we continue to try to improve our shared vocabulary.

Some people may question why we need such standardization when our institutions are so different, our programs unique, and our goals for our students so varied. Our need for precise definitions stems directly from this variety. We cannot build a body of research across such variety of places, programs, and students without such definitions. If we wish to inform ourselves about our field as whole, when measurements are applied, it must be clear to all what the results mean. Semantic ambiguity can skew data in ways for which we cannot retroactively compensate.

The chapter editors confronted their own definitional challenge in deciding between terms such as *international education*, *education abroad*, *study abroad*, and *foreign study*. Foreign study allows the slight negative connotation that the word *foreign* may have to attach itself to the meaning, and so we discarded it. Study abroad excluded programs such as internships, which can be part of education abroad. However, in the interests of varying language and making the text less repetitive, in the end we kept study abroad in some instances. International education really refers to everything that organizations do to foster cross-cultural educational experiences and is not limited to education abroad. The team felt that education abroad encompassed all the variety of programs while still being specific enough to describe students going from their home institution to another country for educational purposes. Despite this consensus, the text uses international education and education abroad interchangeably to make the texts more varied. This simple process of trying to come to consensus on meaning for this text, and to balance different needs for clarity of meaning and variety of wording, illustrates the complexities of attaining a much broader consensus on terms for items that we actually wish to measure.

Ideally, the authors of this work hope that our outcomes assessment studies communicate ideas that lead to positive changes in international education; and that our work not only discovers answers to our immediate questions but also contributes to the international dialog on what constitutes successful cross-cultural sojourns. What constitutes success? How do we measure it? When should we measure it? These questions have different answers depending on our goals, but sharing data of how we answered these questions helps everyone understand the complexities of international education in a deeper and richer fashion. This would be very difficult to accomplish without some consensus on the vocabulary in which to express these ideas.

Of course, we can have the best of everything—frameworks, topics, methods, instruments, and definitions—but if we cannot find the resources to pursue the research, the best-laid plans will not suffice. Chapter 9 looks at different avenues for funding projects. This work can often take as much time as the project design itself, and finding help can save many hours of labor. The chapter describes using databases to narrow down funding sources, working with offices of research and funding agencies, and employing other means to jumpstart the process of making a project financially viable. One avenue that we should not ignore is international funding sources such as the German Academic Exchange Service(DAAD) or other granting organizations based outside the United States, which support multinational work.

Now we have designed, funded, and conducted our study. What's next? The final chapter looks at ways to use such data for advocacy efforts. The chapter describes various audiences to whom we might wish to communicate results, including participants, parents, faculty, administrators, professionals in the field, government officials, and the general public. It looks at the types of data we might want to communicate as well as vehicles for publication and places to seek help in efforts to effectively disseminate data.

As happened in the writing of the guide, teamwork is emphasized. Such projects require a wide variety of expertise, and no one person usually has all of it. Success can often depend on finding the members of the team and partnering with a number of people at different stages of the project. Unless we are professionally trained researchers, this may be the most important use of the guide for international educators. This guide can give you a broad overview of the issues involved in completing projects and the places or people you may coordinate with in order to do so. At the very least, you will have some knowledge with which to evaluate the proposals and decide where you want to invest time and energy.

Chapter 1

The Place of Outcomes Assessment in Higher Education Today and the Implications for Education Abroad

Michael Steinberg

Education abroad is rooted in undergraduate education and has been attracting a growing number of students from colleges and universities of every variety. Some institutions define study abroad as an important if not essential component of undergraduate education, and most students spend at least a semester overseas. At other institutions, a relatively small minority of students participates. Forty years ago, many students studied abroad without credit from their home institutions; today, most institutions award credit for their students' study abroad programs. Further, colleges and universities have adopted education abroad as an important aspect of many of their students' education.

The Report on the Harvard College Curricular Review is one of the more recent examples of the view that international education should be central to the curriculum. Harvard's task force recommends "there be an expectation that all Harvard College students pursue a significant international experience during their time in the College, and that completion of such an experience be noted on the transcript."[1] Harvard, like many other institutions, has put significant financial resources behind this effort.[2] In making this kind of commitment, colleges and universities have clear goals. As the Harvard report states, students are expected to graduate with global competency. In today's climate, there is an implicit expectation that this competency will be assessed in some way, and that students will be directed to activities that ensure this kind of personal growth. Further, if credit is involved, the students' colleges will expect academic progress and achievement.

A growing percentage of undergraduates participate in a study abroad experience. As assessment of outcomes becomes a standard feature of US college life, study abroad will be scrutinized both on its own terms and as part of the total educational experience. Because students frequently enroll in programs not sponsored by their own campuses, colleges will seek to study the outcomes of study abroad for their own students and to what extent these outcomes contribute to what they deem desirable for graduates. Similarly, if disciplines adopt outcomes that are acceptable across colleges, they will be interested in what students gain in their disciplines when they are overseas. The experience of study abroad students thus complements the international movement to develop equivalencies across borders, which has been most prominent in Europe but is likely to be a trend in the rest of the world.

By definition, the three kinds of outcomes assessment are individual, programmatic, and institutional.[2] Individual assessment is an intrinsic part of education throughout the world. Students at all levels are examined and evaluated to determine whether they have mastered the curriculum. This serves as the basis for degree attainment. Programmatic and institutional assessment are related to individual assessment, in that programs are held responsible for group mastery of a discipline, and institutions are accountable for the level of achievement of their overall student body. In a broader sense, educational institutions are held responsible for how well they serve the needs of society for educated citizens and workers. Assessment on the individual and programmatic level should be an essential requirement in study abroad and should inform institutional assessment at institutions that include study abroad as part of their programs.

The modern assessment movement is international and closely linked with economic and social change. The growing importance of technical and service sectors in economies demands a more highly educated work force. Therefore much of the impetus for the contemporary assessment movement in the United States and abroad arose in part from the business community. Businesses expect graduates to be well prepared in skill-based learning as well as critical thinking to take on the roles that contemporary industry demands. Moreover, all organizations are held more accountable for producing and assessing results. The expressed interests of the business community have greatly impacted state governments, which play a crucial role in funding higher education. The business community has a strong commitment to international competence in this age of globalization and can be expected to support the inclusion of the assessment of international study as part of the overall assessment program.[3]

The United States is not alone in developing interest in programmatic and institutional assessment. Britain has long had an implicit assessment system at the university level by employing outside examiners, rather than its own teachers, to test students at the end of their studies. In Germany, the prevalence of state examinations in various disciplines establishes a basis for programmatic and institutional assessment. In recent years, the British government has gone quite far in introducing an assessment system. Since 2000 the Quality Assurance Agency (QAA) has established benchmarks for subjects throughout the curriculum that students are expected to achieve and that are used to evaluate programs.[4] The European Credit Transfer System that developed with the Erasmus program after 1988, and more recently the Bologna process, has prompted educators throughout Europe to examine their curricula against those of other countries and to develop common outcomes for students.[5] US educators, observing the Bologna process, have begun to consider how the United States might be better integrated with this international movement.

In the United States in the mid-1980s, a number of major reports stimulated interest in assessment in higher education—notably the 1984 National Institute of Education Report, Involvement in Learning, and Ernest Boyer's 1987 report for the Carnegie Foundation, College: the Undergraduate Experience in America.[6] US federal and state governments have spearheaded the assessment movement for a number of reasons. Legislators recognize that a well-educated workforce is necessary to maintain competitiveness in a global economy and is also a key factor in furthering high employment levels. The growing cost of education has also had political impact. Taxpayers expect that if their taxes are put to good use, universities can demonstrate that they are doing an effective job. Given rising tuition costs, parents are demanding that their students are well prepared for the job market and that their education is worth the expense.

The contemporary US assessment movement developed political legs in the mid-1980s. William Bennett, secretary of education in the Reagan administration, was an early, vocal advocate of assessment in US higher education. In 1988, he issued an executive order to the accrediting agencies "that institutions or programs confer degrees only on those students who have demonstrated educational achievement as assessed and documented through appropriate measures."[7] Amendments to the Higher Education Act that year specifically required the agencies to "enforce assessment criteria."[8]

In the 1990s, the concept of accountability reinforced the assessment movement. Institutional effectiveness with students could be demonstrated by internal and externally evident measures such as graduation rates, graduates' employment success, and passage rates on licensing exams.[9]

Many in the academic community agree that assessment of student learning needs to be central to accreditation. The Association of American Colleges and Universities organized a Project on Accreditation and Assessment with the expressed aim to focus accreditation on student learning. The project, which drew together the accrediting associations, stressed "liberal learning outcomes and the demonstration by institutions of students' sophisticated intellectual capacities."[10] The project achieved consensus on "the mission of a twenty-first-century liberal education, the desired outcomes from a liberal education, curricular design principles that can help students reach these desired outcomes, and criteria for good practice in assessment of such outcomes.[11] The project report, *Greater Expectations*, explicitly includes global competence among the outcomes goals for all students and employs a number of overseas experiences as examples of good practices, including Michigan State's efforts to increase student participation in overseas programs to 40% by 2006; Eckerd College's study abroad programs for nontraditional students; and Davidson College's Third-World medical internship program."[12]

Student outcomes have become an important part of the accreditation process, and global competence is commonly an expected outcome. The Higher Learning Commission of the North Central Association's guidelines stress continuous evaluation of programs. The commission requires institutions to provide evidence of student learning and to detail the means by which that learning is tested. An institution's success with its students is evaluated in a variety of ways, including accountability measures such as graduation rates and results on licensing exams. Students should be assessed at the course, program, and institutional levels. By definition, the North Central guidelines require that assessment lead to continuing educational improvement. North Central's guidelines do not limit learning to courses with credit but extend explicitly to noncredit aspects of an institution's programs.[13] North Central mandates, "Learning outcomes demonstrate that graduates have achieved breadth of knowledge and skills and the capacity to exercise intellectual inquiry [and that] learning outcomes demonstrate effective preparation for continued learning."[14] North Central views global education as part of the college experience and asks that assessment document that students are prepared to function in a global society. The Commission advises colleges to examine "the usefulness of [their] curricula to students who will live and work in a global, diverse, and technological society."[15]

Similarly, the professional accrediting associations generally posit outcomes as central to accreditation and frequently include global understanding as an important outcome. For example, the American Assembly of Collegiate Schools of Business (AACSB) has elevated student-learning outcomes to a central place in accreditation. Expected outcomes include foundation knowledge in math, statistics, and accounting; skills like effective writing and communications; and understanding of ethical, environmental, technological, political, social, and legal "perspectives that form the context for business." The AACSB fosters assessment in regular workshops and seminars. Members are encouraged to add their own outcomes objectives. Like North Central, the AACSB expects global competence.[16] Similarly, the Accreditation Board for Engineering and Technology (ABET), the chief accrediting organization for programs in applied science, computing, engineering, and technology, defines its mission as "outcomes-based accreditation," and the National Council for Accreditation of Teacher Education (NCATE), focuses on "student performance." ABET's Engineering Criteria 2000 for "outcomes and assessment" states that engineering programs "need to demonstrate that their graduates have "the broad education necessary to understand the impact of engineering solutions in a global and societal context."[17]

Both major accreditation associations, the Council for Higher Education Accreditation (CHEA) and the Association of Specialized and Professional Accreditors (ASPA), place student learning at the center of accreditation.[18] Both associations have given priority to international accreditation issues by focusing mainly on looking at equivalencies across countries and the involvement of U.S accrediting agencies in accreditation of overseas institutions. ASPA's preconference workshop in fall 2005 was titled, "The World is Flat: Globalization of Professional & Specialized Accreditation."[19]

The Bush Administration's No Child Left Behind policy has reinforced both the assessment movement and the mood of accountability. A 2002 Department of Education strategic plan included higher education among the targets of future legislation with respect to accountability. "While noting the excellence of American higher education, the report expressed concern about rising costs and "'the effectiveness of postsecondary institutions' in retaining students and graduating them 'in a timely fashion.'"[21] According to the *Chronicle of Higher Education*, the Bush administration toyed with the idea of making accountability in tertiary education an issue in the 2004 campaign.[20]

In a similar vein, Congress has quizzed accrediting organizations about the extent to which they take student outcomes into account. The possibility of minimum standards for achievement has been raised at Congressional hearings. New amendments to the Higher Education Act may require accrediting agencies to set minimum standards as well as require accrediting bodies to look closely at student learning.[21] The draft reauthorization legislation mandates a study of "the best practices of States in assessing undergraduate postsecondary student learning, particularly as such practices relate to public accountability."[22]

The public and private sectors have also played a continuing role in the assessment movement. In 2001, the Pew Charitable Trusts sponsored a conference for business executives, governors, and leaders in higher education to study the "'desirability' of a 'national indicator of student learning.'"[23] The meeting frankly focused on the economic justification for support of higher education by summing up the results with the question—"What is the educational capital of a state?"—illustrated with four more specific questions:

"What are the current levels of advanced abilities of the citizens residing in our state?

What contributions do our own colleges and universities make to this stock of educational capital?

How good are the resulting learning outcomes in comparison to national standards or the outcomes achieved by graduates in other states?

What do our colleges do to promote better learning?"[24]

Five states followed this up with a pilot study in which they compared results on a wide variety of indices on student learning. The pilot study was funded by the Pew Charitable Trusts and had the cooperation of the National Center for Higher Education Management Systems (NCHEMS). The success of higher education in Illinois, Kentucky, Oklahoma, Nevada, and South Carolina was assessed on the basis of three criteria: the abilities of the college-educated population; the institutional contributions to educational capital; and the performance of college graduates.

The first criterion pertaining to abilities was tested through the use of the 1992 Adult Literacy Survey (NALS), which involves solving real-life and employment problems. The second, institutional contributions to educational capital, was measured by results of licensing exams and the percentage of students taking and passing exams such as MCAT, GRE, and LSAT and pursuing graduate education. To test the performance of college graduates, the study used two testing instruments, the Collegiate Learning Assessment (CLA) for four-year institutions and the ACT Work Keys assessment for two-year colleges. The CLA uses real-life situations that graduates might face on their jobs. The ACT is a reasoning exam focused on student learning in general education.[25] Since 1992, global competence has become an increasing focus of undergraduate education and will likely develop as an important factor in tests like these in the future. The events of 9/11 and its aftermath have raised the consciousness of the federal government, in particular, about our national shortfall in globally competent and linguistically prepared young people entering the job market and available for crucial government work. Business interests as well have continued to push for trained young people who can work in an international context and also manage an increasingly diverse, multiethnic work force in this country.[26]

Many states have also taken individual initiative. By 2000, six states—Florida, Georgia, Tennessee, Arkansas, Texas, and South Dakota—had introduced a common statewide test for all college students as a means of assessing student outcomes. Fifteen additional states, including Illinois, New York, and North Carolina, required assessment but left the test up to the universities. Eight other states were in the process of developing policy.[27] It seems likely that most states will adopt a policy that expects universities to have assessment programs but leaves developing their approach up to them. Instruments such as CLA will likely be the most commonly employed, and international educators need to find means to impact these approaches. It is also essential that international educators sit at the table when state tests are being developed, and that they insist on the assessment of global competency as a factor in these tests.

The popular press, in particular *US News and World Report*, has its own approach to comparing colleges and universities, combining some outcomes metrics such as graduation rates with subjective assessments. Ratings of universities is a worldwide preoccupation, illustrated by similar reports in *Asia Week*, *The Sunday Times Good University Guide*, and the *Guardian's Guide* in the UK, *McClean's Magazine* rankings in Canada, the DAAD-*Die Zeit* rankings of departments in Germany, and *El Mundo's* rankings in Spain. Higher education researchers have attempted to offer a counterweight to the popular press approach. The most notable of these is the National Survey of Student Engagement headed by George Kuh of Indiana University, which utilizes an extensive student survey and focuses on such factors as the level of academic challenge, active and collaborative learning, student-faculty interactions, enriching educational experiences, and supportive campus environment in assessing colleges. Students are asked about their reading habits, study habits, personal development, and the academic atmosphere at their institutions.[28] The survey includes study abroad as an important "enriching educational experience" and finds that while many students indicate interest in study abroad as first-year students, they are most likely to study abroad if they attend institutions that generally score well on the NSSE scale.[29] A Faculty Study of Student Engagement (FSSE), produced by the same research team, examines faculty perceptions along similar lines as well as faculty involvement with students.[30]

Robert Zemsky of the University of Pennsylvania has taken a longitudinal approach to outcomes that should be extrapolated to international education; indeed, he asked questions similar to those in a longitudinal survey undertaken by the Institute for the International Education of Students (IES). Zemsky and his colleague, Susan Shaman, developed the Collegiate Results Survey (CRS), which questions students who are six to nine years out of college. Thirty-four thousand alumni replied to questionnaires that asked them about their "occupations, skills used in the workplace, educational activities since graduation, personal values, and current activities. Alumni were also asked to self-evaluate their ability to perform a variety of tasks derived from real-life scenarios and to indicate whether they would like to learn more about those tasks they felt less confident in performing."[31] The results indicated clear differences among colleges, and could be used by students and their parents to help select colleges that produced outcomes congruent with their goals.

Expanding this questionnaire to identify students in the sample who had studied abroad would provide valuable comparative information on the specific outcomes of study abroad. The US Department of Education has in fact surveyed three cohorts of university students on a longitudinal basis to look into the impact of study abroad and other indications of "global preparedness," including second-language facility and completion of international studies courses. The Department of Education studies demonstrate that students with high levels of global preparedness are significantly more likely to enter careers in such fields as editing and reporting, engineering and architecture, office management and supervision, financial services, and art and performance.[32]

The Education Trust and the National Association of Systems Heads (NASH) are cooperating with Georgia State University in developing standards and expected outcomes for six undergraduate majors: biology, chemistry, English, history, mathematics, and physics. Through the program, funded by the Pew Charitable Trusts and headed by Georgia State Provost Ronald Henry, departments from ten public institutions in four states are collaborating to develop standards of student proficiency that majors will have reached on graduation, as well as assessment procedures for documenting these outcomes.[33] These outcomes are still in development, but so far there are positive signs that international objectives will be included. One of the first, history standards developed in Atlanta, puts international understanding and recognition of global differences at the beginning of the list of disciplinary objectives for lower-division courses.[34] Chemistry standards, developed at Nevada-Reno, expect majors to have developed a broader social knowledge outside of chemistry "that is necessary to understand the impact of science in a global ... context."[35] The development of standards in academic disciplines will likely serve to encourage study abroad but demand tangible and testable results from the experience.

The assessment movement has greatly impacted private liberal arts colleges. Since study abroad is generally an important aspect of liberal arts education at these institutions, this is likely to spill over to closer assessment of study abroad programs. The Association of American Colleges and Universities, with financing from the Teagle Foundation, has enlisted six liberal arts college consortia to look at assessment and the outcomes of liberal arts education. Each consortium is seeking ways to measure the outcomes central to the goals of the participating institutions and practices.[36]

The studies focus on outcomes such as writing, critical and analytical thinking, civic engagement, and global understanding—all areas that could theoretically be enhanced by an overseas experience. Some of the approaches taken might well provide a model for study abroad programs. For example, one of the collaborative projects, undertaken by Beloit, Knox, Lake Forest, Monmouth, and Ripon Colleges and focusing on faculty development, could be applicable to overseas study programs that rely on program faculty rather than full integration in overseas universities. Among the facets of the project are "educating faculty in assessment methods and approaches, including assignment design and grading to improve student learning

... engag[ing] faculty in the discussion of course goals and outcomes in relation to larger departmental and institutional missions; ...to share best practices ...to tailor assessment strategies and feedback mechanisms to the particular needs and culture of individual institutions."[37] Practically, study abroad staff and faculty might benefit from participation in this kind of dialog and examine how their own efforts contribute to the outcomes goals of colleges.

The Teagle Foundation is supporting the development of a model study by the Associated Colleges of the South, the Associated Colleges of the Midwest, and the Great Lakes College Association to look at differing models of study abroad programs and "measure their learning outcomes."[38] The study will analyze the goals of study abroad experience and how these relate to college goals, and then measure learning outcomes. The consortia have advanced from a planning grant in 2004 to an assessment grant in 2005, which will involve interviewing a broad section of their academic communities along with student participants in study abroad to develop new instruments for assessing student growth on study abroad programs.[39]

Practically, institutions have developed a broad variety of approaches to assessing student outcomes from study abroad. Darla Deardoff in 2003 surveyed 73 institutions with a commitment to study abroad and received responses from 38% of them. All were employing methods to assess the development of students' intercultural competence. These institutions were using a variety of methods, ranging from surveys and interviews to portfolios, papers, journals, and tests given before and after study abroad.[40] Most institutions were employing more than one method of assessment.

Portfolios are a widely used liberal arts approach to assessing student development and outcomes. While portfolios grew out of teacher education, they have been adopted with increasing frequency by colleges and departments to monitor both individual development and programmatic success. Portfolios are useful because students choose what to include, incorporate personal reflections on their work, and become personally conscious of their own academic growth. Portfolios also provide a medium for continued feedback to students.

When portfolios are used for programmatic assessment, generally a sampling is reviewed because of the enormous effort it would take to review a large number of portfolios. An evaluation team decides on common criteria and then reviews the sample as a group.[41] Portfolios adapt well as an assessment tool to study abroad programs because they encourage use of a variety of media as well as personal reflections and thereby reflect the holistic nature of the study abroad experience.

Departments and disciplines are also developing outcome standards and tools for assessment. A capstone course is frequently used as an assessment tool in which the students' mastery of the discipline's curriculum and their achievement of programmatic outcomes goals can be tested.[42] In departments where large numbers of students study abroad, the capstone course can be an important locus for the integration of the overseas academic experience with major courses taken at home.

When departments interpret their educational mission broadly, study abroad can be an important means of furthering students' achievement of these broader goals. Barbara E. Walvoord points out in her guide to assessment, "Assessment does not limit itself only to learning that can be objectively tested. It need not be a reductive exercise. Rather, a department can state its highest goals, including goals such as students' ethical development, understanding of diversity, and the like. Then it can seek the best available indicators about whether those goals are being met."[43]

It is therefore not surprising that the assessment movement has also impacted the student affairs field, with its emphasis upon personal growth. Upcraft and Schuh, in a 1996 guide to assessment in student affairs, used similar arguments to those coming from the academic arena to explain the need for assessment: private unrest with costs, the quality of education, and the failure of higher education to produce "educated persons"; and added discrepancies in achievement of different ethnic groups and the pressures of accrediting agencies. They encouraged student services research to cover, among other things, the assessment of "individual and collective outcomes of programs and services" and the assessment of the "developmental impact of individual programs and the total collegiate experience."[44] Upcraft and Schuh noted, "There is substantial evidence that the out of class environment is an important factor in learning, development, academic achievement, and retention."[45] The Council on Academic Standards in Higher Education, an umbrella organization for the nonacademic professional associations in higher education, posits "intellectual growth ... effective communication ... enhanced self-esteem ... realistic self-appraisal ... clarified values ... career choices ... leadership development ... healthy behavior ... meaningful interpersonal relationships ... independence ... collaboration ... social responsibility ... satisfying and productive lifestyles ... appreciating diversity ... [and] spiritual awareness" as desirable outcomes for higher education and defines indicators for all of these attributes.[46]

The holistic nature of the study abroad experience serves the outcomes expectations of these professional associations well. In fact, the study of outcomes in international education can be a model and pacesetter for assessment in US higher education today. The IES MAP© for Study Abroad, for example—the guidelines that the Institute for the International Education of Students developed for its programs—devotes a section to "student learning: assessment and intercultural development."[47] This section focuses on students' "intellectual development ... development of language and communication skills … cognitive growth … interpersonal growth … and intrapersonal growth" and examines programs for activities that reinforce student development in all of these areas.[48] The Forum on Education Abroad's draft guidelines of standards require institutions in study abroad to have "formal review and evaluation processes" and "clearly defined outcomes."[49]

The higher education community, in examining study abroad, is likely to look at both academic and personal outcomes. Academic outcomes include the development of foreign language proficiency, linguistic development, academic learning both in general education and in students' major fields, and global competence, which involves a more rounded intellectual view of the world arising from the contact with foreign science and scholarship as well as the cultural, intellectual, and political milieu of the country where the student is studying. With respect to personal outcomes, the US academic community is likely to look for intercultural competence, the ability to be comfortable in societies other than one's own, career preparation for international work, and personal growth along the lines that are suggested by the Council of Academic Standards in higher education.

Assessment of these outcomes is difficult. Students are abroad for a relatively short period of time, often less than a semester, rarely for a year anymore. It is naturally more difficult to gauge growth in this short a period as compared to the four or more years that a student spends in undergraduate work. Yet the experience abroad is often an intense one. Cultural shock is the norm rather than the exception, and students have to address an onslaught of new experiences, including a different study milieu, different faculty expectations, language immersion in non-English-speaking countries, peers and adults who think and act in different ways than what they have taken as the norms, and looking at the world from different perspectives. The IES longitudinal study of the long-term outcomes of study abroad appears to indicate that the impact on students, even of relatively short study abroad experiences, is profound and long lasting.[50]

US institutions will have a range of expectations with respect to assessment of international programs. The National Center for Post-secondary Improvement (NCPI) at Stanford, which plays an active role in assisting institutions in undergraduate assessment programs, has identified how differing kinds of institutions have reacted to the assessment movement. In 1996, the NCPI carried out a national study on assessment. From this study, the center developed a toolkit that administrators and faculty can use in developing assessment programs. The center's study indicated that associate of arts institutions, in their assessment programs, were likely to have responded to public mandates and to take a centralized approach; baccalaureate institutions were far less influenced by state requirements and tended to focus on "students' cognitive domains (higher-order skills, general education, competence in major field, etc.), and student's experiences and/or satisfaction with the institution." Comprehensive institutions appeared to have been influenced by regional accreditation requirements, stressed academic improvement, and took a decentralized approach. Doctoral and research institutions were more likely to "report being required to use state-mandated student performance indicators," were less likely to be influenced by accreditors, and tended to study "the relationship between students' institutional experiences and student performance."[51]

These differences suggest that the international education community should test a variety of approaches for outcomes assessment that will have validity in different settings. Public expectations of accountability suggest longitudinal studies in which programs look at graduation rates, career choices, and graduate school entrance exams and enrollment. This kind of information is likely to be convincing for parents as well as students who are looking toward postgraduation plans. Comparisons of students who have studied abroad with those who have not on an examination like the Collegiate Learning Assessment developed by the Rand Corporation will help to reinforce information about career-preparation outcomes. The NSSE approach is likely to appeal to faculty, especially those with strong commitments to undergraduate programs, who will be interested in cognitive development, student faculty interaction, and enriched academic experience. Language faculty will be interested in test results and studies of placement when students return to their home colleges. University administrators are likely to favor testing programs that they can use to show accreditors and government officials tangible results.

Assessment is essential to teach us how we can improve what we are doing and assist our students to make the most of their time abroad. As study abroad involves a larger percentage of US undergraduates, we will need to develop new and effective ways to engage students and to ensure that they will meet the goals we are setting for them.

Assessment is also crucial for raising the standards of the field as a whole. Study abroad is regulated today only by the standards of the sending institutions, and many colleges and universities have a *laissez faire* attitude to the programs chosen by their students.

The international education community has a stake in assessing outcomes that transcends the need to tell the world that we have a tangible impact. Assessment begins with setting goals for outcomes, and it is important that international education professionals have the central role in setting these goals. It is also important that we set these goals in dialog with the broader academic community. The Forum on Education Abroad's project to develop standards for the field of study abroad rightly stresses the essentiality both of clearly focused goals and of recurring assessment in study abroad programs based on these goals.[52] The best study abroad programs consciously define their objectives and test their accomplishment through student evaluations, program reviews using outside examiners, and learning assessment instruments.

These aims are in part academic: Students need to develop mastery in their fields of interest. But they also reflect a central value of US higher education that students should grow in a broad variety of ways during their college years. In particular, international educators need to demonstrate that the students on our programs return home having grown intellectually and personally, having developed a greater measure of global and intercultural competence and, when relevant, having developed greater fluency in languages other than English. We also need to demonstrate that they are much better prepared for careers in a global environment. While we feel confident that this happens because our students and our former students tell us what happened to them, we need to demonstrate empirically that these outcomes would not have been achieved to the same degree if these students had stayed home.

Notes

[1] Harvard University Faculty of Arts and Sciences. *A Report on the Harvard College Curricular Review,* April 2004, p. 40.

[2] I am grateful to Dr. Shelly Bannister and Dr. Angeles Eames of Northeastern Illinois University for providing me with a general introduction to the literature on assessment.

[3] William D. Hunter. Got Global Competency? *International Educator.* Washington, DC: Spring 2004. Vol.13, Issue 2, pp. 6–13. A 2002 survey by Cendant Mobility concluded that global competence is essential for employees of institutions working across borders.

[4] Lee Harvey. The British Experience in Assessing Competence. In Catherine A. Palomba and Trudy W. Banta. *Assessing Student Competence in Accredited Disciplines,* Sterling, VA: Stylus Publishing, 2001, pp. 217–243.

[5] Peter T. Ewell. Tomorrow the World: Learning Outcomes and the Bologna Process. *Assessment Update,* November–December 2004. Vol. 16, No. 6, pp. 11–13.

[6] M. Lee Upcraft and John H. Schuh. *Assessment in Student Affairs: A Guide for Practitioners,* San Francisco: Jossey-Bass, 1996, p. 5.

[7] Trudy Banta. Assessing Competence in Higher Education, p. 9. In Catherine A. Palomba and Trudy W. Banta. *Assessing Student Competence in Accredited Disciplines.* Sterling, VA: Stylus Publishing, 2001, pp. 1–12.

[8] *Ibid.*

[9] *The Higher Learning Commission Handbook of Accreditation.* The Higher Learning Commission, a commission of the North Central Association, Chicago, third edition, 2003.

[10] http://aacu.org/issues/assessment

[11] *Ibid.*

[12] *Greater Expectations National Panel Report,* p. 23. Association of American Colleges and Universities, c.2002.

[13] *Ibid.*

[14] *Ibid.*, core component 4b, page 3.1–5.

[15] *Ibid.*, core component 4c, page 3.1–5.

[16] Neil A. Palomba and Catherine A. Polomba. Assessment of student competence in business. In Catherine A. Palomba and Trudy W. Banta. *Assessing Student Competence in Accredited Disciplines.* Sterling, VA: Stylus Publishing, 2001, pp. 121–139.

[17] Weichert, D. (Editor). *Educating the Engineer for the 21st Century. Proceedings of the 3rd Workshop on Global Engineering Education,* Secaucus, NJ: Kluwer Academic Publishers, 2001, p 23. http://80 site.ebrary.com.proxy.alumni.jhu.edu/lib/knowledgenet2/Doc?id=10067355&ppg=3

[18] Catherine A. Palomba and Trudy W. Banta. *Assessing Student Competence in Accredited Disciplines,* Sterling, VA: Stylus Publishing, 2001, p. xi.

[19] http://www.aspa-usa.org/meetings/Fall%202005-Overview%20Schedule-rvsd.doc

[20] *Ibid.*

[21] Peter Ewell. Reauthorization. *Assessment Update.* September–October 2003, Vol. 15, No. 5, pp. 8–10.

[22] *Policy Matters: A compendium.* Vol. 1, No. 4, October 2004. American Association of State Colleges and Universities, p. 14.

[23] Ewell. Going for Broke: The National Forum on College-Level Learnings Multistate Demonstration Project. *Assessment Update,* May–June 2003, pp. 8–9, 14.

[24] *Ibid.*, p. 8.

[25] http://measuringup.highereducation.org/ the national report card on higher education, 2004. The National Center for Public Policy and Higher Education. The Teagle Foundation is also sponsoring a study in which "33 small and mid-sized private colleges and universities are administering the CLA." See www.teagle foundation.org/grantmaking/grantees/outcomes.aspx

[26] See, e.g., International and Foreign Language Studies Act of 2005 May Mean Important Changes to Higher Education Act, Spending Increases. *Foreign Language Annals.* Vol. 38, No. 2, Summer 2005, p. 314.

[27] *Policy Matters: A compendium*, Vol. 1, No. 4, October 2004. American Association of State Colleges and Universities, p. 14. For a more detailed discussion, see Peter Ewell and Paula Ries, Assessing Student Learning Outcomes: A Supplement to *Measuring Up 2000*." National Center for Public Policy and Higher Education, c.2000.

[28] http://www.indiana.edu/~nsse/, The National Survey of Student Engagement.

[29] http://nsse.iub.edu/pdf/NSSE2005_annual_report.pdf, National Survey of Student Engagement, Annual Report 1995, p. 49. At the date of this writing, the Forum is in discussion with NSSE with respect to surveying students more broadly about study abroad.

[30] http://websurvey.indiana.edu/fsse2005/Demo/

[31] About the Collegiate Results Survey, National Center for Postsecondary Improvement. www.stanford.edu/group/ncpi/unspecified/students_parents_toolkit/cri.html; See also Mary M. Dwyer, Charting the Impact of Study Abroad. *International Educator,* Winter 2004, pp. 14–20.

[32] Clifford Adelman 'Global Preparedness' of pre-9/11 college graduates: what the US longitudinal studies say. *Tertiary Education and Management* 10: 243–260, 2004.

[33] http://www2.gsu.edu/~wwwque/

[34] http://www2.gsu.edu/~wwwque/standards/history/historylowerdiv.htm

[35] http://www.chem.unr.edu/undergraduates/standards.pdf

[36] www.teaglefoundation.org/grantmaking/grantees/vaa.aspx

[37] www.teaglefoundation.org/grantmaking/grantees/vaafull.aspx

[38] www.teaglefoundation.org/ grantmaking/ grantees/ outcomesfull.aspx

[39] http://www.teaglefoundation.org/grantmaking/grantees/outcomesfull.aspx#ACS/ACM/GLCA

[40] Darla K Deardorff. International Educator. Washington: May/June 2005. Vol.14, Iss. 3; pp. 26–32.

[41] Catherine A. Palomba and Trudy W. Banta. *Assessment Essentials,* San Francisco: Jossey-Bass, 1999, pp. 131–147.

[42] Barbara E. Walvoord. *Assessment Clear and Simple: A Practical Guide for Institutions, Departments, and General Education.* San Francisco: Jossey-Bass: c.2004, p. 3.

[43] Barbara E. Walvoord. *Assessment Clear and Simple*, op.cit.

[44] Assessment practice in student affairs: An applications manual. San Francisco: Jossey-Bass. Cited in The role of outcomes assessment and program evaluation. *CAS Professional Standards for Higher Education.* Theodore K. Miller (Editor). Washington, DC: Council for the Advancement of Standards in Higher Education, 2003, pp. 239–240.

[45] Upcraft and Schuh. *Assessment in Student Affairs…*, op. cit., p. 8.

[46] Outcomes Assessment and Program Evaluation Services, CAS Standards and Guidelines. *CAS Professional Standards for Higher Education.* Theodore K. Miller, editor. Washington, DC: Council for the Advancement of Standards in Higher Education, 2003, pp. 246.

[47] *The IES MAP for Study Abroad*, c.1999, 2001, 2003, pp. 20–21

[48] *Ibid.*

[49] http://www.forumea.org/pdfs/ForumStandards.pdf, p. 13; revised edition, unpublished draft.

[50] Mary M. Dwyer and Courtney Peters. The Benefits of Study Abroad: New Study Confirms Significant Gains. *Transitions Abroad*, March/April 2004; More is Better: the Impact of Study Abroad Program Duration. *Frontiers*, Vol. X, August 2005, pp.121–142; Mary M. Dwyer, Charting the Impact of Study Abroad, op.cit.

[51] National Center for Postsecondary Improvement. Student Assessment by Differing Institution Types. http://www.stanford.edu/group/ncpi/unspecified/assessment_toolkit1/inst_type.html. The NCPI webpage provides a variety of publications on assessment in different types of institutions.

[52] The Forum on Education Abroad. *Standards of Good Practice for Education Abroad.* www.forumea.org, 2005.

Chapter 2

Research Design in Assessing Learning Outcomes of Education Abroad Programs

Richard C. Sutton, Ann N. Miller, Donald L. Rubin

Introduction

Higher education has finally reached a consensus that a meaningful college education should include a substantive international component (Dennis, 2004). This expectation is expressed in many ways, but typically it involves some measure of undergraduate students who study abroad. Target rates of 25% for US undergraduate study abroad participation are not uncommon, with some institutions proclaiming goals of 50% or more (Sutton & Rubin, 2004; Vande Berg, 2004; Bollag, 2004). The number of US students earning credits abroad tripled during the last 15 years of the 20th century and it continues to grow, with expectations of more than one million US students abroad within the next decade (Chin, 2003; Lincoln Commission, 2005). Study abroad has shifted from a marginal opportunity originally confined to an elite group of students to a cornerstone of US higher education instructional strategy (Vande Berg, 2004).

Although one million US students abroad in 2017 would constitute only about 6% of the country's projected higher education undergraduate student population (16,865,000 in 2015; NCES, p. 125), it still represents significant growth in participation rates. That expansion of students abroad will continue to draw greater attention and critical scrutiny to the study abroad field. Education abroad professionals should be prepared to document the strengths and weaknesses of study abroad programs with rigorous evidentiary research, and they should be particularly attentive to questions of the value that study abroad adds to a college education.

The increasing number of students studying abroad has been accompanied by decreasing duration of their study abroad programs. The largest enrollment increase since 1990 as documented by the Institute for the International Education of Students (IES) has been in programs of less than one academic quarter; full-year enrollments have correspondingly declined (Dwyer, 2004a). The prototypical study abroad program—supplanting the traditional semester-long immersion experience—is now composed of four- to eight-week sojourns led by home institution faculty and enrolling groups of sufficient size to be economically viable, often consisting of students from various majors and institutions (Chin, 2003; Kinginger & Farrell, 2004).

No doubt the proliferation of such programs reflects positive change, since it expands their availability and appeal to a broader swath of US college students. Yet key questions about the academic outcomes of this plethora of overseas experiences remain barely explored (Stronkhorst, 2005). Do students really learn anything by studying classical rhetoric in Athens, Greece, for a month that they would not have internalized in the same course back in Athens, Georgia? Do students learn more about Renaissance painting, sculpture, and architecture—even when one includes aesthetic response in a definition of fine arts knowledge—in a three-week course in Florence, Italy, than they could learn in a semester in Florence, South Carolina? Beyond some documented gains in personal development factors such as self-efficacy (e.g., Stronkhorst, 2005) and flexibility (e.g., Rundstrom Williams, 2005) that may under certain circumstances accrue from time spent in unfamiliar places and cultures, does the cost of study abroad justify its perceived benefits? And even in terms of those well-documented increments in personal development outcomes, is exposure to host-national peers for a US undergraduate in Kent, United Kingdom, qualitatively equivalent to host-national peers in Tashkent, Uzbekistan? To what extent do differences in study abroad destinations and program configurations lead to differences in learning outcomes?

Typical indices of institutional effectiveness to which colleges and universities have been held accountable in the past, not only in study abroad programming in particular, but in higher education in general, have included almost everything *but* student learning (Wellman, 2001). Reports to governing boards and accrediting agencies compile information about a host of input measures (e.g., entering SAT scores, faculty credentials, conformance of curricula to disciplinary standards, adequacy of library resources) and output measures (e.g., year-to-year student retention, graduation rates, efficiency of the bursar's office). Although these are all useful factors in looking at the productivity, efficiency, and effectiveness of the educational enterprise, at best they can only approximate student learning outcomes through corollary data, rather than assessing learning directly.

Study abroad programs, too, have traditionally relied on institutional indicators of effectiveness such as number of credit hours generated, number of student participants, and records of student health and safety (Gillespie, Braskamp & Braskamp, 1999). In addition, many study abroad administrators compile exit interview data (e.g., Cash, 1993) collected from student participants. Exit questionnaires often ask students to rate their satisfaction with various aspects of the program: *My home-stay family was friendly and helpful*; or *I would recommend this program to other students at my college*. Some also ask participants to evaluate the broad impact that the experience has had on their goals and personal traits: *How has this program affected your intention to get involved in improving the environment?* or *I am more confident of my leadership ability as a result of studying abroad.* (See, for example, British Columbia Centre for International Education, 2002; Handel & Grove, 1986; Laubscher, 1994). Although this sort of student opinion data may be useful for recruiting students and solidifying institutional support, it is often anecdotal and is less than optimal in identifying specific student academic gains. The critique by Deiter Brietenbach (cited in Smith, 1983) remains uncomfortably current:

> If one looks at the numerous "evaluation reports" which have been written on exchange programmes, one cannot avoid the impression that major survey and research institutes adopt unthinkingly and without even a minimal degree of scientific preparation the line of questioning suggested by their sponsors. . . they then proceed to eulogies which throw positive light on the institutions concerned with the administration of such programmes ...but have little to do with academic credibility. (p. 140)

The currently ascendant trend in higher education accountability calls for a more central role for student learning outcomes assessment (Allan, 1996; Commission on Institutions of Higher Education, 1998; McDaniel, Felder, Gordon, Hrutka & Quinn, 2000). Chapter 1 in this guide, by Michael Steinberg, elaborates on the variety of ways that higher education has responded to demands for assessment focused more clearly on learning outcomes. Undoubtedly ever more intense competition for student enrollment fuels some of the heightened stress on accountability, with parents and funding organizations looking for hard evidence that their investments have yielded palpable educational dividends (Milleret, 1990; Wellman, 2001; Zernike, 2002). Beyond such market-driven motivations for documenting learning outcomes, student learning is the *raison d'être* for the entire higher education enterprise, and therefore of study abroad programming as well. Measures of student outcomes for study overseas that assess only student satisfaction with programming—by one estimate (Vande Berg cited in Stronkhorst, 2005), fully 60% of published studies on the topic—can offer only indirect evidence of program effectiveness, leaving designers open to skeptical criticism regarding their value-added. For example, absent data regarding learning outcomes, some critics have contended that short-term study abroad programs are at best tourism with a college course number attached, and at worst, excursions in self-exploration that simply confirm an inaccurate US-centric view of the world (Freinberg, 2002). Carefully designed evaluation is a critical need.

A Framework for Study Abroad Assessment

Study abroad assessment is a relatively young field of inquiry. One of the challenges of this immaturity is to articulate a structure in which emerging research studies connect with each other and fit within a broader context. The research agenda is vast, and many professionals have conducted or are beginning to conduct analyses across a wide spectrum of issues and methodologies. These studies vary greatly in their scope, substance, and findings, but they are all driven by a single, critical question: What value does education abroad add to higher education?

This chapter offers a foundational framework for designing study abroad learning outcomes assessment research projects. We suggest a research design matrix that captures three key sets of learning outcomes (i.e., clusters of dependent variables) associated with the study abroad experience and identifies three primary sets of independent or mediating variables that may interact to influence those outcomes. The model can be expanded and tailored, but its central purpose is to provide a basic structure in which to place current and forthcoming studies. In concert with other chapters, we attempt to help entry-level researchers frame their approaches to core issues that need further investigation.

From this elemental inquiry, a fountain of other questions flows. The next chapter in this guide looks at the variety of fields that invite closer examination. As a segue to that conversation, we conclude our chapter with a list of potential inquiries that future research might wish to pursue. What are the key questions that researchers need to answer? How are these questions translated into verifiable hypotheses? Which research methodologies are most likely to yield evidence that answers a given hypothesis? The list of questions is long; answers convincing to skeptical audiences are short; energy, time, and resources to resolve these issues are much in demand.

Challenges Implicit in Assessing Study Abroad Programs

Preliminary to presenting our study abroad learning outcomes framework, it is necessary to lay a foundation regarding some of the generic challenges of research in our field. In this section we therefore begin by presenting brief general guidelines for planning assessment efforts and move on to noting some issues of validity that are especially salient to study abroad research, based on Campbell and Stanley's (1966) seminal statement about experimental and quasi-experimental designs in educational research.

Program Objectives and Stakeholder Needs as the Impetus for Measuring Learning Outcomes

Planning adequate assessment of study abroad learning outcomes should be based on three basic criteria. First, like any educational assessment, assessment in study abroad must begin with the establishment of program objectives (see, for example, US Office of Management and Budget, 2005). This is an obvious statement, but all too many reports of study abroad impact make no mention of specific program goals regarding value-added to *academic* learning (Gray, Murdock & Stephens, 2002). That is, what specific academic learning objectives do the program planners believe will be met better by offering a given course on location overseas rather at the home campus?

Taxonomies of such study abroad objectives are already available. Two decades ago, Smith (1983) offered a comprehensive listing of impacts of study abroad programs that were ripe for assessment, categorizing them into four major types: cultural, linguistic, educational, and professional. More recently, the *IES MAP for Study Abroad* (IES, 2003) offered guidelines for assessment of study abroad programs in four areas, one of which was "student learning and development of intercultural competence." General objectives under student learning included demonstration of knowledge and understanding of course material; development of critical thinking skills through programmed exposure to host country political, social, and cultural institutions; development of learning strategies toward integration into host culture; development of ability to critique home culture value system; development of host culture language and communication skills; increased ability to recognize cultural difference; greater respect for persons of other cultures; and knowledge of comparisons between home and host cultures.

Once program objectives are clearly stated, learning outcome measures must be explicitly linked to them. We take the admittedly stringent position that assessing the generic impact of study abroad programs such as student satisfaction, or documenting psychosocial outcomes like increased sense of independence and self-confidence, often does not qualify as learning outcomes assessment per se. Such studies can provide data that may be useful for other theoretical and institutional purposes, but they offer no direct evidence of academic learning. This is a critical point with respect to evaluation of study abroad outcomes, because changes in psychological traits and attitudes of student participants are among the most commonly touted benefits of the study abroad experience (Carlson & Widamon, 1988; Lindsey, 2005; Sell, 1983). However, those variables cannot be construed as learning outcomes per se. Target changes in modes of thinking and processing may be viewed as learning outcomes, but only if they map onto previously defined program learning objectives. For example, measured increases in student multicultural identity or decreases in ethnocentrism should be deliberately geared to specific program inputs or design features that were intended to bring about such change among students in a mindful fashion (Langer, 1989; Thomas, 2006).

Learning outcomes assessment methodologies must be selected not only with consideration of the programmatic learning objectives, but also with the target audience or stakeholder in mind. Results of learning assessments can be beneficial to students, faculty, and/or university administrators, but the same instruments will not necessarily address concerns of all stakeholders at once. Students will benefit little from simple pretest and posttest research designs; they need ongoing input into their progress toward defined educational goals (Milleret, 1990). On the other hand, instructors may be more interested in comparative assessment on the effectiveness of different pedagogical approaches, while institutional program planners may in addition be concerned about the impact of larger design features such as level of immersion, duration of stay, and participant screening procedures (see Smith, 1983). In general, the needs of stakeholders with more local concerns—study abroad student participants or directors of single study abroad programs—will be most satisfied by thick, qualitative data. Stakeholders with more broad-based agendas—campus directors of international education or members of institutional accreditation teams—may find more value in data that can yield valid comparisons between settings of interest or that can reveal broad patterns of best practices.

Validity in Program Assessment

Like all research and program evaluation efforts, attempts to assess the outcomes of overseas study are subject to a number of distinct threats to validity. The concept of validity is most conventionally applied in a psychometric sense to specific measures or instruments. In Chapter7, Michael Paige addresses the psychometric validity of major instruments utilized in study abroad outcomes assessment. Our concern in this chapter is with validity judgments not about specific instruments and measures, but *apropos* entire research designs that assess the outcomes of educational interventions. These experiment-wise validity judgments are, like assessment methodologies in general, contingent on the *uses and users* of the assessments. In other words, the validity of a study abroad research design depends on how well that design is tailored to the specifics of the program, students, and decision-making context in which that research will be applied.

The classic statement of validity criteria for research designs is Campbell and Stanley's *Experimental and Quasi-Experimental Designs* (1966; see also Cook & Campbell, 1979). This approach to analyzing and organizing research designs has been widely applied to program evaluation studies and has lost none of its currency over the years (Barnette & Wallis, 2005). The taxonomy establishes two categories of threats to the validity of experiments or program evaluations: external and internal.

Four threats to external validity

Threats to external validity affect the researcher's ability to generalize results. The first such threat to external validity accrues from participants' possible *reactivity to pre-tests* that we may administer. In a typical time series design, a researcher might hope to ascertain changes in study abroad participants' culture shock over the course of a semester. But the very act of asking about culture shock during week 1 may have sensitized students to culture shock and therefore induced higher levels of that phenomenon than might spontaneously be the case. The antidote is to include at least one comparison group of program participants who are *not* tested at week 1 but only at some later point. By comparing the scores of these previously untested program participants with their peers who did receive pretesting, researchers can estimate the impact of program participation *versus* the impact of test sensitization on the measured outcome.

The second threat to external validity arises from an unanticipated (and often difficult to detect) *interaction between the experimental treatment and biases in recruiting assessment participants.* The most obvious example is a situation in which only a relatively small subset of a study abroad cohort volunteers to fill out evaluation questionnaires (for an example, see DeDee & Stewart, 2003). These volunteers are likely to hold more extreme views—either favorable or unfavorable—than would a random sample of participants. Another example might arise from collecting data about interaction within a study abroad group using an online questionnaire. Online data collection could introduce a subtle sampling bias favoring individuals who enjoy online interaction rather than face-to-face interaction. Are these participants who are motivated enough to fill out the assessment questionnaires representative of *all* study abroad students or of *all* students from the domestic comparison group?

The Hawthorne Effect—similar to the observer's paradox—comes into play when individuals react in a particular way simply because they know they are part of a research study. Without using deceptive methods, it is difficult to know if research participants are behaving as they would were they not aware of their status as research participants. These *reactive effects of experimental arrangements* constitute the third threat to external validity. In a study abroad evaluation, for example, participants might pad their journals with accounts of host-culture interaction if they know that program assessors are reading the journals.

In educational settings, students are exposed to multiple treatments in sequence, and *prior (or even simultaneous) interventions often interact with the primary experimental intervention* in unpredictable ways. For example, all participants in a particular French language immersion program may have completed a required third semester of French on campus. To reach that level prior to the junior year, perhaps a large proportion of these students had taken a high school Advanced Placement class that emphasized written rather than oral language. Therefore the sample of study abroad students in such a program might be skewed against students whose introductory French classes had been more communicatively oriented.

Eight threats to internal validity

Internal validity pertains to the warrant for drawing causal inferences about the effects of a program intervention on an outcome. Sometimes a coincidence of *history* can dramatically affect a program outcome in such a way that data collected contemporaneously with that historical event are useless. The invasion and occupation of Iraq created such perturbations of public opinion worldwide that study abroad outcomes for US students during the winter and spring of 2003 were overwhelmed by that singular event (McMurtrie, 2003). If one used spring 2003 data to conclude that study abroad enhances world-mindedness, the conclusion would be suspect because of the historical events that cohort experienced provide a plausible rival explanation.

Maturation effects can also threaten internal validity of study abroad program assessments. For example, changes in self-efficacy that study abroad participants experience during the course of a semester's exchange might equally be attributable to the rapid personal development that occurs during the college years. Similarly, evaluation studies that investigate the long-term impact of study abroad experiences on lifespan career and mobility choices are prone to error due to maturation effects (for an example, see Alred & Byram, 2002). Comparison, or nonexperimental, groups are necessary to account for the percent of variance in change scores that is due to maturation absent any particular educational intervention. Hadis (2005), however, has recently proposed that data derived from participants' own retrospective reflections might serve as a means for isolating the effects of program impact versus maturation.

Just as the reactivity of *testing* can impair external validity (generalizability), so can testing constitute a threat to internal validity. Sometimes the very instruments that are used to assess cross-cultural competency, such as cultural assimilators, are also used for training that very trait (Brislin, 1986). Once again, if a comparison group of nonparticipants in study abroad is subjected to the same testing regime as the program participants, this threat to internal validity can be contained. Better yet, one (or more) comparison group(s) should be exposed to the entire testing regime, and another (or several) comparison group(s) should be subjected only to a single testing episode. By contrasting the scores of students who have not studied abroad, but who have been exposed to varying waves of testing, researchers can estimate the cumulative impact attributable merely to multiple exposures to the measurement instrument.

Internal validity is also jeopardized when researchers change *instrumentation* from pretesting to posttesting. Of course few researchers would commit the error of administering one measure of intercultural competence at pretest and then comparing it with a different measure, say of world-mindedness, at posttest. [Technical note: Under some circumstances it could make sense to use a test administered at *Time 1* as a covariate when comparing postintervention scores. In that situation, the covariate may not need to be the same instrument as the posttest instrument.] Yet instrumentation can change from pretest to posttest in less obvious ways. For example, if raters were judging the quality of analytic essays as an index of a learning outcomes in, say, a history class, those raters might become less or more stringent when reading postintervention essays as compared to pretest essays. To avoid confounding variance due to time of *rating* (a nuisance variable) with variance due to time of *testing* (the primary variable of interest), raters in such situations should be presented with pretest and posttest essays to score all at one time and in random order.

Another threat to internal validity is the general tendency for *regression to the mean*. If one were to measure global mindedness among students who previously had little cosmopolitan exposure, no doubt their scores would rise from pretest to posttest no matter what kind of cultural intervention they experienced. After all, their scores have no place to go but up. By the same token, a high-scoring group might display no further gain or even show some minor decline from pretest to posttest. One should not infer in either case that these changes across time were the result of any intervention; they are just statistical artifacts.

In general, inferences about causality require comparisons among groups that are exposed to different treatment regimes. (Our author team tries to avoid the terms *control group* or *zero treatment group*, because they imply that nothing is happening to members of that group. But of course members of the nonexperimental group are undergoing *some* experience, and it is important to inform research consumers about the nature of that comparison group treatment condition, rather than just dismissing it as a so-called control group. Readers would want to know, for example, if a so-called control group back on campus were required to take a sequence of multicultural courses.) In a true experiment, participants are randomly assigned to these regimes, but in study abroad assessments, random assignment might be to a three-week residence abroad as opposed to a year-long exchange program. *Biased assignment of treatments to individuals* and a related problem of *unintended bias in interactions between treatments and groups* are two additional threats to internal validity that are to be avoided.

Inadvertent *interaction between treatments and groups* could occur if, for example, it turned out that a semester-long exchange were more expensive than a three-week residence. In that case, a comparison between the two levels of duration abroad could be confounded with an unintended comparison between wealthier and less wealthy students, or between nonscholarship students and scholarship students. Perhaps wealthier students would have the financial resources to take advantage of more host-country excursions, and those excursions—not program duration per se—comprised the mechanism that wrought measured change.

An especially insidious selection bias seems inherent in most conventional comparisons between students studying abroad and those studying on campus. One cannot very well randomly assign students to study abroad, nor prevent them from doing so on a random basis. Those who *elect* to study abroad may very well possess attributes that would mature into traits like self-efficacy or global mindedness whether they were afforded a study abroad opportunity or simply remained on campus. In terms of experimental design, one solution to this fundamental selection bias would be to measure disposition to study abroad well prior to conducting a field study. One could compare the amount of variance in some learning outcomes accounted for purely by that disposition, relative to the amount of variance accounted for by actual participation status.

The final threat to internal validity, according to the classic Campbell and Stanley account (1966), is differential experimental *mortality*. This factor pertains to who drops out of which treatment conditions. Thus, suppose researchers were interested in determining whether studying a foreign language abroad was more efficacious (higher gain scores) for beginning or for intermediate learners. The drop-out rate for beginning language learners in the on-campus comparison groups might be higher than for intermediate-level learners on campus and higher than for any of the language learners studying abroad (after all, students spending a semester in St. Petersberg skip their Russian language classes at their own peril). Who will be left among the on-campus beginners group after the less robust learners drop out? It could be that the survivors of this on-campus beginners group are the most efficacious learners of all, and that their gain scores will therefore eclipse those of their peers studying abroad.

Mixed Qualitative and Quantitative Approaches to Valid Research Designs

The Campbell and Stanley (1966) account of threats to experimental validity presumes that data are quantitative in nature. One cannot speak of *regression to the mean* for qualitative data, of course. In recent years, however, enormous strides have been made in methodologies for qualitative program evaluation (Patton, 1987). These methodologies have been applied to evaluating study abroad outcomes in general (e.g., Gray, et al., 2002), and although less often, study abroad learning outcomes in particular (Hill & Woodland, 2002).

Qualitative methodologies typically eschew concerns about external validity; they are avowedly intended to explore context-specific ideographic models. Generalizability beyond the immediate data source is not a priority. Alternatively, qualitative studies may include several safeguards to help assure accuracy of data analyses. These safeguards include the process of member checking, in which participants who are the subject of study are explicitly asked to affirm the accuracy of the researchers' findings (Patton, 1987).

Another key contribution of qualitative methodology to research study validation is the notion of triangulation. One can be confident of a finding if it can be independently derived from several different concurrent data sources. For example, a qualitative study of the impact of study abroad on subsequent career and life decisions (e.g., Alred & Byram, 2003) might collect data via focus groups, in-depth interviewing, and life narrative analysis. Alternatively, one might use a similar data-collection technique, interviewing for example, and seek corroboration among several different constituencies. That was the tack Schmidt-Rinehart and Knight (2004) took in establishing the value afforded to homestay experiences by students, housing directors, and host families. If the findings from each of those data sources all pointed toward the same conclusions, confidence in those conclusions would be substantial.

Despite some purist concerns arising in the philosophy of social sciences that quantitative and qualitative methodologies are epistemologically incompatible, a more pragmatic turn in program evaluation practices advocates for adopting mixed qualitative and quantitative methods (e.g., Greene & Caracelli, 1997; Frechtling & Sharpe, 1997). For example, it is often held (a bit simplistically—see Rao & Woolcock 2003) that qualitative studies are primarily hypothesis *generating*, while quantitative studies are primarily hypothesis *testing*. Therefore researchers often adopt qualitative methods like focus groups in initial phases of a study to identify and explore central constructs and propositions in a formative manner. These formative findings are in some later phase of research operationalized as questionnaire scales and experimental tasks that are subsequently deployed in more summative research.

Rao and Woolcock (2003) offer an especially comprehensive and thoughtful account of relations between quantitative and qualitative data and analyses. Their account can inform mixed methods research, particularly in intercultural settings. As they point out by way of illustration, qualitative methods can help detect sources of measurement error and bias in quantitative instruments. Thus one might discover that what a group of US college juniors would mark as *appropriate amount of out-of-class work* might not correspond to the same referent that host-national college faculty would associate with that descriptor. By the same token, ethnographic observations are more likely than quantitative measurement to illuminate disruptive internal social dynamics in a study abroad cohort that might explain some aberrant learning outcome data for that particular group. Qualitative data can often be especially enlightening about *process factors* affecting outcomes in specific settings.

Qualitative data can help researchers contextualize quantitative findings, making them less reductionist. A finding that expert ratings revealed higher average reflectiveness scores for essays written in study abroad than in domestic classes is rather abstract. Such a finding could be made more meaningful to consumers of that research by augmenting that quantitative result with qualitative textual analyses that explicate and support it. (See Wu & Rubin, 2000 for an example of quantitative findings augmented by textual analysis.) In short, Rao and Woolcock (2003) propose that in program evaluations, qualitative and quantitative data collection should occur in parallel or better yet, iteratively and not merely sequentially, with initial qualitative findings feeding into more summative quantitative phases.

Assessment Methodologies for Key Study Abroad Objectives

We now turn to an examination of assessment methodologies explicitly used for study abroad objectives. Anticipated learning outcomes for students studying abroad may be broadly divided into three categories roughly paralleling cognitive, affective, and behavioral learning: knowledge and skills, attitudinal development, and resultant life choices (c.f., Immetman & Schneider, 1998). Assessment of these outcomes will seek to determine whether they are different among study abroad participants than among comparable student populations who have not gone abroad for study. Perhaps more importantly, addressing these outcomes thoroughly will often involve investigating additional influences on study abroad learning outcomes—factors that may explain why some individuals and programs meet more learning objectives than do others. Research on the full set of learning outcomes should help identify key moderating factors that are responsible for individual and programmatic differentials in outcomes achieved.

We have classified these moderating factors into three categories as well: individual differences in sojourners, program design features, and differences in host culture attributes. The first two—individual differences and program design features—will be familiar to educational researchers who are inspired by the extensive research base on aptitude x treatment interactions (ATI) (Cronbach & Snow, 1977; Snow, 1989). The ATI paradigm recognizes that certain instructional environments benefit one type of student more than another. Efficient instruction occurs when educators can match students with instructional methods that are optimal for those students' aptitudes. To this classic ATI educational paradigm we add a third dimension: cultural context. Our commitment is to identify instructional models that match student traits with the particular instructional methods that are optimal *in specified contexts* (e.g., in specific national cultures).

Combining the set of outcome categories with the set of moderating factors graphically yields a three-by-three matrix of researchable impacts of the study abroad experience on academic performance (see Table 1).

Table 1: Classification of Study Abroad Learning Outcomes and Influences

		I: Learning Outcomes		
		A. knowledge/ skills	B. development	C. life choices
II: Moderators	*a. individual differences*	1	4	7
	b. program features	2	5	8
	c. host culture	3	6	9

We examine each of the three learning outcome categories, noting strengths and weaknesses of available instruments for each one, as well as highlighting some existing research about moderating influences on each. Based on literature reviewed for all nine cells, we then note some limits in current scholarship and make suggestions for future research questions and appropriate methodologies for addressing them.

I-A: Knowledge and Skills

The central assessment question with respect to cognitive learning component is whether students who study abroad attain higher levels of achievement in terms of knowledge of course content and assimilation of associated skills than students who take the same courses at their home institution. The type of achievement most often addressed in this way is language learning.

Educators can find a number of instruments and methods to assess linguistic progress, as referenced in Chapter 4. Standardized written and oral tests of language proficiency are commonly administered pre- and post-sojourn (Milleret, 1990; Segalowitz, Freed, Collentine, Lafford, Lazar, et al., 2004), sometimes with a mid-program administration as well (Engle & Engle, 2004). One advantage to using these tools is that they have been refined by years of use, and their validity for specified populations is generally quite high. Because they assign a level to student performance, they can serve as a baseline for later assessments (Milleret, 1990; Wright). In addition, testing companies can make available norm-referenced scores and thus provide local evaluators with evidence for the need to improve program curricula. The *Standards for Foreign Language Learning in the Twenty-first Century* developed by the American Council on Teaching of Foreign Languages also provides a variety of indicators of foreign language competence for all levels of language learners. A major disadvantage to these instruments is that they require extensive, expensive training for the instructors administering them.

Pretesting and posttesting may also be conducted using locally produced tests. Although developing a test specific to the program at hand requires more time on the part of the instructor and sacrifices the possibility of comparing with other institutions, it does allow for greater content validity through shaping items to the specific content of the study abroad course. Locally developed tests may also be less expensive to use and enable educators to be more flexible in administration (Wright).

Other quantitative approaches to assessment of language learning include the use of hypothetical scenarios in which students select the appropriate linguistic response (Kinginger & Farrell, 2004; Vande Berg, et al., 2004), computer-based assessment of reaction time for visual word recognition and lexical access (Segawitz, et al., 2004), and student self-report surveys of language learning (Ingraham & Peterson, 2004). However, we caution that despite their adaptability to a variety of situations and relatively low cost, self-reporting surveys can at best be regarded as providing indirect evidence of knowledge and skills gains. As Wright (p. 6) has observed, ". . . typically [self reports] measure satisfaction and impressions but do not generate information about deeper learning." Surveys should be used only as supplements, not alternatives, to direct testing of learning. Assessments employing a combination of language learning assessment techniques can yield a particularly rich picture of student language gains (e.g., Segawitz, et al., 2004).

Language proficiency may also be assessed qualitatively. Conversation analysis of students with host families combined with ethnographic techniques has yielded unexpected and somewhat disturbing results (Wilkinson, 2002). Student progress can also be assessed by means of audiotaped recordings of class interaction (Talburt & Stewart, 1999); by categorizing of strategies used in the case of communication breakdowns or gaps in conversation (Segalowitz, et al., 2004); and by journal writing in the target language, which instructors can evaluate with respect to syntax, grammar, and writing style (Mendelson, 2004; Milleret, 1990). Although the practice has not been widely applied to study abroad assessment, portfolios of student work provide an additional means of tapping into student learning outcomes (Cambridge, 1996;

Gillman & Rafferty, 1995; Wright). Faculty case study reports and postprogram reports, as well as faculty and student interviews and focus groups, have also been examined for evidence of linguistic achievement in overseas study (Ingraham & Peterson, 2004). Like surveys, however, interviews and focus groups can provide only indirect evidence of academic learning and should be combined with other measures.

Extensive precedence exists for measuring study abroad academic learning outcomes in foreign language classes, but assessments focusing on other types of academic knowledge and skills acquired through study abroad have been relatively rare. With respect to nonlanguage learning outcomes, the most common method at present appears to be simply asking students how much they feel they learned from their experience (e.g., Chieffo, 2006; Stronkhorst, 2005). Although an argument can be made that perceived impact from the perspective of the student is worth studying (Chieffo & Griffiths, 2004), such an approach is not actually measuring either change over time or difference from on-campus students. The dependence on student self-reports of learning is a particular concern in the area of cross-cultural communication competence, an area rarely measured outside of self-reported development. A few promising studies have incorporated instruments designed to evaluate general culture learning, such as formatted worksheets, interviews with the instructor, and even knowledge tests (Milleret, 1990).

One generic knowledge indicator that has been used only infrequently in study abroad research is course grades. Comparisons between student grades in study abroad versus home campus classes, or between different treatment conditions in study abroad programs, could be a straightforward way of assessing learning outcomes. An excellent example of the possibilities of this sort of comparison has been provided by DiBiasio and Mello (2004), who described a carefully formulated procedure for assessing learning outcomes among engineering students. These students, whether studying abroad or domestically, were involved in project-based learning and assessment. The assessment system included performance contract reviews, peer evaluation forms, weekly advisor feedback, graded students reports, and external evaluation of student reports by reviewers recruited and trained for the purpose, as well as a comparison of summative grades. Engineering students who conducted their projects abroad scored significantly better in a number of subject areas than those who did not.

I-A/II-a: Influence of Individual Differences on Knowledge/Skills

To match students with programs that play to their individual learning styles and strengths, it is useful to explore factors that may be associated with variation in individual outcomes. Existing assessments of study abroad language learning that have incorporated individual difference measures into research design have located a number of effects. Gender and previous language background have been found to impact language achievement in overseas programs (Ginsberg, 1992; Rivers, 1998; Stronkhorst, 2005), as has innate language processing ability (Segawitz et al., 2004). Personality factors such as extroversion, as manifested in willingness to make social contact with nationals outside the classroom, have also been demonstrated to impact language learning abroad in some studies (Kinginger & Farrell, 2004; Langley & Breese, 2005; Stronkhorst, 2005), although other studies have shown no association between host culture contact hours and language gains (Mendelson, 2004). Mendelson (2004) has suggested more sensitive measures are needed determine whether language learning is best promoted through specific types of host culture contact.

It is more difficult to locate model studies with respect to individual differences in learning nonlanguage skills abroad. Chieffo (2006) found small differences in subject matter learning between freshman and sophomore college students studying abroad, but used self-report of learning as a measure. The application of learning style or personality inventories to study abroad learning outcome research offers a promising, if underutilized, avenue for future research.

I-A/II-b: Influence of Program Design Features on Knowledge/Skills

Key programmatic features evaluated with respect to study abroad and language learning include: program duration, amount of previous language study, housing arrangements, and context of the course. Contextual factors examined in this regard have included home-institution classes taught by home-institution faculty, special host university courses for study abroad participants taught by host-country faculty, regular university courses taught by host faculty, or a combination of these options (Vande Berg, et al., 2004).

The assessed results of these program design features are sometimes surprising. Educators have supposed, quite naturally, that students who interact frequently with native speakers in authentic situations will have distinct advantages over those whose language learning is limited to the classroom. Although some studies have indeed yielded findings consistent with the immersion hypothesis (e.g., Yager, 1998), particularly with respect to oral fluency (Segawitz, 2004), other studies have concluded that study abroad can actually undermine grammatical accuracy in the target language; students immersed in homestay situations sometimes achieve lesser gains in language proficiency than students who reside in international program residence halls (e.g., Ginsberg, 1992; Rivers, 1998; Veguez, 1984). Similarly, intensive domestic language learning environments have been shown in some cases to yield results comparable to or greater than those achieved by studying abroad, at least in certain specific skill sets such as grammatical abilities (Freed, Segalowitz, and Dewey., 2004; Segalowitz et al., 2004).

Studies exploring the effect of program duration have found (among other things), that although one-year experiences resulted in greater overall linguistic gains than semester-long exposure, student learning curves were steeper during the first semester of language study in a residential program than during the second (Engle & Engle, 2004). Ingraham and Peterson (2004) examined the correlation of length of sojourn with language learning, academic performance, and a set of indicators that they grouped under the term *professional development* that included "choice of a career, awareness of how a student's intended profession may be viewed and practiced differently in different cultures, as well as the acquisition of attitudes and cross-cultural skills that help a person be an effective professional" (p. 96). The longer the program, the stronger the response was in all three areas of learning.

With respect to design of the experience abroad, structured learning activities have been found to be more effective in promoting student language learning than unstructured free time (Van de Berg et al., 2004). Institutional support also seems to be associated with language gains (Stronkhorst, 2005). Although it is presumed that students who choose to study abroad enjoy high levels of internal motivation, external motivation may also play a powerful role. Merva (2003) assessed the difference in student performance between programs in which grades for study abroad were averaged into students' cumulative GPA and those who took courses abroad on a pass/fail basis, controlling for academic ability and other variables. She concluded that the latter policy adversely affects academic incentives and presumably, by extension, achievement of learning outcomes. More recently Trooboff, Cressey, and Monty (2004) came to the opposite conclusion.

Although numerous studies have explored the influence of program design on language learning, a need remains for additional research on questions relating program design features to other learning outcomes.

I-A/II-c: Influence of Host Culture Attributes

Finally, it might be expected that host culture attributes would impact student learning of course content. This expectation has been explored with regard to language learning to some degree, with attitudes and responses of host families toward study abroad participants being shown to affect student language learning outcomes (Wilkinson, 2002), and linguistic distance from home to host culture negatively associated with language learning (Stronkhorst, 2005). Once again, however, the impact of host culture attributes has been little explored outside the subject area of linguistics and language. For example, one might hypothesize that students immersed in cultures with strong traditions of vigorous political debate among citizens would be influenced in the direction of greater civic consciousness; however, empirical verification of such a hypothesis remains incomplete.

In any case, the above findings regarding factors moderating study abroad language learning gains serve to remind educators that learning outcomes from study abroad—just like outcomes on domestic campuses—can be highly variable: Study abroad is no guarantee of satisfactory learning. Carefully designed assessments are essential for discovering whether results are in line with planner expectations.

I-B: Attitudinal Development

International educators predicate objectives with respect to attitudinal outcomes on the assumption that studying abroad accelerates student development along some continua of cognitive and/or affective development. As we have noted, although measures of shifts in individual personality traits such as individual autonomy, cognitive flexibility, and sociability do not necessarily qualify as learning objectives for many study abroad experiences, it is possible that in certain cases courses offered abroad—in fact, almost any courses tagged with the modifier *international*—might identify attitudinal objectives (e.g., Koskinen, 2004; Orahood, Kruze, & Pearson, 2004).

At an institutional level, the attitudinal benefit of study abroad has often been addressed in exit questionnaires that ask participants to evaluate the broad impact the experience has had on their goals and personal traits (e.g., British Columbia Centre for International Education, 2002; Handel & Grove, 1986; Laubscher, 1994), but these self-report satisfaction scales may not measure true learning outcomes. Scales designed to tap specific skill sets related to cognitive and affective outcomes of study abroad provide a measurement option that is less subjective than satisfaction questionnaires, although they retain the inherent weaknesses of all self-report measures. Examples of these instruments include the cross-cultural adaptability inventory (CCAI; Kelly & Meyers, 1995), the Multicultural Personality Questionnaire (Van der Zee & Van Oudenhoven, 2001), the Intercultural Sensitivity Inventory (ICSI; Bhawuk & Brislin, 1992), the Global Competency and Intercultural Sensitivity Index (ISI; Olson & Kroeger, 2001), and probably most frequently used in study abroad research, the Intercultural Development Inventory [IDI] (Hammer & Bennett, 2001). A different approach targeted on academic variables has been proffered in the Intercultural Learning Outcomes scales (Sutton & Rubin, 2004).

These and other similar measures (see review by Paige in Chapter 7) may be used as pretest/posttest measures or for comparing students who have gone abroad with those who have remained on the home campus (e.g., Carlson & Widamon, 1988; Lathrop, 1999; Medina-Lopez-Portillo, 2004; Nash, 1976; Ryan & Twibell, 2000), frequently in conjunction with various demographic factors, personality trait measures, or situational characteristics as moderator variables. Several studies have compared study abroad students not only to nonsojourning colleagues but also to students who intended to go on a study abroad tour but had not yet done so (Drews & Meyer, 1996; Sutton & Rubin, 2004). Such comparisons allow for conjectures regarding whether changes reported are a result of study abroad, or of a selection bias resulting from a preexisting personal dispositions toward continued development of world-mindedness and other qualities.

The affective learning category of outcomes has also been assessed qualitatively by using free association combined with semantic differential scales to tap into stereotypes of other cultures (Drews & Meyer, 1996), by individual interviews of participants pre- and postsojourn (Dolby, 2004), and by student journals and reflection papers (Gray et al., 2002; Lindsey, 2005).

I-B/II-a: Influence of Individual Differences

A number of studies have explored the impact of individual differences on affective changes during study abroad. Among other characteristics, students' individual motives for study abroad (enhance cross-cultural skills, learn subject matter, join with friends; Kisantas, 2004; see also Stronkhorst, 2005), levels of uncertainty and anxiety (Hullet & Witte, 2001), and cultural empathy and open-mindedness (Stronkhorst, 2005) have been found to influence cognitive and affective learning outcomes. Traits of experience-seeking and need for achievement have also been shown to have small effects on outcomes of study abroad (Schroth & McCormack, 2000). In some studies, attitudinal and affective outcomes have varied by student race and ethnicity (Martin, Bradford, & Rohrlich, 1995). Personality traits have also been shown to be associated with emotional expectancy about study abroad programs (Kim & Goldstein, 2005).

I-B/II-b: Influence of Program Design Features

Findings regarding the impact of program design features have generally confirmed expectations. Affective outcomes of study abroad have found to be in direct proportion to program duration (Dwyer, 2004a; Lancaster, 2006; Medina-Lopez-Portillo, 2004; Zorn, 1996). Also, higher levels of cultural immersion in study abroad programs have been shown to promote greater affective learning outcomes (Sell, 1983). Meyer-Lee and Warfield (2006) have proposed that a quantification of the frequency of intercultural engagements (e.g., number of cultural events, other events and establishments catering to locals attended, number of visits to local homes, number of on-campus informal conversations with locals, amount of reading or listening to local news) should also be associated with attitudinal gains, although results of their analysis are at present preliminary.

I-B/II-c: Influence of Host Culture Attributes

Researchers have documented limited connection between affective learning gains in study abroad and attributes of the host culture. One study did find that when members of the host culture violate student expectations, this can detrimentally affect both affective and cognitive learning (Martin et al., 1995). Once again, differences in context likely modify affective growth that results from study abroad experience (see Gudykunst, 1993, 1995). Intuitively we might predict that greater cultural distance between host and home cultures would incline students toward more dramatic affective changes in either positive or negative directions, and that study abroad in a developing nation in Africa might impact students quite differently than study abroad in the developed context of Western Europe. Since cultures differ in their host receptivity or group permeability to foreigners, that factor would also likely exert impact on emotional well being and affective outcomes.

Finally, it should be mentioned that although all learning gains may erode over time, when we speak of changes in attitudes, worldview, and the like, it is particularly important to establish that these gains are not temporary. Several researchers (see review by Sell, 1983; Nash, 1976) have reported that initially recorded changes did not appear to persist after return from overseas. Claims regarding attitudinal shifts apparently need to be reassessed by delayed posttesting after some time has passed to ascertain whether they dissipate as the student reacculturates to life back home, and the memory of the stretching effect of foreign travel recedes. Longitudinal studies of these issues, complicated as they are to conduct, are essential to a full understanding of the role that study abroad plays in the attitudinal development and maturation of participants.

I-C: Life Choices

International educators build on the conviction that real learning, particularly of affective components associated with study abroad, should result in students making life choices that reflect such changes (e.g., Akande & Slawson, 2000; Nash, 1976). A reasonable hypothesis is that alumni of study abroad programs would choose characteristic academic majors, career paths, lifestyles, and residence patterns. This type of assessment attempts to determine whether changes are fleeting or long-term, and whether shifts in attitude translate into transformation in behavior.

Obtaining this sort of data in the medium term is relatively easy; as long as returned study abroad students still reside within the university setting, they are accessible for follow up. Comparative data may be gathered, for instance, on involvement by study abroad alumni versus other students in extracurricular activities on the home campus geared toward increasing international awareness (Gray, et al., 2002) or on shifts that occur in long-term plans following the study abroad experience (e.g., Orahood, Kruze, & Pearson, 2004; Stronkhorst, 2005; Warfield, Ellis, & Cavender, 2006). Once individuals have left the university, however, life choice research entails particular challenges. Locating long-departed alumni can in itself be a daunting task, and getting them to respond to requests for information can be even more difficult.

Alumni survey research is often conducted by organizations like IES, which have a ready roster of alumni and many more years of data available than most university programs. In recent years some universities have also begun to explore long-term impact of their own study abroad opportunities (e.g., DeDee & Stewart, 2003; Messer & Wolter, 2005; Orahood, Kruze, & Pearson, 2004; Sutton & Rubin, 2004), an exercise that we believe is especially critical if a full understanding of the impact of study abroad programs is to be realized. Typical measures in alumni questionnaires include Likert-type items asking respondents to rate the impact of the study abroad experience on a set of life variables (Akande & Slawson, 2000; Dwyer, 2004b), including whether the alumni uses a second language regularly in the workplace, whether they have ever worked overseas or for a multinational corporation, their highest level of education, and so on.

This method is, of course, subject to several empirical objections. It is difficult to obtain a true nonexperimental group for such an effort and nearly impossible to ensure that such a group is truly comparable with the experimental one. Selection bias no doubt influences who chooses to participate in such surveys. Conversely, even without a non-study abroad comparison group, it is possible to draw contrasts among those who studied abroad with respect to the effect of moderating variables of individual, programmatic, and host-cultural differences. A possible alternative to surveys is the use of qualitative methodology such as interviews or focus groups of past study abroad participants (Alred & Byram, 2002; Tonkin & Quiroga, 2004), methods that do not make the claims to generalizability that alumni surveys do.

I-C/II-a: Influence of Individual Differences and Host Culture Attributes on Life Choices

Undoubtedly in large measure because of difficulty of accessing large numbers of study abroad alumni in many organizations and the constraints related to locating an equivalent group for comparison, no examples of life choice outcomes studied in association with individual differences were located for purposes of this chapter. We suggest, though, that it would be valuable to test the effects of individual difference variables such as dogmatism vs. tolerance for ambiguity or academic major on susceptibility of subsequent lifestyle choices to studying abroad.

I-C/II-b: Influence of Program Design Features

Some studies have addressed the influence of various program design features on study abroad alumni lifestyle choices. Duration of program (Dwyer, 2004a), housing and resultant degree of cultural immersion (Dwyer, 2004b), and participation in internships (Dwyer, 2004c) have all been found to impact alumni years later in their lives.

I-C/II-c: Influence of Host Culture Attributes

Research linking life choices made as a result of the study abroad experience with host culture attributes is anecdotal at best. Literature from other fields suggests a number of host culture traits like economic status and ethnic identity of host families, size of emigrè community, and individualistic versus collectivistic orientation of the host culture at large might also impact future lifestyle decisions (see Gudykunst & Lee, 2003; Kim, 2001). To assume, for example, that a study abroad program in Paris would influence the same life choices as a program in Kigali, Rwanda—even though university courses in both nations would be conducted in French—is surely naïve. Thoughtful exploration of the impact of the influence of a wide array of host cultural traits could provide critical information for the design of study abroad opportunities across the disciplinary spectrum.

Although for purposes of discussion, we have split out the cells of the matrix separately, the assessment of study abroad outcomes can be particularly interesting when skills, attitudinal, and life choice indicators are all examined for a single population and the effects of multiple moderators tested conjointly, as in Stronkhort's (2005) examination of learning outcomes of study and work abroad programs at two Dutch universities, Ingraham and Peterson's (2004) multiphased longitudinal investigation of a range of study abroad programs at Michigan State University, and the GLOSSARI project's (Sutton & Rubin, 2004) analysis of an array of student abroad effects across the entire University System of Georgia.

Some Questions and Hypotheses for an Emerging Research Agenda

As preceding sections of this chapter have indicated, much good research work has been conducted (or is in process) to help advance our understanding of how study abroad influences student learning. Much more, however, remains to be done. Although it is beyond the scope of this chapter to formulate a research agenda for the education abroad community, we can suggest some lines of inquiry that may help guide future studies. We premise these suggestions with the recognition that this is a relatively new field of investigation, that its infancy invites varied exploration, and that every piece of research (large-scale and small, quantitative and qualitative, theoretical and practical) helps contribute to a broader understanding of this collective enterprise.

Within the framework of the assessment matrix that we have provided in this chapter, a number of fundamental research questions invite further exploration. The topics below are by no means exhaustive, but they may help guide researchers to promising areas of investigation and help them formulate additional questions. Mapping study abroad objectives and moderating factors onto the assessment matrix has highlighted several broad gaps in current knowledge of learning outcomes of study abroad programming.

In general terms, it is evident that individual differences have captured a great deal of interest as predictors of learning outcomes, as indeed they have received a great deal of attention in literature on intercultural adjustment at large. Structural characteristics of study abroad programs have also been analyzed fairly extensively. What has not been addressed much is the area of features of host culture attributes. Recognition of how study abroad learning outcomes differ in line with host culture characteristics can readily be used to develop site-specific orientation and monitoring procedures and, ultimately, to inform program development efforts.

Also notably scarce in the literature are studies that examine nonlinguistic knowledge and skills, and those that attempt to do so often rely primarily on students' self-reported gains. In terms of assessing the value added to education by a study abroad experience, this is a considerable omission in current scholarship. Excepting institutional benefits of tabulating large numbers of student sojourns every semester, we cannot truly know whether sending students abroad to study is preferable to teaching that student on his or her home campus until we frankly assess whether the actual objectives of the course are fulfilled better in the former context. A prerequisite for such investigation, of course, is the location of adequate learning assessment tools. We believe that such tools, if not immediately available, can be readily developed. Perhaps more to the point is that the will to make such comparisons must also be present, because findings may challenge certain aspects of the status quo.

Future Research Focused on Student Learning Outcomes

Student Learning Outcomes: Knowledge and Skills

The authors of this chapter believe that the single biggest obligation of assessment research in education abroad is to determine whether students acquire substantive knowledge and skills through participation in study abroad programs that they might not otherwise acquire without the study abroad experience. There are many layers of investigation imbedded in this hypothesis, but the fundamental question of qualitatively improved learning of knowledge and skills is central to any discussions about the value of study abroad, the benefits of integrating it into degree programs, the justification for greater institutional investment in study abroad programs, and other bedrock issues in the profession. This is particularly important when those discussions take place between advocates of study abroad and those who are less convinced of (or even hostile to) the presumed intrinsic value of education abroad.

- Do students learn the content of their coursework more effectively, more easily, with greater retention, or with deeper reflection than they do in a domestic classroom setting? Is the content of coursework in fact comparable?

- Do faculty teach better (or worse) in an overseas environment? Neither the education abroad community or the broader higher education assessment community has devoted much serious effort to evaluating the quality of instruction in overseas programs, despite the dominant importance of teaching quality at most US colleges and universities.

- Do students learn more effectively from US faculty abroad or from host national instructors?

- Does the presence (or absence) of learning resources abroad contribute to improved student learning? Do instructors abroad effectively employ authentic sources to strengthen the quality and impact of their teaching, and does this result in greater knowledge gains by students?

- How has access to ubiquitous electronic information changed the learning process abroad? Does the ability to view a computer model of Michaelangelo's David sufficiently simulate seeing the actual sculpture for learning purposes?

- What learning skills do students acquire or improve during an overseas academic program? Do they perfect learning behaviors (navigating new libraries, persisting in completing difficult projects, etc.) that enhance future academic performance?

Student Learning Outcomes: Attitudinal

Much existing research has focused on the changes in students' attitudes toward other peoples and cultures that can result from studying abroad. Intercultural awareness, development, and sensitivity are among the most commonly acknowledged outcomes of many study abroad programs. Other areas of personal growth and development, however, are less documented. Questions along these lines include:

- Do students exercise a greater level of civic engagement as a consequence of studying abroad?
- Do students develop a stronger sense of social responsibility?
- Does the study abroad experience contribute to any greater commitment toward social or economic justice?
- Do students achieve any deeper level of spiritual understanding?

We anticipate that many of the answers to questions like these will vary according to the country in which the student lives and learns. More sophisticated awareness of social responsibility and economic justice may emerge in a country like India, for example, while stronger commitments to civic engagement may develop in European societies.

Student Learning Outcomes: Life Choices

One of the most intriguing areas of research in education abroad is the impact of studying abroad on a person's subsequent life choices in career, further education, community involvement, personal lifestyle, and other decisions that may reflect values acquired from a study abroad experience. Although we are all familiar with the many heartwarming stories of students who met abroad and subsequently married, very limited research exists on this or other life choices and their associations with study abroad. Admittedly this is a very complicated research construct, since there are many variables to consider and many challenges in locating and tracking research subjects.

Two studies funded separately in 2006 by the US Department of Education and by the Council for International Educational Exchange are investigating some of these issues: one, by looking retrospectively at the lives of persons who studied abroad over the past 40 years; the other, by following the lives of current study abroad students during the next three decades. These major investigations will yield important new information about some of the enduring outcomes of the study abroad experience. Still, there are a number of questions that individual researchers can pursue to complement these studies, including:

- Are there intergenerational linkages between the overseas experiences of parents and the study abroad participation of their children? Are these stronger than sibling or peer influences on the decision to go abroad?
- Are study abroad alumni more loyal to their home institutions for providing an overseas component to their education, and are they more generous in contributing funds to support those programs?
- Are a person's affinities for a particular country or culture resulting from study abroad participation sustained over time? Do individuals continue to engage with that culture in other subsequent contexts, or is the experience limited by static parameters and perceptions?

Future Research Focused on the Variables that Influence Student Learning Outcomes

Moderators: Individual differences

Researchers need to focus much greater attention on the influence of individual differences among the study abroad population. A frequent criticism of research in this field is the presumed self-selection of superior students who go abroad and who would therefore naturally achieve greater learning outcomes.

- What are the differences in learning outcomes for students who are going abroad for the first time in their lives, compared to those whose study abroad experience was preceded by a previous overseas stay? Are there learning outcomes that may be attributed to the initial experience of leaving one's homeland that are not subsequently repeated? Conversely are there learning outcomes that only reach significance after a second (or third) venture to a foreign country?
- Do study abroad learning outcomes vary by personality type? The integration of personality inventories (Myers-Briggs, etc.) with learning outcomes assessment may offer important insights.
- Do heritage students process the study abroad experience in different ways than students who lack a familial affinity to the host country, and does this affect their learning outcomes?
- Are there significant differences in learning outcomes among students of different majors, academic aptitude, gender, race, or ethnicity?

Moderators: Host Culture

One of the greatest challenges for education abroad researchers is to determine the extent to which a student's gains in learning outcomes are attributable to the experience of living abroad as opposed to the study abroad program itself. If residence in a foreign country is a primary driver of improved student learning outcomes, researchers still need to identify the components of that experience that have the greatest influence on these results. Any number of overseas environmental factors could account for these gains, including:

- country of residence (considered not just in standard geopolitical regions, but employing other indexes of economic or social development used by agencies such as the World Bank or United Nations);
- demography and geography of residence (rural/urban, country/city size, availability of public transportation, etc.);
- degree of Westernization in the host culture; or
- level of English-language penetration in the host culture (particularly for nonforeign language students).

Moderators: Program Design Features

Conversely, if study abroad programs are decisive in transforming the overseas experience from passive/reactive to active engagement/reflection (which is certainly the founding principle of the education abroad profession), researchers need to conduct rigorous studies that identify which intentional design elements of study abroad programs have the greatest influence on these results.

The identification of particular design features responsible for particular student learning outcomes is problematic, since study abroad programs vary significantly in style and scope. Although some common generic elements appear to spread across certain genres of programs (exchange, study tour, study abroad center, etc.), even here the differences may be more important than their similarities. For example, is a mandatory homestay on a summer program in Germany equivalent to a mandatory homestay on a summer program in Kenya? Even within the same country, different program providers may screen and structure homestays quite differently. And even within the same program, one student's homestay experience may differ greatly from another's, simply because of the personalities, family structures, and amenities involved. So at three separate levels, the identification of a homestay as a causal factor in a student's improved learning outcomes can be misleading.

Thoughtful development of program design taxonomies is a key part of this research process (Engle & Engle, 2004). Among many factors that invite repeated examination across the spectrum of academic programs abroad are:

- Time variables, such as program length, amount of time dedicated to curricular and co-curricular activities, periods of structured immersion in the host culture, periods of unstructured exploration in the host culture, etc.;
- Styles of residence abroad (independent, collective, homestay, hostel, etc.), with primary attention to the qualitative elements of host-culture engagement that attend to each living situation;
- Variety and quality of instruction, evaluated both by student learners and by independent peer faculty;
- Variety and quality of instructional resources, including the use of local resources and authentic materials.

Closing Thoughts

The research questions and hypotheses that we have suggested here do not require large research teams or massive resources. Although large-scale assessment projects have certain benefits that help shape our understanding of the study abroad learning process, smaller scale research can illuminate many particular issues and specific topics. Such research is likewise not limited to any prescribed methodology. Quantitative, qualitative, and mixed method studies can all inform these discussions. The primary responsibility of the researcher is to design a project that is free from unintended bias to the maximum extent possible, and then to execute the research and analysis with honesty and integrity.

There are many reasons why educators have not conducted thorough assessments of study abroad learning outcomes, just as they have for many years resisted learning assessments in higher education generally. Pressures for assessment from accrediting and funding bodies, as described in Chapter 1, can tempt practitioners to tack assessment onto an existing process without spending the time to do it well. This often results in assessment that is not tailored to program-specific learning outcomes, as well as the common use of measures and designs off-the-shelf that do not address appropriate research design strategies.

Study abroad program designers typically do not specify expected learning outcomes that should result from participation on their overseas programs. Consequently, any attempt to measure what these programs achieve may be seriously impaired from the beginning of the investigation. The current expansion of interest in the assessment of study abroad learning outcomes should encourage much greater attention to these issues at the front end of the program development process.

Many of the most prized learning outcomes— advanced critical thinking, cultural understanding, and communicative competence—are often the most difficult to articulate and assess. Educators have for years struggled with these concepts as demonstrable outcomes of the learning process, and academic programs abroad are no exception. Education abroad professionals have a unique opportunity to learn from other assessment movements and, perhaps more importantly, to contribute important new dimensions to this ongoing conversation.

Many educators may fear the possible consequences should a well-planned learning assessment fail to demonstrate meaningful value-added academic experiences in study abroad. We should realistically anticipate that some cherished assumptions about this enterprise may not find support in assessment research. It speaks well of the profession that we are prepared to confront these challenges in a forthright, empirical manner and seek improvements that are driven by our research findings. Well-planned, objective-linked assessment is critical for all stakeholders involved with study abroad efforts. For students to obtain maximum benefit, for faculty to implement effective pedagogy, and for administrators to create optimal program design, we must treat assessment as skilled research design. If study abroad is all that we hope and say it is, it is well worth the effort.

References

Akande, Y., & Slawson, C. (2000). A case study of 50 years of study abroad alumni. *International Educator, 9,* 12–16.

Allan, J. (1996). Learning outcomes in higher education. *Studies in Higher Education, 21,* 93–108.

Alred, G., & Byram, M. (2002). Becoming an intercultural mediator: A longitudinal study of residence abroad. *Journal of Multilingual and Multicultural Development, 25,* 339–362.

American Educational Research Association, American Psychological Association & National Council on Measurement in Education (1999). *Standards for Educational and Psychological Testing.*

Washington, DC: American Educational Research Association.

Bhawuk, D. P. S., Brislin, R. (1992). The measurement of intercultural sensitivity using the concepts of individualism and collectivism. *International Journal of Intercultural Relations, 16,* 413–436.

Barnette, J. J., & Wallis, A. B. (2005). The missing treatment design element: Continuity of treatment when multiple post observations are used in time-series and repeated measures study designs. *American Journal of Evaluation, 26,* 106–123.

Bollag, B. (2004, November 19). Get out of the country, please. *Chronicle of Higher Education, 51, (13).*

Brislin, R. (1986). A cultural general assimilator: Preparation for various types of sojourns. *International Journal of Intercultural Relations, 10,* 215–234.

British Columbia Centre for International Education (2002). *Study abroad impact outcomes report.* Victoria, BC: author.

Cambridge, B.L. (1996). The paradigm shifts: Examining quality of teaching through assessment of student learning. *Innovative Higher Education, 20,* 287–297.

Campbell, D.T., & Stanley, J.C. (1966). *Experimental and quasi-experimental designs for research.* Chicago: Rand McNally College Pub. Co. [Originally published 1963.]

Carlson, J.S., & Widaman, K.F. (1988). The effects of study abroad during college on attitudes toward other cultures. *International Journal of Intercultural Relations, 12,* 1–17.

Cash, W.R. (1993, May). *Assessment of study-abroad programs using surveys of student participants.* Paper presented at the Annual Forum of the Association for Institutional Research, Chicago. [EDRS #ED360925]

Chieffo, L. (2006). The freshman factor: Outcomes of short-term education abroad programs on first-year students. Poster presentation at NAFSA Annual Conference, Montreal.

Chieffo, L., & Griffiths, L. (2004). Large-scale assessment of student attitudes after a short-term study abroad program. *Frontiers: The Interdisciplinary Journal of Study Abroad, 10,* 165–177.

Chin, K. K. (2003). *Open doors: Report on international educational exchange.* New York: Institute of International Education.

Commission on the Abraham Lincoln Study Abroad Fellowship Program (2005). *Global competence and national Needs: One million americans studying abroad.* Washington, DC.

Commission on Institutions of Higher Education of the New England Association of Schools and Colleges. *Summary of the survey on enhancing institutional effectiveness through student outcomes assessment at the undergraduate level.* <http://www.neasc.org/cihe/summary.htm> accessed August 14, 2002.

Cook, T. D., & Campbell, D. T. (1979). *Quasi-experimentation: Design and analysis for field settings.* Chicago: Rand McNally.

Cronbach, L. J., & Snow, R. D. (1977). *Aptitude and instructional methods.* New York: John Wiley.

DeDee, L. S., & Stewart, S. (2003). The effect of student participation in international study. *Journal of Professional Nursing, 19,* 237–242.

Dennis, M. (2004). Looking ahead: Mega-trends in student enrollment. *Administrator, January,* 4, 7.

DiBiasio, D., & Mello, N. A. (2004). Multi–level assessment of program outcomes: Assessing a nontraditional study abroad program in the engineering disciplines. *Frontiers: The Interdisciplinary Journal of Study Abroad, 10,* 237–252.

Dolby, N. (2004). Encountering an American self: Study abroad and national identity. *Comparative Education Review, 48,* 150–173.

Drews, D. R., & Meyer, L. L. (1996). Effects of study abroad on conceptualizations of national groups. *College Student Journal, 30,* 452.

Dwyer, M. M. (2004a). More is better: The impact of study abroad program duration. *Frontiers: The Interdisciplinary Journal of Study Abroad, 10,* 151–163.

Dwyer, M. (2004b). Charting the impact of studying abroad. *International Educator, 13,* 14–17.

Dwyer, M. (2004c). The internship effect: Academic? *International Educator, 13,* 18–20.

Engle, L. & Engle, J. (2004). Assessing Language Acquisition and Intercultural Sensitivity Development in Relation to Study Abroad Program Design. *Frontiers: The Interdisciplinary Journal of Study Abroad,* X, 219–236.

Frechtling, J., & Sharpe, L. (1997). *User-friendly handbook for mixed method evaluations.* Bethesda, MD: National Science Foundation Directorate for Education and Human Resources. Retrieved March 9, 2006 at http://www.nsf.gov/pubs/1997/nsf97153/start.htm

Freed, B.F., Segalowitz, N., & Dewey, D.P. (2004). Context of learning and second language fluency in French: Comparing regular classroom, study abroad, and intensive domestic immersion programs. *Journal of Second Language Learning, 26*, 275–301

Freinberg, B. (2002, May 3). What students don't learn abroad. *Chronicle of Higher Education, 48 (34).*

Gillespie, J., Braskamp, L., & Braskamp, D. (1999). Evaluation and study abroad: Developing assessment criteria and practices to promote excellence. *Frontiers: The Interdisciplinary Journal of Study Abroad, 5,* 101–127.

Gilman, D. A., & Rafferty, C. D. (1995). More than work folders: Using portfolios for educational assessment. *NASSP Practitioner, 21,* ED391836.

Ginsberg, R.B. (1992). *Language gains during study abroad: An analysis of the ACTR data.* (National Foreign Language Center Working Papers), Washington, DC: Johns Hopkins University. [EDRS #ED358717].

Gray, K. S., Murdock, G. K., & Stebbins, C. D. (2002). Assessing study abroad's effect on an international mission. *Change, 34,* 44–51.

Greene, J. C., & Caracelli, V. J. (Eds.) (1997). *Advances in mixed-method evaluation: The challenges and benefits of integrating diverse paradigms* (New Directions for Program Evaluation, No. 74). San Francisco: Jossey-Bass.

Gudykunst, W. B. (1993). Toward a theory of effective interpersonal and intergroup communication: An anxiety/uncertainty management (AUM) perspective. In R. L. Wiseman and J. Koester (Eds.), *Intercultural communication competence* (pp. 33–71). Newbury Park, CA: Sage.

Gudykunst, W. B. (1995). Anxiety/uncertainty management (AUM) theory: Current status. In R. L. Wiseman (Ed.), *Intercultural Communication* (pp. 8–58). Thousand Oaks, CA: Sage.

Gudykunst, W. B., & Lee, C. M. (2003). Cross-cultural communication theories. In W. B. Gudykunst (Ed.), *Cross-cultural and intercultural communication* (pp. 7–34). Thousand Oaks, CA: Sage.

Hadis, B. F. (2005). Gauging the impact of study abroad: How to overcome the limitations of a single-cell design. *Assessment and Evaluation in Higher Education, 30,* 3–19.

Hammer, M. R., & Bennett, M. J. (2001). *The Intercultural Development Inventory (IDI).* Portland, OR: Intercultural Communication Institute.

Handel, B., & Grove, N. (1986). International student exchange programs—Are the educational benefits real? *NAASP Bulletin,* 84–90.

Hill, J., & Woodland, W. (2002). An evaluation of foreign fieldwork in promoting deep learning: A preliminary investigation. *Assessment and Evaluation in Higher Education, 27,* 539–555.

Hullett, C. R., & Witte, K. (2001). Predicting intercultural adaptation and isolation: using the extended parallel process model to test anxiety/uncertainty management theory. *International Journal of Intercultural Relations, 25,* 125–139.

Immetman, A., & Schneider, P. (1998). Assessing student learning in study-abroad programs: A conceptual framework and methodology for assessing student learning in study-abroad programs. *Journal of Studies in International Education, 2,* 59–80.

Ingraham, E.C., & Peterson, D.L. (2004) Assessing the impact of study abroad on student learning at Michigan State University. *Frontiers: The Interdisciplinary Journal of Study Abroad, 10,* 83–100

Institute for International Education of Students. (2003). *The IES MAP for study abroad: Charting a course for quality.* Retrieved on January 6, 2006 from http://www.iesabroad.org.

Kelley, C., & Meyers, J. (1995). *Cross-cultural Adaptability Inventory.* Minneapolis, NV: National Computer Systems.

Kim, R. I., & Goldstein, S. B. (2005). Intercultural attitudes predict favorable study abroad expectations of US college students. *Journal of Studies in International Education, 9,* 265–278.

Kim, Y. Y. (2001). *Becoming intercultural: An integrative theory of communication and cross-cultural adaptation.* Thousand Oaks, CA: Sage.

Kinginger, C., & Farrell, K. (2004). Assessing Developments of Meta-Pragmatic awareness in study abroad. *Frontiers: The Interdisciplinary Journal of Study Abroad, 10,* 19–42.

Koskinen, L., & Tossasvainen, K. (2004). Study abroad as a process of learning intercultural competence in nursing. *International Journal of Nursing Practice, 10,* 111–120.

Lancaster, B. (2006). *Changes that occur abroad: Assessing student outcomes on short-term and long-term study abroad programs.* Poster presentation at NAFSA Annual Conference, Montreal.

Langer, E. (1989). *Mindfulness.* Reading, MA: Addison-Wesley.

Langley, C. S., & Breeze, J. R. (2005). Interacting sojourners: A study of students studying abroad. *The Social Science Journal, 42,* 313–321.

Lathrop, B. J. J. (1999). *The influence of study abroad programs on United States students' psychological development.* Unpublished doctoral dissertation, University of Georgia.

Laubscher, M.R. (1994). *Encounters with difference: Student perceptions of the role of out-of-class experiences in education abroad.* Westport, CN: Greenwood Press.

Lindsey, E. W. (2005). Study abroad and values development in social work students. *Journal of Social Work Education, 40,* 229–250.

Martin, J. N., Bradford, L., & Rohrlich, B. (1995). Comparing pre-departure expectations and post-sojourn reports: A longitudinal study of US students abroad. *International Journal of Intercultural Relations, 19,* 97–110.

McDaniel, E.A., Felder, B.D., Gordon, L., Hrutka, M.E., & Quinn, S. (2000). New faculty roles in learning outcomes education: The experiences of four models and institutions. *Innovative Higher Education, 25,* 143–157.

McMurtrie, B. (2003, March). Iraq conflict sparks protests around the globe. *Chronicle of Higher Education, 49:29,* A10–A11.

Medina-Lopez-Portillo, A. (2004) Intercultural learning assessment: The link between program duration and the development of intercultural sensitivity. *Frontiers: The Interdisciplinary Journal of Study Abroad, 10,* 179–200.

Mendelson, V. G. (2004). Hindsight is 20/20: Student perceptions of language learning and the study abroad experience. *Frontiers: The Interdisciplinary Journal of Study Abroad, 10,* 43–63.

Merva, M. (2003). Grades as incentives: A quantitative assessment with implications for study abroad programs. *Journal of Studies in International Education, 7,* 149–156.

Messer, D., Wolter, S. C. (2005). Are student exchange programs worth it? *IZA Discussion Papers 1656.* Institute for the Study of Labor. Retreived January 10, 2006 at http://ideas.repec.org/cgi bin/ref.cgi!handle=RePEc:iza:izadps: dp1656&output=0.

Meyer-Lee, E., & Warfield, C. (2006). Assessing impact: Study abroad at two institutions. Paper presented at the AIEA Annual Conference, San Diego.

Milleret, M. (1990). Evaluation and the summer language program abroad: A review essay. *The Modern Language Journal, 74,* 73–78.

Nash, D. (1976). The personal consequences of a year of study abroad. *The Journal of Higher Education, 47,* 191–203.

National Center for Education Statistics (2006). *The Condition of Education 2006.* Washington, DC: US Department of Education.

Olson, C. L., & Kroeger, K. R. (2001, Summer). Global competency and intercultural sensitivity. *Journal of Studies in International Education, 5,* 116–137.

Orahood, T., Kruze, L., Pearson, D. E. (2004). The impact of study abroad on business students' career goals. *Frontiers: The Interdisciplinary Journal of Study Abroad, 10, 117–130.*

Patton, M. (1987). *How to use qualitative methods in evaluation.* Newbury Park, CA: Sage.

Rao, V., & Woolcock, M. (2003). Integrating qualitative and quantitative approaches in program evaluation. In F. J. Bourguignon & L. P. da Silva (Eds.), *The impact of economic policies on poverty and income distribution: Evaluation techniques and tools* (pp. 165–190). New York: The World Bank and Oxford University Press.

Rivers, W.P. (1998). Is being there enough? The effects of homestay placements on language gain during study abroad. *Foreign Language Annals, 31*, 492–500.

Rundstrom Williams, T. (2005) Exploring the impact of study abroad on students' intercultural communication skills: Adaptability and sensitivity. *Journal of Studies in International Education, 9,* 356–371.

Ryan, M. E., & Twibell, R. S. (2000). Concerns, values, stress, coping, health and educational outcomes of college students who studied abroad. *International Journal of Intercultural relations, 24,* 409–435.

Schmidt-Rinehart, B. C., & Knight, S. M. (2004). The homestay component of study abroad: Three perspectives. *Foreign Language Annals, 37,* 25–262.

Schroth, M. L., & McCormack, W. A. Sensation seeking and need for achievement among study-abroad students. *The Journal of Social Psychology, 140,* 533–535.

Segalowitz, N., Freed, B., Collentine, J., Lafford, B., Lazar, N., & Diaz-Campos, M. (2004). A comparison of Spanish second language acquisition in two different learning contexts: Study abroad and the domestic classroom. *Frontiers: The Interdisciplinary Journal of Study Abroad, 10,* 1–18.

Sell, D. K. (1983). Research on attitude change in US students who participate in foreign study experiences. *International Journal of Intercultural Relations, 7,* 131–147.

Sideli, K. (2001). Outcomes Assessment and Study Abroad Programs: Commentary on the Results of a SECUSSA/IIE Electronic Sampling. *International Educator, X*: 2, 30.

Smith, A. (1983). International communication through study abroad: Some priorities and pitfalls for future research. *European Journal of Education, 18,* 139–150.

Snow, R. (1989). Aptitude-Treatment interaction as a framework for research on individual differences in learning. In P. Ackerman, R. M. Sternberg, & R. Glaser (Eds.), *Learning and individual differences.* New York: W. H. Freeman.

Stronkhorst, R. (2005). Learning outcomes of international mobility at two Dutch institutions of higher education. *Journal of Studies in International Education, 9,* 292–315.

Sutton, R. C., & Rubin, D. L. (2004). The GLOSSARI Project: Initial findings from a system-wide research initiative on study abroad learning outcomes. *Frontiers: The Interdisciplinary Journal of Study Abroad, 10,* 65–82.

Talburt, M. S., and Stewart, M. A. (1999). Race, gender, and "living culture." *The Modern Language Journal, 85,* 175–173.

Thomas, D.C. (2006). Domain and development of cultural intelligence: The importance of mindfulness. Group and Organization Management, 31, 78–99.

Tonkin, H., & Quiroga, D. (2004). A qualitative approach to the assessment of international service learning. *Frontiers: The Interdisciplinary Journal of Study Abroad, 10,* 131–149.

Trooboff, S., Cressey, W., & Monty, S. (2004) Does study abroad grading motivate students? *Frontiers: The Interdisciplinary Journal of Study Abroad, 10, 201–217.*

U. S. Office of Management and Budget. (2005). *Performance Assessment Rating Tool.* Accessed May 2, 2006 at http://www.whitehouse.gove/omb/part/.

Van der Zee, K. I., & Van Oudenhoven, J. P. (2001). The multicultural personality questionnaire: Reliability and validity of self- and other ratings of multicultural effectiveness. *Journal of Research in Personality, 35,* 278–288.

Vande Berg, M. J. (2004). Introduction. *Frontiers: The Interdisciplinary Journal of Study Abroad, 10,* xii–xxii.

Vande Berg, M. J., Balkcum, A., Scheid, M., & Whalen, B. J. (2004). The Georgetown university consortium project: A report from the halfway mark. *Frontiers: The Interdisciplinary Journal of Study Abroad, 10,* 101–116.

Veguez, R. (1984, April). *The oral proficiency interview and the junior year abroad: Some unexpected results.* Paper presented at the Annual Northeast Conference on the Teaching of Foreign Languages, New York. [EDRS #ED253075]

Warfield, C. L., Ellis, J. F., Cavender, D. H. (2006). Assessing institutional impact of study abroad at two institutions. Paper presented at the AIEA Annual Conference, San Diego.

Wellman, J.V. (2001, March). Assessing state accountability systems. *Change, 33,* 47–55.

Wilkinson, S. (2002). The omnipresent classroom during summer study abroad: American students in conversation with their French hosts. *The Modern Language Journal, 86,* 157–173.

Wright, B. D. (n.d.) *Strengths and weaknesses: Tests, surveys, interviews, portfolios, and inventories.* Washington, DC: American Council on Education. Retrieved March 6, 2006 at http://www.acenet.edu/AM/Template.cfm?Section=Home&Template=/CM/ContentDisplay.cfm&ContentID=2834

Wu, S-Y., & Rubin, D.L. (2000). Evaluating the impact of collectivism and individualism on argumentative writing by Chinese and North American college students. *Research in the Teaching of English, 35*, 148–178.

Yager, K. (1998). Learning Spanish in Mexico: The effect of informal contact and student attitudes on language gain. *Hispania, 81*, 898–913.

Zernike, K. (2002, August 4). Tests are not just for kids: Accountability hits higher education. *New York Times Education Supplement* (Section 4A), 26–29.

Zorn, C. R. (1996). The long-term impact on nursing students of participating international education. Journal of Professional Nursing, 112, 106–111.

Chapter 3

Areas of Study in Outcomes Assessment

Elaine Meyer-Lee, Joy Evans

Introduction

Quality research on international programs is crucial to understanding their impact on student learning and informing their designs. All quality research must begin with thoughtful research questions. Before we can dive into considering methods, research designs, or measures for assessing outcomes as described in the last chapter, we need to carefully decide exactly what type of outcomes to assess. While this may seem obvious, it can be very tempting to simply follow the current best-practice method for assessing outcomes, which then constrains the areas one can study. As Maslow once wrote, "If the only tool you have is a hammer, everything looks like a nail."

The question of what outcomes we want to assess may be largely determined by why we are assessing them, and who we are—whether we are primarily scholars of the topic or education abroad practitioners. We assess some outcomes in a basic research sense for pure theory building or charting the terrain of student growth, and the field is blessed to have an increasing number of academicians and graduate students who have the luxury of doing so. Most of us, though, are probably educators who are responsible for carrying out some aspect of international programs. We thus want to assess their outcomes and apply what we learn to further our work in fairly concrete ways.

In the case of either scholar or practitioner, it is wise to first allow oneself to generate and articulate possible assessment ideas as if anything were possible. Engaging in lively dialog with respected colleagues to define and refine these ideas can be most useful at this point. (The bulk of this chapter outlines many areas of potential study in outcomes assessment to facilitate this brainstorming process, but it is by no means exhaustive and should not be seen as limiting.) After this unedited visioning, one can turn to narrowing down these options by taking into consideration the realities of the situation, including audience(s) for or commissioners of the assessment, and the resources available.

Possible audiences were described in detail in Chapter 1, but it is important to note here that the outcomes one chooses to assess would vary considerably if one were conducting the assessment, for example, to promote the benefits of education abroad to students, their parents, or prospective students; convince a skeptical science professor of its merits; showcase to the president or a donor the effectiveness of some recent improvements; point out areas needing improvement to onsite staff members; contribute to a self-study for reaccreditation; or seek publication in a specific scholarly journal. Carefully considering the intended audience should help identify the most promising outcomes to assess.

Another reality shaping the outcomes that can be assessed is the amount of available resources, including time, money, expertise, and the nature of the students and programs in the particular institutional context. Excellent outcomes assessment can be very resource-intensive, and so this phase of the assessment design can be painful. Important outcomes to assess almost always outstrip the resources available to assess them, and setting aside worthy ideas to focus on just a feasible few, though necessary, can bring grief.

Before enumerating various types of outcomes one could assess, it is important to define an *outcome*. An outcome most generally can be any kind of end result, impact, effect, or consequence of something; in this case, of education abroad. We have divided these possible areas of study into two major categories: direct impact of education abroad on individual participants (students, alumni, or faculty and staff); and indirect impact of education abroad on participants' contexts. The first category of direct outcomes for individual participants brings us into the complex area of individual change, which requires a bit more definition.

An outcome of an experience for an individual could technically be as simple as becoming angry or gaining weight; however, individual change in an educational context usually refers to more complex and directional processes of growth, learning, or development. Some scholars use the terms *growth* and *learning* quite distinctly, with growth referring to primarily maturational changes, and learning referring to changes that are explicitly instilled from the outside context. We would argue from a developmental perspective that this dichotomy is largely false, however, especially in an experiential learning environment such as education abroad, where content learning can trigger immense personal growth, which in turn leads to more openness to content learning.

We will therefore use the terms *development*, *learning*, *growth*, and *impact* throughout this chapter almost interchangeably and quite broadly to mean any directional patterns of change over time. Directionality goes beyond just cause and effect to suggest patterns of movement along pathways from earlier starting points toward later, at least theoretical, endpoints, with change processes in between. Implicit in this definition of development is the fact that labeling certain directional changes over time as positive (or growth or progress), such that later positions are seen as more desirable, involves enormous value judgments. There seems to be sufficient consensus in the field of international education about kinds of thinking, feeling, and behaviors that are to be encouraged, however, to warrant explicitly adopting those values in this chapter.

Direct Impact of Education Abroad on Participants

When considering what areas of outcomes to assess in international education, often the first question asked is, How did studying abroad affect the students? This is actually a very large question. A way to subset this question is by asking, What are the direct impacts of studying abroad? Then we determine which directly impacted population we are most interested in assessing. Students are an obvious place to start, but faculty and staff either lead or participate on study abroad programs as well. Thus, the direct impacts of international education can be measured with three discrete populations: currently enrolled students, alumni, faculty and staff.

Determining the population of a study is one way of organizing how to approach the possible areas of study. Of the three populations, currently enrolled students are the most accessible. However, contacting alumni to assess the longer-term impacts may be possible through collaborations with on-campus departments that routinely contact alumni, such as the development, alumni relations, or institutional research offices. While faculty and staff may also be an accessible on-campus population, do consider the political repercussions of faculty assessments such as who will have access to the results. Factors such as these have traditionally made assessing current students' outcomes the most frequent place to begin an assessment of education abroad.

Current Students: What immediate direct impacts does study abroad have on students?

The areas for assessing how study abroad immediately and directly affects current students can be broadly categorized into four categories of development: language learning, intercultural competence (including host-culture specific knowledge), disciplinary knowledge, and social growth. These categories serve as a way to further refine the research questions within the area of direct impact of education abroad. For the purposes of assessment, the more we refine the area or question of research, the easier it is to identify appropriate methods of study. While some scholars argue that language skills are an integral component of intercultural competence and would not separate the two (Byram, 2000), we would argue that not all study abroad programs involve language acquisition. People can also develop intercultural competence within domestic or host environments that may not require foreign language skills.

Language Learning

Studying abroad can have a significant impact on student's ability to learn another language as opportunities to use the language outside the classroom can abound. Consider whether you are interested in students' self-assessment of their proficiency levels in relation to activities of daily life abroad or in objectively measuring students' oral, written and aural skill.

Intercultural Competence

As students learn and live in another culture, they have the opportunity to develop new levels of intercultural competence. Many characteristics could be involved in people's capacity for intergroup relating, and theorists and researchers have parsed, named, and grouped these components or dimensions in many different ways. Clearly, all administrators, scholars, and international professionals do not define even *competence* in the same way (Deardorff, 2004), and agreeing on a working definition of intercultural competence for the field of study abroad is an imperative (see chapter 8 on defining terms). Broadly constructed, intercultural competence can be subdivided into three areas: cognitive/knowledge, affective/attitudes, and behavior/skills. Some empirical evidence indicates that the feeling or affective (and perhaps even unconscious) aspect of attitude is slower to change than the abstract beliefs or cognitive aspects, and perhaps more directly linked to a person's actual behavior (Meyer-Lee, 1995). Considered all together, these three areas help educators assess the complex and interconnected development that can take place when students have daily opportunities to experience intercultural engagement.

Cognitive/knowledge

Studying abroad directly affects students' understanding of cultural differences and cultural interactions, often reported as a life-changing, epiphanal experience. In addition to knowledge about culture in general, students may also acquire rich, culture-specific knowledge pertaining to the host culture or cultures, which can help to overcome prior stereotyped thinking. Student outcomes can also include new levels of broader global awareness, also sometimes referred to as international perspective or world-mindedness. And finally, studying abroad can affect students' general ability to think critically and to reflect on personal learning experiences.

Affective/attitudes

The primary outcomes of education abroad in terms of attitudes can be subdivided into attitudes toward self (identity) and attitudes toward others. At the level of self, consider assessing students' national, cultural or citizenship identity. Erikson

(1968), charted the general territory of formation of identity—developing a coherent sense of who one is, who one is not, what one stands for, and how one is seen. Tajfel (1981) then built on that, defining ethnic identity as that part of an individual's identity that derives from his or her membership in a social group, together with the value and emotional significance attached to that membership. Many theorists have mapped out specific models of ethnic identity development (White & Burke, 1987; Phinney, 1990; Smith, 1991; Rowe, Bennett Atkinson, 1994), and also racial identity development (Cross, 1971; Jackson, 1976; Hardiman, 1979; Helms, 1984; Ponterotto, 1988). In assessing attitudes towards self, one could explore everything education abroad participants think and feel about their own culture, nationality, and place in society. This might include critical self-awareness or intrapersonal knowledge, as well as personal values, worldview/belief systems, and vocation.

At the level of *other*, we would assess changes in students' attitudes toward other cultures. Attitudes—specifically, cultural attitudes—have been defined many different ways and have been much studied with whole books charting the terrain. In general, attitude refers to a person's value position in regards to something else; in this case how favorably or unfavorably a person thinks or feels about those of a different culture or country. Although attitudes are primarily affective, referring to how a person feels about relating to those of other culture, they are interrelated with cognitive aspects such as stereotyped thinking about specific cultural groups, or abstract beliefs about or explanations of intercultural relating. Specific attitudes toward others that could be affected by education abroad might include curiosity, openness, de-centering, intercultural sensitivity, respect, empathy, prejudice, and bias, to name just a few.

Behavior/skills

Behavioral outcomes may be some of the most desired by international educators. Unfortunately, real-life behaviors are also some of the hardest to assess economically, since self-report or even laboratory behavior is not necessarily an accurate indicator. Consider exploring the following skills that study abroad can impact: adaptability or tolerance for ambiguity; communication style (the ability to apply cognitive learning); observation skills; development of new styles or strategies for learning information; the ability to effectively function in multicultural groups (sometimes called *transnational competence*), and increased academic achievement.

Disciplinary Knowledge

Within every study abroad experience in addition to intercultural knowledge, the student may gain new levels of disciplinary knowledge as a result of the location. This could also include the ability to apply disciplinary knowledge such as within the field of international business. Normally, assessment of learning outcomes in disciplinary knowledge such as art history in Rome or biology in Ecuador would take place within the course context, through assignments and grades, but it could also be done through research projects, work by students with faculty upon return, or sharing this learning with others in presentations, course modules, or other exhibits.

Social and Emotional Growth

The final area of direct impact of education abroad on current students is social and emotional growth. Education abroad may increase students' independence, maturity, social development, general interpersonal relating skills, and confidence levels, whether these are explicit goals or not. Students themselves as well as their parents often report dramatic outcomes in these areas. Keep in mind the level of independence afforded to students varies considerably in different education abroad programs. For example, short-term programs may allow students less free time to travel on their own or make decisions away from the group.

Alumni: What long-term direct impacts did study abroad have on students?

There are four areas for assessing long-term direct impacts of study abroad on alumni. First, all of the student outcomes mentioned above to assess the immediate impact could also be assessed for longer-term effects. The other long-term direct outcomes of education abroad include affecting the following: student's careers, students' academic progression, and students' institutional loyalty to their home campus.

Language Learning, Intercultural Competence, Disciplinary Knowledge, and Social Development

To understand the long-term or lasting impacts on students' personal learning, one can assess alumni's language skills, intercultural competence, disciplinary knowledge, and social/emotional development as detailed above for current students. This follow-up data collection is a crucial area of research, as education abroad is certainly intended to have permanent outcomes. Ideally, assessment both immediately after education abroad as well as some years later could establish whether the immediate outcomes diminished over time, stayed about the same, or even increased.

Career Impact

Education abroad can impact students' career development in several ways. Employers who value the skills developed during education abroad may be willing to pay for those skills, so that the students' investment in studying abroad has long-term economic returns in terms of salary. In addition, students may obtain their job of choice because of skills developed abroad, which will affect their levels of satisfaction with their career. Finally, they may gravitate toward lines of work with an international dimension or a multicultural dimension.

Academic Progression

Studying abroad can directly impact a student's desire, as well as ability, to succeed in graduate or professional school. Assessing whether education abroad impacts students' academic progression can include exploring students' motivation to do graduate work, their confidence in their academic abilities, or the actual matriculation rate of study abroad participants into graduate programs.

Institutional Loyalty

Understanding the long-term effects that participating in education abroad has on alumni loyalty to their home institution may be of interest to multiple administrative audiences. Exploring how the bonds students made with students from their home institution affect alumni participation rates in alumni clubs and activities, as well as how alumni's attitudes shifted toward the home institution over time after their experiences abroad, could yield useful data.

Faculty and Staff: What direct impacts has education abroad had on faculty and staff who participated?

Again, while researchers often overlook this area in study abroad assessment, the direct impacts that academics and professionals experience from their involvement with education abroad can and should be assessed, since the more they develop their own international knowledge and skills, the more they can teach these to others. Several of the areas of personal learning that can be assessed in current students and alumni can also be explored with faculty and staff, including language learning and intercultural competence. In addition, particularly in regard to faculty but possibly staff as well, we can assess changes in the faculty member's professional approach.

Language Learning and Intercultural Competence

For faculty and staff, practicing another language or intercultural skills provides opportunities to improve these skills. It is extremely important to assess outcomes for faculty members' own development (as detailed above under current students); their level of intercultural competence cannot be assumed, and their own growth can trickle down to affect many students over the course of their careers. However, outcomes for faculty or staff may not show the same patterns as for students.

Changes in Professional Approach

Education abroad can directly impact faculty members' academic focus and direction in several ways. As a result of their involvement with education abroad, they might develop new courses, which could be offered at the home institution or abroad. Faculty members might employ new pedagogies or teaching styles within existing courses to expose their home-campus students to different ways of learning. A shift in the research agenda of faculty members could occur after their involvement with education abroad. Their advising behavior might change (positively or negatively) after being engaged with the institution's education abroad programs. A faculty member's amount of service on internationally focused committees could shift. The number of international grants a professor receives might be affected, and his or her willingness or ability to work in cross-disciplinary approaches might change as well. All of these areas could be explored that would lead to further documentation of the direct affects of education abroad on the faculty and staff of the home institution.

Indirect Impact of Education Abroad on Participants' Contexts

Beyond these many significant outcomes for individuals participating in education abroad, potential indirect or secondary outcomes also exist for the program's broader contexts. Some of these might result from conscious intercultural leadership efforts by transformed individuals, and others might just occur almost by osmosis. For example, one could examine various aspects of home departments or institutions that send large numbers of students abroad for ripple effects, including policies, finances, and the campus climate. Policy outcomes might be evidenced in mission statements, curriculum requirements, or even the criteria for hiring, promotion, and tenure. Campus climate outcomes could be seen in changes in students and faculty or staff who do not participate in education abroad but relate to many others who do.

Given the current, economically difficult times, there are many compelling reasons to assess the promising outcomes of education abroad for the financial health of the institution. First, especially for tuition-driven schools, documenting the outcome of a strong education abroad program for admissions is extremely helpful. Similarly, effects on retention and time to graduation would be very important for enrollment management. Turning to the other major revenue sources, assessing the outcome of education abroad in terms of alumni giving rates, and whether the possible increased alumni loyalty discussed above translates into dollars, can be informative. And finally, one could assess the outcome of international programs in motivating other donations or corporate or foundation grants.

Beyond even the participants' home institution, outcomes for the local community exist in areas such as employers' report of value in the workplace, or as participation rates in service-learning or civic engagement. We would expect these community outcomes to grow as educators increasingly try to explicitly facilitate them. At the state and national level, one could examine the voting records of politicians who studied abroad for evidence of outcomes. One could also study education abroad alumni for participation rates in federal programs such as the Fulbright, and for any application of language and culture skills for national security. Finally, one could even study the host country community for outcomes, including changes in the host family or roommates.

Conclusion

This chapter has illustrated the wide range of areas that could be assessed within education abroad to help generate ideas and clarify research questions. A good place to start is deciding exactly what aspects of direct and indirect outcomes of education abroad for participants and their contexts you are most interested in assessing. However, one does not need to stop with assessment of outcomes in isolation; one can go on to use these data to answer relevant comparative questions.

Often the most useful assessments of education abroad are in looking at how outcomes correlate with other variables. One might want to explore the differential impacts (both direct and indirect) of international programs in different host countries, with various program models, lengths of program, etc. Currently, taxonomies within the field are being developed to help think about and organize research in relation to program design (Engle and Engle, 2003). Alternatively, it is instructive to correlate outcomes with various individual student characteristics such as age, previous experience, motivation, major, or personal intercultural engagement. Finally, as we build a corpus of data on outcomes, we will increasingly be able to compare impacts (direct and indirect) across generations or at least time periods: For example, are outcomes the same as they were before the events of 9/11, and if not, how do they differ?

Discerning what outcomes one is trying to assess, as well as what variables one might want to be able to correlate with them, is essential before plunging into assessment design. In other words, the refining of assessment questions must be driven by *what* outcomes one wants to understand before deciding *how* to gather the information.

References

Byram, M. (2000). Assessing intercultural competence in language teaching. *SPROGFORUM*, No. 18, Vol. 6, 2000, pp. 9. Available Online: http://inet.dpb.dpu.dk/infodok/sprogforum/Espr18/byram.html

Cross, W.E. (1971). The Negro-to-Black conversion experience: Toward a psychology of black liberation. *Black World.* 20(9), 13–27.

Deardorff, Darla K. (2004). The identification and assessment of intercultural competence as a student outcome of internationalization at institutions of higher education in the United States. North Carolina: North Carolina State University. EdD. 2004. xi, 324 p. Includes bibliographical references. Dissertation Available Online: http://www.lib.ncsu.edu/theses/available/etd-06162004-000223/unrestricted/etd.pdf

Engle, Lilli & Engle, John. (2003). Study abroad levels: Toward a classification of program types. *Frontiers: The interdisciplinary journal of study abroad*, Volume IX, Fall, pp 1–20.

Erikson, Erik. (1968). *Identity: Youth and Crisis*. New York: Norton.

Hardiman, R. (1979). *White identity development theory.* Unpublished manuscript, University of Massachusetts, Amherst.

Helms, J. (1984). Toward a theoretical explanation of the effects of race on counseling: A black and white model. *Counseling Psychologist, 12*, 153–165.

Jackson, B. (1976). Black identity development. In Golubschick, L. & B. Persky (Eds.), *Urban social and educational issues* Dubuque, IA: Kendall/Hunt.

Meyer-Lee, Elaine. (1995). White adults moving beyond ethnocentrism: A critical review of the literature. Qualifying Paper. Harvard University.

Phinney, J. (1990). Ethnic identity in adolescents and adults: Review of research. *Psychological Bulletin, 108,* 499–514.

Ponterotto, J. (1988). Racial consciousness development among white counselor trainees: A stage model. *Journal of multicultural counseling and development, 16,* 146–156.

Rowe, W., Bennett, S., & Atkinson, D. (1994). White racial identity models: A critique and alternative proposal. *Counseling Psychologist, 22*(1), 129–146.

Smith, E. J. (1991). Ethnic identity development: Toward the development of a theory within the context of majority/minority status. *Journal of Counseling & Development, 70*(1), 181–188.

Tajfel, Henri. (1981). *Human groups and social categories.* Cambridge: Cambridge University Press.

White, C., & Burke, P. (1987). Ethnic role identity among Black and White college students: An interactionist approach. *Sociological Perspectives, 30*(3), 310–331.

Chapter 4

How to Begin: Key Decision Points in the Assessment Process

Lee Sternberger, Bruce LaBrack, Brian Whalen

To Assess or Not to Assess: Issues and Implications

As with other forms of research in international education, the act of assessing student learning outcomes is both an art and a science. It requires a clear understanding of research design and methods, an appreciation for the contributions of relevant professional expertise, an informed understanding of the human condition, a willingness to bear scrutiny, and an openness to feedback and approaches that may be unfamiliar. Because the various phases of assessment are interdependent and complex, it is important to have sufficient understanding of how an assessment project is best designed on the front end, so that the data that are eventually gathered are actually able to answer project questions.

This chapter provides an overview of the major assessment issues that you—an administrator, faculty member, program director, or project coordinator—need to know if you are contemplating or planning to conduct an assessment of an international learning experience. By the end of this chapter, you will know something of the dos and don'ts that are integral to high-quality assessment, and why assessment and research are inextricably linked. You will also become aware of the questions and issues you will have to address along the way, and the kinds of people, processes, steps, and resources that will be necessary to execute a successful assessment project. This chapter does not answer detailed questions on assessment methods, research design, data analysis, or statistics. In addition to the references we include in this chapter, we also recommend that you consult experts in appropriate areas who will be best positioned to recommend materials that are relevant to your specific needs and circumstances.

Successful engagement in an effective assessment program or research project requires planning, time, skill, and resources. But it also requires the willingness to engage in complex and challenging discussions and decision-making regarding the nature and form of research itself, and the analysis, implications, and reporting of the concomitant results. Ultimately, the process of assessment is iterative; with each successive round of refinements and inquiry, we learn more about the relevance of identified outcomes, the effectiveness of our measures, and the meaningfulness of the information generated. Thus, perhaps the first and most basic message here is:

in order to complete an assessment project that will be recognized as credible by the larger professional community, one must be willing and able to commit deeply, knowingly, and for the long haul. If you make such a commitment, the design, implementation, and analysis of a well-conceived assessment project can be fascinating, relevant, and immensely rewarding, both personally and professionally.

Although the effects of assessment within higher education may be revolutionary, the causes are not particularly surprising. In an age of accountability, it is not unexpected that legislators, accreditors, and those who administer funding systems increasingly are asking, "What are we getting for our higher education dollars?" and "Are we doing what we say we are doing?" Administrators and faculty who recognize the inevitability, if not legitimacy, of such questions and obtain assessment data to support educational endeavors enhance the likelihood of demonstrably improving their particular programs and providing evidence of their effectiveness to those ultimately responsible for authorizing necessary resources. Note the deliberate inclusion of two standards here: *demonstrably improve* and *provide evidence.* Quality assessment offers much more than data to prove that a program is worthy; it also provides information that can be used to modify and improve various aspects of the program design.

The assessment movement also arises from the need for institutions and administrators to respond flexibly and with agility to changing student interests and societal needs. International education in general, and study abroad in particular, are not immune to these expectations for increased responsiveness as well as accountability and effectiveness. As anyone who works within this field can attest, some administrators and faculty members still view study abroad as suspect, no more than junkets for drinking and shopping, and in rare cases, this is unfortunately true. Yet, those who work seriously in the field of study abroad have abundant anecdotal evidence as well as intuitive awareness that study abroad is powerfully transformational for the vast majority of participants. However, few of us have systematic data to support our claims. Thus, the need for the assessment of learning outcomes is as essential, if not more essential, to international education as it is to other programs within higher education.

As with other processes and decisions within higher education, the potential downsides of assessment should not be underestimated. It takes considerable time, energy, and resources to do assessment well. Moreover, assessment results may not be favorable; they may be instructive but not necessarily positive. Complicating matters, when done poorly, assessment processes can easily generate hostility and mistrust—particularly among the faculty who typically are responsible for the actual process of gathering information—without providing meaningful results. In the final analysis, the *con* argument is not particularly persuasive, mainly because it is predicated on either the hassle factor or the fear of what may be discovered. The pressure to assess is not going to abate anytime soon, and is likely to increase over the long term; the most adaptive response is not to avoid the issue, but to face it squarely and acquire—or hire—the knowledge and skills that are necessary and sufficient to complete a competent assessment process.

The Beginnings of a Plan: Knowing Enough to Get Started

To assess any set of student learning outcomes effectively and efficiently, you will need adequate information and expertise. Perhaps the best place to start is to ask yourself this question: Do I know enough to get started? Many international education administrators may have engaged in research in graduate school, but few are assessment experts. Rarely does one not specifically trained in this area have the breadth of expertise and knowledge necessary to make informed choices regarding research design and methods, the development of student learning outcomes, the choice of instruments and procedures, the analysis of data, and the implementations of assessment results. However, assessment research requires some knowledge of the topics just listed; you simply must put aside time from an already overburdened schedule to read enough on assessment and research design to be able to think through the major issues. And certainly, with a number of publications on the assessment of student learning outcomes in press, there are materials with which to start.[1]

A second and accompanying question to consider at the outset is: Do you need to engage the talents of an assessment consultant, whether internal or external to your institution? Faculty members and colleagues who are trained in the art and science of assessment—as psychometricians, statisticians, methodologists, and in other related disciplines—can be of enormous help in the design, implementation, and analysis processes. Assessment consultants can provide invaluable help as support people, facilitating the design, process, and cycle of assessment over time. Most universities and colleges have faculty members with this sort of expertise who are willing (with some wooing or a small stipend) to assist in the development of an assessment program. However, it may be more effective to engage an external consultant who has specialized skills or can provide information from an outsider's perspective. Regardless of whether you choose a colleague in your organization or someone from an external institution, seeking insights from others with assessment and research expertise is always beneficial.

In selecting such an individual, we must emphasize one very important caveat: assessment may mean different things to different people. Although a detailed explication of this issue exceeds the scope of this article, the most basic point here is that if your project is designed to assess the effectiveness of various international learning experiences and/or will involve the development or appraisal of actual assessment measures (e.g., questionnaires, surveys, or instruments), it is essential that the assessment consultant you engage has demonstrable relevant expertise with research and assessment design, development, and analysis. Assessment experts come in all shapes and sizes; make sure that at least one of the consultants you engage has such expertise.

Assuming you have armed *yourself* with enough of an understanding to begin considering the details of assessment, the next step is to decide what you want to assess and why. What is your motivation for implementing an assessment program? What do you want to learn from the process? Most of us would agree that the improvement of student learning is our primary goal in assessment; we want to understand better how students learn, which facets of our programs are effective or not, and whether our programs achieve their desired outcomes. And, as noted above, in resource-hungry environments, assessment and proven effectiveness may serve as leverage in negotiation processes to justify continued support for programs and to generate greater investment in study abroad and other international programs. The many reasons for engaging in assessment and other research initiatives are complex and interrelated. To ignore the often-politicized nature of assessment is foolhardy. Therefore, you will want a thorough analysis of the reasons for, and possible results of, engaging in an assessment program at the outset.

When opportunities for initiating research present themselves, another major consideration is the development of an assessment or research team. Who needs or wants to be involved, and how should you approach key players? The question of who should be involved in an assessment process partially depends upon whether the impetus for the assessment arose from within the study abroad office or from outside. If internally generated, the major goals include building consensus that assessment is necessary and meaningful; developing concise goals for the assessment process (again, the question of what do you want to assess and why); seeking support from campus leaders and departments who may need to assist with, or contribute to, the assessment process; and creating clear statements about what the project will involve and the potential benefits that will accrue to the organization by generating assessment data.

However, as noted above, the motives to implement assessment procedures are varied and come from multiple sources. What if the impetus to engage in assessment is external to the study abroad office?

Key Players and Clear Communication

If externally generated, the need or desire for program assessment can originate from institutional sources (e.g., president or provost) as well as external organizations. In any case, a successful assessment process significantly depends upon both the degree of administrative support and clear communication about the goals of the assessment. Assessments can be externally driven due to outside events in the international arena (e.g., a crisis event involving external program providers or unrest overseas), or by normal, periodic reviews by agencies (e.g., accreditation visits). In addition, personnel changes and office reorganizations often precipitate a fresh evaluation strategy or the acquisition of new data. More specifically, key moments that often provide a climate supportive of program review and assessment frequently include the following:

- Changes in major leadership personnel ranging from a new president or provost to a new head of the international study abroad office. Any alteration in key support personnel within study abroad programs or closely allied departments (e.g., student life, foreign language centers) often provides such opportunities.

- National and regional accreditation visits and consultations that include study abroad activities and/or concerns about language gain and cultural competency, intercultural communication skill acquisition, etc.

- University self-study surveys and program evaluations as part of curriculum review, budget allocations and financial priorities, degree requirements, and internationalization efforts.

- Policy discussions between the administration and study abroad office regarding the role of direct-exchange, direct enrollment, expanding or reducing island programs, and any other major shift in program emphases or cost-allocation models can provide an excellent opportunity to revisit the how, what, and why of study abroad assessment.

Large-scale research projects initiated by higher education consortia are also becoming more common in the field of international education. In this case, organizations often begin by polling their members and inquiring who might be interested in participating. Member institutions can then choose to join in the research project(s) and form a community who can collectively provide assistance to one another in the areas of design, data collection, and analysis and comparative statistics. Although joining in such an effort may present some challenges and loss of flexibility for partners (e.g., in that there must be some project standardization across institutions), the benefits almost always outweigh the difficulties that accrue to the project as a whole.

Cooperative projects may enhance the validity and significance of results because those results are based on larger samples than more limited, single-unit studies can generate. Consortium research can arise from a number of circumstances. As a first example, statewide system projects exist that involve multiple campuses and programs such as recent initiatives by the University of California and the University of Texas systems. Other projects often originate as partnerships between study abroad providers and their feeder organizations to address program quality and satisfaction issues. As a final example, colleagues working at different universities (e.g., across states or institutional types) may collaborate often with the support of external funding. [2]

Within most institutions, natural collaborators with an affinity for and an interest in the assessment of study abroad exist. These include faculty, administrators, and staff members across different offices and departments, all of whom can assist at some stage of the process, including providing data collected within their units that may augment that collected within study abroad programs. Of course, the core of any assessment team, and often the most highly motivated, usually includes faculty and staff actively involved in study abroad operations, as well as those in allied units such as offices of international programs and services, international student and scholar services, and those delivering international student programming. All of these units probably gather basic information already and may be open to collaborating on an assessment research project that has the potential to add new or more accurate data they can use in some pragmatic way.

Other groups that may compile information potentially useful as a part of a study abroad assessment protocol include academic majors with international emphases including international/foreign affairs, international studies, modern languages, anthropology, international development, area/regional studies, and ESL/TOEFL programs. Campus offices dealing with student affairs or residential life—especially those involved with international students, language residence halls or floors, and activities that have a multicultural and/or international dimension— likely house natural allies. Campus offices that address diversity issues or multicultural affairs may also collect basic data in focused ways that may be useful to augment study abroad demographics.

Career and alumni offices may have data (i.e., graduate school and career choice) that might be useful for documenting longitudinal outcomes of international learning. Admissions offices may have data about students' choices when entering college, including their desire to study abroad. That data could be compared with actual participation rates to examine which students study abroad and why. In short, the act of engaging in a research project or assessment program on study abroad requires the support of many different units and offices on campus; you need to consider at the outset who might serve as natural allies and collaborators, and where more dialog will be required to generate a sense of commitment to the project.

However, collaboration can rarely be assured simply because collaborators exist who can provide answers to certain questions or who possess knowledge that might be of interest. Organizations that take research seriously and pursue it regularly almost universally offer tangible rewards for participating in research-related projects. For faculty, the range of these considerations includes course release time, funding for graduate students or research assistants, compensation for professional expertise and consulting related to the project, publication authorship, public recognition, small stipends, and a whole host of other compensatory mechanisms, many of which are no or low cost to the institution but deeply appreciated by individuals. For staff, such rewards could include the use of flextime, additional vacation or comp time, recognition as part of the team and, frequently, inclusion in the final report as contributors or co-authors.

In any event, it is crucial to consider how to motivate already busy people to take on additional (and possibly quite new and daunting) tasks related to research. One way administrators can promote such research is to be absolutely clear that doing so is an important and central part of the organization's mission. This is most directly accomplished when senior administrators agree that as a matter of public policy, such activities should count toward important matters such as performance reviews, promotions, tenure deliberations, professional development, and institutional service. Policies promoting research are also the quickest and most effective mechanisms to encourage and reward people appropriately for engaging in research over time.

Research Basics

Given that most of us would agree that the improvement of student learning is the top priority for research regarding study abroad, the development of appropriate and measurable student learning outcomes is key to an effective assessment program. What do you perceive students learn from your programs? Do you have any evidence for such learning, even if it is informal and anecdotal? How can such learning be more formally assessed? Is the current curriculum working? Aside from what you believe they currently learn, what other outcomes could or should they be learning? How might that learning change in the months and years after the completion of study abroad?

In addition to issues relating to curricular reform, the list of potential topics to investigate is vast. However, it can be summed up in a few overarching themes such as, "What is the immediate impact of study abroad on such areas as language learning, cultural competence, disciplinary knowledge, academic progress, affective and cognitive development, and emotional intelligence and growth?" Longer-term effects to investigate might include increasing institutional loyalty, career and professional development, alumni support, and further international involvement.[3] What, if anything, does a review of such research in these areas reveal about what other colleagues found when investigating such learning processes and outcomes? These comprise just a few of the questions that you and your colleagues may wish to ask at the outset of any discussion regarding your project. Such discussions should include a wide range of stakeholders: faculty members involved in leading study abroad programs, international program staff members, and students who have studied abroad.

Moreover, as implied above, publications on the development of student learning outcomes contain useful guidelines for generating your own outcomes. A growing body of literature on international student outcomes, and several initiatives in progress at the time of this writing, do as well. For example, the American Council on Education (ACE) is sponsoring a three-year, six-institution project on the assessment of international student learning outcomes, entitled *Lessons Learned in Assessing International Learning*. The faculty members engaged in the project have identified nine learning outcomes across the knowledge, skills, and attitudes students might gain through international experiences (at home and abroad), and have selected two assessment measures in a comprehensive and mixed methods (i.e., quantitative and qualitative) research design.[4] Anyone contemplating an assessment of international learning project would do well to become familiar with this and other such projects, as the questions to be asked are likely to overlap considerably with those that you and your colleagues must answer.[5] In short, although modifications and adaptation may well be necessary, you may save considerable time and resources by not completely reinventing the assessment of international learning wheel.

Study abroad offices and organizations almost universally collect some form of data on study abroad. This data includes such information as basic demographics, student self-assessments, pre- and post-experience interviews, and questionnaires dealing with program satisfaction. When considering an assessment process, you may be able to integrate the information you are already gathering by altering the format to fit your research questions, without creating entirely new processes. Increasingly, faculty and administrators within the field of study abroad are taking a closer and more nuanced look at the experience of study abroad, considering in more detail the cognitive, emotional, and developmental changes that may occur as a result of the experience. In some cases, it is even possible to make testable predictions in advance about who will be likely to benefit from an international learning experience, to what degree, and under what circumstances.

More and more studies are implementing measures that examine the impact of study abroad on intercultural communication, beliefs and values, issues of maturation, etc. Yet many of the collection methods still do not follow best practices in research design, nor do the researchers collect data in ways that are consistent over time. Even when internally coherent, the data categories used may not easily lend themselves to cross-institution comparisons. It is beyond our scope here to deal with data comparability issues; however we encourage those involved in data gathering to read Mell Bolen's position paper on *Data Collection and Outcomes Assessment*, available at the Forum website.[6] We must actively consider how we in the study abroad field can work toward developing reasonable standards of how we collect data and report our outcomes. The cumulative impact of assessment studies will be enhanced when those working in the field better understand the complexities and nuances of research design and assessment practices, and when demographic and research results are reported in comparable forms or frameworks. This guide provides some guidelines and suggestions for beginning to do this work.

As you move forward in planning an assessment project on study abroad, decisions regarding the type of data you want to collect and measures or processes for doing so are crucial. At the very least, you should have access to a professional consultant who has sufficient expertise in statistical analysis *and* can discuss these issues in a way that is accessible and relevant. If you work at a university, you most likely will have such individuals on staff as faculty members, but you may also wish to hire an external consultant to serve in this role. In other types of organizations, collaboration with a university or hiring an external consultant will provide the necessary expertise. In either case, you will likely have specific questions regarding your programs that require additional mechanisms for gathering data.

While we will not provide an exhaustive discussion of issues of measurement here, there are a few basics to consider.[7] First, many if not most assessment experts would agree that research designs that include qualitative and quantitative measures are ideal, in that each methodology can provide different but complementary information. You will also need to consider issues of the reliability (Is the measure consistent over time and/or across raters?) and validity (Does it actually measure what is purports to measure?) of the instrument or questionnaire, as well as costs and ease of administration, scoring and/or rating, and analysis. A plethora of instruments and processes—both quantitative and qualitative—exist within the social sciences that address issues of intercultural communication and range of beliefs and values (e.g., openness toward other belief systems, altruism and volunteerism, and stereotypes regarding other cultures). Moreover, there are well-established standards and practices for assessment in general from the American Psychological Association[8] and measuring foreign language skills in particular.[9] Such guidelines and measures may help inform various decisions you must make along the way, including but not limited to the selection of specific measures. Creation of a reliable, valid, and effective measurement tool requires years to complete and great expertise.

Using an instrument that has already been developed, is demonstrably relevant for your purposes, and has evidence of reliability and validity, may save you a great deal of time, effort, and resources over the long run. Sometimes the author of an instrument may be willing to work directly with you and your team so that the instrument can be adapted to, modified for, or accessed by your institution. On the other hand, some instruments may require a great deal of resources to access and/or earn certification for usage, and these issues should be understood and investigated early in your process. Finally, the accessibility of an instrument (e.g., in terms of administration, scoring, and database management) is a significant factor to consider before selecting the measure(s) that you and your team will use. The advice of your assessment expert or an external consultant can be insightful as you wade through the number and types of measures and consider the pros and cons of selection and implementation.

Sensitive Information and Sophisticated Statistics: Information Management

Engaging in research regarding students' perceptions on any topic, including study abroad, must conform to the research guidelines of your institution. Typically all research projects using students as subjects, in which students are asked to disclose potentially sensitive information about themselves, must have the approval of your institutional research review board.[10] The issue here is one of ensuring consent, safety, and confidentiality; if students are asked to reveal information about themselves, you must consider these issues before any research begins in order to develop explicit policies to ensure these criteria are met. As you plan your research project and consider which measures you would like to implement, you must think through such ethical issues as privacy, confidentiality, and informed consent (e.g., that students understand what they are being asked to do, and have the right to withdraw from the project without consequence).

If you are unfamiliar with the research review board and the types of processes that must be in place to protect research participants, a dialog with the faculty members serving on your institutional research approval committee or board is imperative. Institutional review processes vary considerably. At some colleges and universities, the process may be fairly simple, while at others, particularly research-intensive institutions, the process may be quite detailed, inflexible, and time consuming. Even if your organization does not have a solid review board in place, various federal regulations regarding research with human subjects may still apply to your particular project. Of course, you cannot gather data until your project is approved, but when your team determines the details of the assessment program, the research review and approval process needs to begin.

Thus it is important in the early stages of research design to determine the degree of anonymity, privacy, and individual attribution you will require in your study. Although most routine study abroad topics are unlikely to be controversial or raise strong emotions, some (e.g., gender roles and behavior, gay and lesbian issues, eating disorders and mental health, ethnic identity concerns, discrimination, etc.) may be extremely sensitive.

The nature of the information you are seeking may necessitate a high degree of confidentiality that in turn will require you to make early decisions about how you will protect a respondent's identity and safeguard the questionnaires or resulting data. There are many accepted ways to accomplish this. For example, when using questionnaires, it is common to implement a numerical or coded identification key to ensure that individuals and their responses cannot be linked. Most importantly, whatever agreements or promises your research team makes to participants must be honored, not only during the study but also permanently, including future dissemination and publication of the data and any future access to the original data.[11]

Once you have developed a rationale for the project, assembled your team to assist with design and the development of outcomes, chosen measures, and gained institutional approval, you are ready to gather data. Ironically, even though you will not be able to gather your data until the project has been developed, approved, and implemented, it is crucial that questions of data analysis be asked and answered early on. The design you and your team develop will determine whether you can even answer these questions down the line. For example, if you want to know how a study abroad program affects learning outcomes, but fail to include a pretest in your design, you will have no way of knowing whether the study abroad experience was responsible for the results you gather, or if these results were due to preexisting factors in your students, which vary across students. Before you even settle these issues and questions, you need to consider who will gather, enter, and analyze your data. That person should be involved in the project from the outset to tell you what design and methodology issues you must address to be able to derive the data you want and therefore answer the questions you have.

Among a plethora of design issues, you need to consider at what point(s) you will capture data, and through what venue or forum? For example, some portion of an orientation meeting can be set aside for the completion of a questionnaire or measure, while a component of a program evaluation or reentry meeting can be set aside for a posttest or exit interview. Increasingly, measures (both quantitative and qualitative) exist online, which can provide much more flexibility in terms of administration. However, study abroad staff at home, faculty accompanying students, and onsite staff likely will need to prompt students to complete questionnaires or turn in portfolios (or other qualitative information) in a timely manner.

A related issue is how to create incentives for participating in this project that are also acceptable to your institutional review board (e.g., extra credit, financial incentives, building into program requirements). Finally, you may wish to consider a longer timeframe for gathering data than simply before and immediately after study abroad. You may want to develop mechanisms to gather data longitudinally, perhaps through a voluntary process later in students' undergraduate career or as alumni, so that student development and the effects of your program(s) can be assessed over time.

If your design uses both a qualitative and quantitative measure, you will likely want to compare the results from these measures. This means your qualitative measure (e.g., a portfolio, survey, or interview) will eventually have be to be translated into quantitative terms. You may need to develop a rating system by which you evaluate qualitative measures; without such ratings, no data points exist to compare to those of a quantitative measure. Again, the statistical and/or test development consultant(s) you have as part of your team can help you address these important issues.

Once gathered, the data will need to be entered into a database. Data entry, while time-consuming, is a relatively easy process that a responsible undergraduate or graduate student can manage. As measures and instruments move to an electronic format, data entry becomes quite manageable as students submit information directly to an electronic repository. A number of companies that market questionnaires and measures will also provide analyses of the data for you, sometimes for an additional fee. If you are using measures that require you physically to enter the data, the format of database and method of data entry will require the assistance of a statistician, psychometrician, or other assessment expert. If your measures are web-based, you will have to integrate the web-based version of your measures with a database that can be analyzed statistically, perhaps using SPSS (Statistical Package for the Social Sciences). Such processes can be labor intensive and costly, and will require someone who understands the complexity of the project to work with various individuals (e.g., a programmer or statistician) to ensure the system functions in a smooth and coherent manner. The benefits of an integrated, well-functioning, and web-based system are enormous, as this significantly enhances administrative and analytic flexibility. Students can now take your measures anywhere in the world, with the data being dumped into a common and secured site that can be readily accessed by data coordinators and statisticians.

In trying to make sense of the data collected, the types of analyses you might conduct will flow directly from your questions regarding the interrelationships between student demographics, student learning outcomes, and other facets of the student experience (e.g., cognitive, attitudinal, and emotional changes) that you have assessed. The measurements themselves focus and frame the analyses you can conduct based on your questions and hypotheses. In most cases, even very simple data collection can provide a wealth of information through basic analyses, including correlations and comparisons between different groups of students.

On the other hand, a well-designed project with good measures and clear outcomes can be subject to an extraordinary array of analyses, demonstrating everything from who learns what under what circumstances, to sophisticated comparisons among different learning experiences, to basic indices of the reliability and validity of the measures selected for your project. While we will not provide an in-depth discussion of statistical methods, analyses, and interpretation here, you should think through your questions carefully and consult experts in measurement and analysis from start to finish as you move through the decision-making process on your project.

Along these lines, a final point should be emphasized again: If you are not an expert in assessment but are coordinating an assessment project, it is your responsibility to gain as much information as possible about the nature of conducting a high-quality assessment project. It is crucial to remember that assessment means different things to different people. The person(s) you ask to serve in a consultative role should have the knowledge and expertise to help you design, implement, analyze, and interpret your project in a way that corresponds with acceptable standards, and is logical, comprehensible, and responsive. It is no less important that you be sure that the consultant knows assessment in the context of research design, methodology, psychometrics, and statistics, and not simply as part of preparation for accreditation, program review, or qualitative analysis. Although it is quite possible that one individual has expertise in both realms of assessment, do not confuse these two forms of assessment expertise. Be explicit that you are looking for someone (or more than one individual) who can work in a collaborative and open manner, has the necessary expertise to design, implement, and analyze both quantitative and qualitative assessment research, and can translate the process and results into terms that are comprehensible, useful, and relevant to project goals and outcomes.

Making Assessment Matter: Communication and Use of Results

The manner in which you communicate your results will depend very much upon the results themselves, the audience, and the purpose of the communication. What do you hope to accomplish through the act of communicating your results?

Communication with senior administrators, government officials, other departments on campus, study abroad faculty and staff, or members of the field may all take different forms and produce differing outcomes. Similarly, the manner in which you use your results for program change will depend in part upon the results themselves and the feasibility and cost of making changes. Your results may point to simple changes in office procedure (e.g., marketing study abroad more effectively to certain students on campus), the addition of certain experiences to enhance study abroad (e.g., a service-learning component), or personnel changes (e.g., recruiting new faculty to lead certain programs). Regardless of the specific changes that may or may not be needed, with a well-designed and skillfully executed research project, any changes you do make can be justified on the basis of evidence rather than on anecdotes and supposition. Here are some questions for you and your team to consider at this point in the process:

- What are the implications of explaining your results to faculty and staff who might make changes in study abroad programs?
- How can you effectively communicate your results to senior administrators (and others) with the goal of leveraging for resources?
- How might you present your results to a state commission or committee as a rationale for international education in general?
- Are there other audiences—internal or external to your institution—that might benefit from your results? If yes, what is the most effective mechanism for communication?
- Once you have completed an assessment cycle, how do you implement the results for program enhancement or development?
- How do you plan to evaluate the assessment process itself? What worked effectively? How might you improve upon the assessment process itself?
- How do you plan to sustain your assessment program? What additional and/or long-term resources will you need?

Credible answers to questions such as these, and the others that will emerge relevant to your specific institution and circumstances, will help you communicate your findings in a manner that is accessible and understandable regardless of the audience. Of course, when results are positive or validate expectations, both interpretation and communication are easier. Regardless of whether the outcomes are positive or point to needed program changes, the overarching goal is clear, concise, and contextualized communication about learning processes and outcomes. Such answers will help you improve your program(s) in the short term, and help establish a transparent culture of assessment that can be integrated into various administrative and programmatic processes.

Conclusion: Considerations in Developing a Step-by-Step Plan

In conclusion, the steps necessary to develop a study abroad assessment program might include:

1. Discussions with appropriate knowledgeable, interested individuals to decide if research is necessary and/or desirable at this point in time
2. Development of a rationale for the project
3. Decisions on what questions to ask and why
4. Identification of project team members to oversee the process
5. Identification of data collection tools while considering:
    - Existing data sources you may already possess or those to which you have access
    - Existing methodologies from similar projects in the same or related fields
    - Existing instruments in this or related fields
    - Your restrictions on time, resources and expertise
6. Completion of the necessary human subject review processes for your institution
7. Decisions on technical issues while considering:
    - Desirable and/or acceptable N (total study sample size)
    - Primary methodology (or methodologies)
    - When and where to best collect the data
    - Development of questionnaires, focus group guides, etc.
    - Development of a database
    - Management of quantitative data
    - Management of qualitative data including content analysis and conversion to quantitative indicators

- Data entry and analysis
- Processes to gain informed consent and maintain confidentiality

8. Implementation of the data collection process
9. Review of types of analyses and results to ensure the assessment protocol and resulting data are providing the information needed to answer questions from step 3 above
10. Interpretation and organization of data
11. Creating and writing a summary of results and project report
12. Developing a communication and dissemination plan(s) for external and internal audiences

As with many processes and decisions in higher education, there are pros and cons to engaging in assessment. It should be clear from this discussion that it takes energy and resources to conduct high-quality assessment projects. Moreover, results are not guaranteed to be favorable; they may be instructive but not necessarily positive. Done poorly, assessment can generate hostility and mistrust, particularly among the faculty who are typically responsible for the actual process of gathering information, without providing meaningful results. Done well, an efficient and effective assessment program can stimulate rich dialog among students, faculty, administrators, and staff; provide evidence of program effectiveness or facilitate meaningful program change; serve as a compelling tool for communication and advocacy; and promote greater understanding of the nature of student learning.

The process and eventual findings will be much more interesting and relevant if you maintain an inquisitive and open mind, a good sense of humor, and a healthy dose of the larger perspective. Never forget that good assessment is good research; your design, measures, and results should permit you to discover something you did not know before the project began. For all its complexity, conducting an outcomes assessment can also be intellectually stimulating, personally satisfying and even fun!

Notes

[1] There are many excellent resources for research design and methodology. For an accessible and comprehensive review of issues of assessing student learning, you may wish to consult *Assessing student learning: A common sense guide* by Linda Suskie (Bolton, Massachusetts: Anker Publishing Company, 2004).

[2] See the discussion of the six-institution American Council on Education Assessment Project later in this chapter.

[3] For a fuller review of suggested research areas, see chapter 3 in this volume.

[4] For more information on the project, see the ACE project website, http://www.acenet.edu/AM/Template.cfm?Section=IntCurrent&Template=/CM/HTMLDisplay.cfm&ContentID=9387.

[5] See chapters 5 and 6 in this guide for more information on projects and current methodologies.

[6] We also refer you to chapter 8 in this guide for a discussion on the consistent definition of research terms. See http://www.forumea.org/outcomes.html

[7] See chapter 2 for some discussion on this.

[8] See division 5, Evaluation, Measurement, and Statistics, of the American Psychological Association, at http://www.apa.org/divisions/div5/.

[9] See, for example, the practices and standards advocated by the American Council on the Teaching of Foreign Languages at its website, www.actfl.org.

[10] The gathering of demographic information or completion of program and course evaluations typically does not require institutional review and approval.

[11] Codes of ethics and links for hundred of organizations can be found at http://ethics.iit.edu/index.html

Chapter 5

An Overview of the Basic Methods of Outcomes Assessment

Darla K. Deardorff, Duane L. Deardorff

One hallmark of effective outcomes assessment is utilizing multiple measures and methods, and in so doing, recognizing that student learning is multidimensional. As one assessment expert states, "Multiple measures are essential because no single measure is perfectly reliable or valid; several measures of the same construct can furnish support for one another as stakeholders draw conclusions about strengths or weaknesses" (Banta, 2004, p. 5). This chapter outlines some of the methods possible; specific examples of how such methods are actually utilized in education abroad assessment can be found in Chapter 6.

There is no one way to do outcomes assessment—no single tool, no method that works across the board. It starts first with knowing what you want to assess: What are your goals and objectives? What are the outcomes you intend to measure and for what purpose? Have those outcomes been explicitly defined (and defined according to whom?) What are the criteria/indicators to be assessed? These questions then determine which methods or tools you would use to measure specific outcomes. These questions also become the first part of creating an assessment plan, as we saw in the previous chapter. It is most important that you not start by asking, "What assessment tool should we use?" but instead ask, "What do we need to assess and why?" Once that is determined, you are ready to select the most appropriate methods/tools that match your objectives and intended outcomes.

So, what assessment methods are used in outcomes assessment? These methods can generally be categorized into direct methods and indirect methods. Direct methods provide evidence of what students learn, while indirect methods involve evidence of the process of learning, including reflection on the process. Both methods can use qualitative and quantitative data collection methods and interpretation. Other terms can also be used to describe assessment methods, including formal and informal assessment, traditional and authentic assessment, and so on. Much of the outcomes assessment literature uses the terms direct and indirect methods.

Direct Assessment Methods

Direct methods of assessment "are those that provide evidence of whether or not a student has command of a specific subject or contact area, can perform a certain task, exhibits a particular skill, demonstrates a certain quality in his or her work, or holds a particular value" (Middle States Commission on Higher Education, Student Learning Assessment, p. 30). Direct methods can include embedded course/program assessment, portfolios, performance (as in the case of an internship or practicum), testing, papers, and a capstone or final project.

Advantages of these direct assessment methods include authenticity (i.e., student-structured, task performance), application of knowledge and skills, and as in the case of embedded assessment, the ability to build them into the program or course. "Direct methods provide stronger evidence about the knowledge and skills that students . . . have learned, value, and are able to demonstrate. . ." (Hernon, 2004, p. 167). The main limitation of using direct methods is that assessment is subjective in most of these cases. Thus, detailed rubrics must be developed based on specific criteria to move toward more objective assessment. The development of such rubrics can be time consuming.

Specifically, some options for direct assessment include:

Embedded Course Assessment: Embedded assessment consists of questions or assignments embedded into the papers, research reports, and exams that relate directly to the intended outcomes. Student responses to these questions often are evaluated differently than the standard evaluation process used for exams, papers, etc., since this is within the context of intended outcomes. Embedded assessment can also include a variety of ways to solicit student feedback such as one-minute papers, in which students reflect on their learning on a focused topic, including remaining questions they may have about the topic, which can then be used to guide further learning.

Portfolios: Portfolios are electronic or print collections of student work—direct evidence of student learning in achieving intended outcomes. These collections may include journal reflections, research reports, essay examinations, and so on. Such collections can document student growth and progress over time. (For further discussion on portfolios, see chapter 1.) It is crucial that these portfolios be built around the intended outcomes, and that appropriate rubrics are developed to effectively assess items in the portfolio.

Performance: Performance assessment can take several different forms, including internship or practicum performance or evidence from videotapes or audiotapes of students engaged in particular tasks. This can also include presentations. In the case of performance assessment, others such as supervisors provide evaluation of the performance based on specific criteria, which are derived from the intended outcomes. Since others serve as assessors, this provides an opportunity for multi-perspective assessment, which is another hallmark of outcomes assessment.

Testing: This method primarily consists of knowledge-based tests that can be locally designed or commercially produced. Testing is popular to use as a pre- and postmeasurement to determine how much a student has learned as a result of an education abroad experience, for example.

Papers/projects: Papers and projects allow students to apply and demonstrate knowledge and skills to a particular focused topic. In assessing these, it is important to have well-developed rubrics keyed to intended outcomes.

Capstone: A capstone paper or project provides students with the opportunity to synthesize the knowledge and skills they have gained through an educational experience. This direct method provides evidence of students' ability to apply a broad range of learning. Critical analysis can be used to evaluate this direct method.

Indirect Methods of Outcomes Assessment

Indirect methods of assessment are "related to the act of learning, such as factors that predict or mediate learning or perceptions about learning but do not reflect learning itself" (Middle States Commission on higher Education, 2003, p. 32). Evidence collected through indirect methods lead to inferences about change. Methods include surveys and other instruments, interviews, focus groups, self-assessment, curriculum analysis, and other review of data such as transcript analysis, retention rates, and job placement data.

Advantages of using indirect methods include the ease of use (for many indirect methods as in the case of surveys and self-report instruments), more objective interpretations for many of these methods and the provision of a more complete picture of the student learning *process.* Limitations to indirect methods include lack of actual evidence of student learning and the self-report nature of many of the indirect assessments, which could lead to bias. "Indirect methods support the desired educational outcomes to a lesser degree" (Hernon, 2004, p. 167). This is due primarily to the lack of documented evidence of actual student learning or performance (as provided through direct measures discussed previously in this chapter). Hence, it is important to utilize indirect and direct methods to provide data on both the actual learning that occurs combined with the perceptions of the learning process and other impacts of such learning.

Specifically, some options for indirect assessment include:

Surveys: Surveys are one of the most popular methods that education abroad administrators use. These can include program satisfaction forms, self-report instruments that may ask students to reflect on their experience and specific knowledge, skills, and attitudes gained (see chapter 7 for an in-depth discussion of specific instruments that can be used within the context of education abroad), and targeted surveys such as those to alumni. Surveys can be locally designed or commercially produced. Some reflection-type questions can be incorporated into program satisfaction surveys that can help provide data beyond program satisfaction. Issues of validity and reliability (as discussed in the following section) should be ensured in whichever instruments are used. When selecting or developing an instrument, it is crucial to understand first what outcomes need to be measured. The outcomes determine the method and the tool, not the other way around. Another key piece to know is exactly what the instrument measures: Does this match the intended outcome? We must remember that surveys and self-report instruments are one method among many to use in determining outcomes assessment results, and that it is incumbent upon us to use multiple measures to gain a fuller assessment picture.

Interviews: Interviews are an indirect assessment method for exploring perceptions into the process of student learning. In addition, interviews provide the opportunity to evaluate students' thought processes in their responses to case studies, critical incidents, and particular cross-cultural situations. Interviews also provide a fuller picture of the learning process that could not be answered through direct assessment methods.

Focus groups: A variation of the interview method, focus groups allow for multiple students to provide insights and perceptions on their learning experiences.

Self-assessment: Self-assessment specifically asks students to address what they have learned, where they would like to be, where their perceived deficits are, and how they plan to overcome perceived deficits. This self-assessment can take the form of a written reflection or can be conducted through an interview; however, it is usually recommended that students are allowed time to reflect upon and learn from their own self-assessments. Self-assessments can also include guided inventories as part of the assessment.

Curriculum and transcript analyses: Analyzing curriculum, syllabi, and transcripts provides yet another method for substantiating content designed to meet intended outcomes. This can be an especially useful tool in assessment across programs or departments.

Documented data (job placement data, retention rates, etc.): Another indirect measure of student learning can be the examination of other data such as job placement data, retention rates, graduation rates, and so on. These data provide yet one more way to offer a fuller picture of student learning. However, it may be difficult to determine the exact relation between education abroad and student learning outcomes in regard to some of these data.

Assessment in Practice

One example of these various assessment methods in use is illustrated through a study conducted in 2004 in which 24 postsecondary institutions were surveyed regarding their assessment of intercultural competence in their students (Deardorff, 2004). Slightly over one-third of those institutions (38%) were currently assessing intercultural competence as a student outcome through a variety of methods, with an average of five methods (range of two to six used per institution).

Figure 1 presents the assessment methods used. Student interviews were the most frequently used assessment method (89%) followed by student papers or presentations (79%). Other assessment methods that the schools cited frequently included observation, student portfolios, professor evaluations (embedded assessment), and use of pre- and posttests. It is interesting to note that while pre- and posttests were popular with administrators, there was not consensus among leading intercultural experts on the use of pre- and posttesting in assessing intercultural competence.

Figure 1. ***Intercultural competence assessment methods used by institutions***

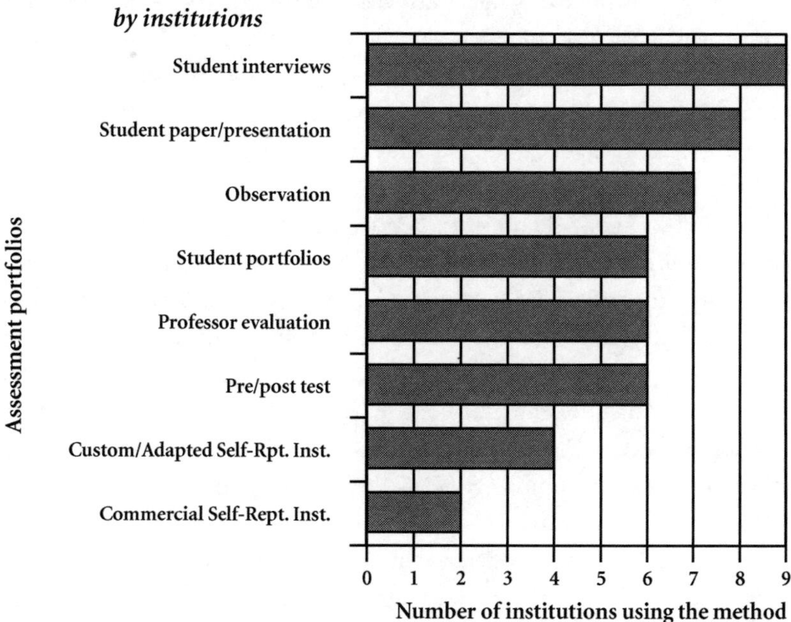

The important observation to make about the results of this study is that multiple methods, both direct and indirect, were used in assessing students' intercultural competence. Direct methods such as portfolios provide documented evidence of progress toward development of intercultural competence, while indirect methods such as interviews provided insights into the process of acquiring intercultural competence, which was found to be a key part of intercultural competence assessment (Deardorff, 2005). Another important part of this study was its focus on first defining what we intend to assess. In this case, 21 leading intercultural experts (including Storti, Kohls, LaBrack, Triandis, Hammer, Pusch, and Bennett) achieved consensus on a definition and elements of intercultural competence. Once the specific outcome has been defined, it can become a starting point for developing specific indicators that lead to the selection of a variety of specific assessment methods as previously discussed.

Considerations

This brief overview of some methods of direct and indirect assessment leads us next to some key considerations when using these methods. Two important considerations for any assessment are the *validity* and *reliability* of the measurement. The *validity* of the assessment is a judgment by the stakeholders as to whether the tool or method being used is an accurate measure of the intended outcomes. This question of relevancy is a subjective determination that is not easily measured but can be decided based on the opinions of experts and stakeholders. An assessment method that users find irrelevant or unhelpful is clearly not valid. However, just because an assessment tool or method has been identified as valid does not mean that it will always yield accurate results. Chapter 2 of this guide identifies a number of internal and external threats to validity, and precautionary measures must be taken to minimize their effects.

The quality of an assessment also depends on its *reliability* or consistency. An instrument that does not yield consistent results cannot be trusted, and any conclusions drawn from the results would be suspect. A certain degree of reliability must be demonstrated for a particular assessment method so that inferences and decisions based on the results can be made confidently. Quantitative methods of assessment often use reliability measures such as the Kuder-Richardson Formula 20 (KR-20) for dichotomous data or Cronbach's alpha for non-dichotomous data to quantify the internal consistency. The reliability of informal measures is more difficult to determine, but repeated administrations of the method under similar conditions can provide a sense of the variability.

Assessments can be administered either at the end of a treatment or throughout. *Formative assessments* are used to gather information about how students are performing while there is still time to make corrections or adjustments to the program if necessary. This is also known as ongoing assessment, and it ideally would be integrated into the program or course. *Summative assessments* are used to determine final outcomes after students have completed their work. It is important to include both formative and summative assessments in your assessment plan.

Depending on the number of students involved in a program, it may be necessary to assess only a sample of the population instead of all of the participants. If this is the case, careful attention must be given to the selection of the sample to ensure that it is as unbiased as possible. Whenever feasible, the sample should be obtained by randomly selecting students. The sample size depends on the reliability of the assessment and the amount of uncertainty that is acceptable in the averaged results. Given the tradeoff between the improved precision of a larger sample and the expense of its higher administration costs, it is important to first consider how the results will be used. Usually the cost to administer an assessment increases linearly with the sample size, but the improved reliability of the results only increases by the square root of the sample size. This means, for example, that doubling the sample size would double the cost but would only yield about a 40% improvement in the confidence of the results.

Conclusion

This chapter briefly outlines a variety of direct and indirect methods that can be used in outcomes assessment, along with some key considerations when engaging in assessment. International educators need to understand the importance of utilizing multiple methods in both formative and summative assessments of outcomes, because a richer, fuller portrait of outcomes emerges through the use of multiple assessment methods.

References

Banta, T. W., ed. (2004). *Hallmarks of effective outcomes assessment.* San Francisco: Jossey-Bass.

Deardorff, D.K. (2004). *The identification and assessment of intercultural competence as a student outcome of internationalization at institutions of higher education in the United States.* Raleigh, NC: North Carolina State University.

Deardorff, D.K. (2005). A matter of logic. In *International Educator*, May/June 2005, Vol. 14, Iss 3, pp. 26-32.

Hernon, P. Selecting from the assessment tool chest. In *Outcomes assessment in higher education: Views and perspectives*, P. Hernon and R.E. Dugan, eds. Westport, CT: Libraries Unlimited.

Middle States Commission on Higher Education. (2003). *Student learning assessment: options and resources.* Philadelphia: Middle States Commission on Higher Education.

Chapter 6

Literature and Resources for Education Abroad Outcomes Assessment

David Comp, Sophie Gladding, Gary Rhodes, Skye Stephenson, Michael Vande Berg

Education abroad assessment research has grown increasingly complex and sophisticated over the past decade. While early research sought simply to demonstrate that a student's knowledge or skills had improved while he or she was abroad—with nearly all early studies focusing on skills associated with a single learning domain, second-language learning—recent research has evolved in several important ways. Researchers have become increasingly aware of the need to design studies that will provide valid and reliable data. Thus current research is much more likely than earlier studies to respond to explicitly stated research questions, to rely on instruments that have been validated prior to the study, to compare the results of student performance abroad with groups of control students on the home campus or abroad, and so on.

As research methods have grown more sophisticated, research questions have also become more complex. This complexity manifests itself in two different types of recent research studies. First, while a considerable number of recent studies continue to yield important insights in investigating second-language acquisition, others are increasingly exploring student learning in other domains, focusing for example on intercultural competence or sensitivity, global awareness and, most recently, on disciplinary learning abroad. Second, a number of recent studies have focused not only on what students are learning abroad but also on the extent to which a variety of specific factors—some related to the learning environment, some to the learner—may inform learning. Thus some researchers are exploring how program duration, home institution grading policy, types of housing abroad, amount of contact with host-country nationals, and other environmental variables impact learning; while other researchers are asking questions about the extent to which factors intrinsic to outbound students—linguistic and other academic training prior to departure, motivation, capacity for learning specific skills—may influence their learning abroad.

In this chapter, we begin by listing general resources in assessment and then move to specific resources for education abroad. We have grouped descriptions of studies around various research foci according to the variables or areas they seek to explore. Each study description includes brief comments on the variables explored, methodologies used, and significant results. We also point out where and why certain studies are particularly good models for specific types of research.

Resources for Assessment in Higher Education[1]

While research and assessment on education abroad have increased and become more complex and rigorous over the decades, it is important for researchers to have grounding in and exposure to the research, evaluation, and assessment literature of the greater higher education community. Researchers who focus on study abroad and campus internationalization efforts can learn a tremendous amount from colleagues across higher education who are engaged in similar research, evaluation, and assessment activities. For instance, the *9 Principles of Good Practice for Assessing Student Learning* (1991) by the former American Association for Higher Education (AAHE) Assessment Forum and the *Ethical Standards of the American Educational Research Association* (1992)[2] are applicable to researchers across higher education and should be known by those researching and assessing student outcomes in education abroad. All education abroad researchers also should have a comprehensive understanding of the functions and importance of the Institutional Review Board (IRB).

In November 2006, the Forum on Education Abroad announced that members of the Outcomes Assessment Committee will collaborate with the annual North Carolina State University Undergraduate Assessment Symposium starting in 2007.[3] Furthermore, the North Carolina State University Undergraduate Assessment Symposium will add a new international education track at the symposium with the assistance of the Forum on Education Abroad.[4]

The publications listed below are examples of the type of literature that would be informative to those conducting research, evaluations and outcomes assessment in education abroad.

Leskes, Andrea. (2002,Winter/Spring). *Beyond Confusion: An Assessment Glossary. Peer Review.*

Leskes, Andrea and Barbara Wright. *(2005). The Art & Science of Assessing General Education Outcomes: A Practical Guide.* Washington, DC: Association of American Colleges and Universities.

Light, Richard J., Judith A. Singer, and John B. Willett. (1990). *By Design: Planning Research on Higher Education.* Cambridge, MA: Harvard University Press.

McTighe Musil, Caryn. (2006). *Assessing Global Learning: Matching Good Intentions with Good Practice.* Washington, DC: Association of American Colleges and Universities.

Palomba, Catherine A., and Trudy W. Banta. (1999). *Assessment Essentials: Planning, Implementing and Improving Assessment of Higher Education.* San Francisco: Jossey-Bass.

Schuh, John H., and M. Lee Upcraft and Associates. (2001). *Assessment Practice in Student Affairs: An Applications Manual.* San Francisco: Jossey-Bass.

Walvoord, Barbara E. (2004). *Assessment Clear and Simple: A Practical Guide for Institutions, Departments, and General Education.* San Francisco: Jossey-Bass.

Resources for Assessment in Education Abroad

Research on education abroad began to emerge during the 1950s, and by the end of the 1960s, a respectable literature base and focus had been established. A review of the major research bibliographies on study abroad demonstrates a significant increase in the number of study abroad research-based articles, reports, books and presentations per decade. The following table shows this steady increase from the 1950s through 2003.

Research-Based Articles/Reports/Books/Presentations in Education Abroad per Decade[5]

Decade	Number of research based articles/reports/books/	Percent increase from previous decade
1950's	34	127% increase from pre-1950s
1960's	117	244% increase from 1950s
1970's	189	62% increase from 1960s
1980's	377	99% increase from 1970s
1990's	675	79% increase from 1980s
2000–2003	315[6]	N/A

While the education abroad research base continues to grow, it is important that education abroad professionals and researchers approach the literature with caution. A body of sound research is available for education abroad professionals to consult to inform their practice or when they need to incorporate data and results into their advocacy efforts or for researchers conducting literature reviews. However, as is the case of all professions and fields of study, many research studies (published and unpublished) are poorly designed and/or provide invalid results. Thus inclusion in such bibliographies may not imply high quality of the study or its results. In consulting these resources, the researcher should conduct a quality review before using the studies as models.

Much of the research on US students abroad has been identified and compiled on three main annotated bibliographies. The following bibliographies on education abroad research are currently available on the Loyola Marymount University Center for Global Education website (http://www.globaled.us/ro/).

Weaver, Henry D. (Ed.). (1989). *Research on U.S. Students Abroad: A Bibliography with Abstracts.* Council on International Educational Exchange; Education Abroad Program, University of California; Institute of International Education; and National Association of Foreign Student Affairs.

Chao, Maureen, (Ed.). (2001). *Research on U.S. Students Abroad, Volume II, A Bibliography with Abstracts 1989–2000.* NAFSA: Association of International Educators/SECUSSA (Section on U.S. Students Abroad).

Comp, David. (Ed.). (2005). R*esearch on U.S. Students Abroad, Volume III, 2001 to 2005 with Updates to the 1989 and Volume II Editions.* Loyola Marymount University.

David Comp has also compiled several additional annotated bibliographies such as Research, Assessment, and Evaluation on International Education; Research on Underrepresentation in Education Abroad; Heritage Seeking in Study Abroad; GLBT Students Abroad; Female Students Abroad; and Education Abroad and its Value in the Job Market. These additional annotated bibliographies are accessible via the websites of The Forum on Education Abroad (www.forumea.org) and NAFSA: Association of International Educators—Teaching, Learning and Scholarship Knowledge Community (www.nafsa.org).

Two additional online resources are worth mentioning. The first is the Database of Research on International Education by Australian Education International – Australian Government (http://aei.dest.gov.au); and the International Higher Education Clearinghouse of the Center for International Higher Education at Boston College (www.bc.edu/cihe/ihec/). Both of these websites offer comprehensive information related to research on comparative and international education with valuable links to resources related to US students abroad.

The three main US organizations that focus entirely or in part on US students abroad are the Forum on Education Abroad; NAFSA: Association of International Educators; and the Association of International Education Administrators (AIEA). The Forum on Education Abroad was established in 2001 and organized around five specific goals/areas to advance the field: standards of good practice, advocacy, data collection, outcomes assessment, and curriculum development and design. The

Forum's Committee on Outcomes Assessment is leading the field in this area. In a few short years, this committee has partnered with *Frontiers: The Interdisciplinary Journal of Study Abroad*, introduced a conference roundtable format to encourage dialog and stimulate new ideas and collaboration, introduced a juried student award competition for integrating research into the education abroad experience, and envisioned this publication on outcomes assessment.

NAFSA's new organizational structure has created a knowledge community devoted to Teaching, Learning and Scholarship (TLS). The goals of the TLS knowledge community are to foster connections among scholarship, policy, and practice by identifying emerging research priorities; engaging international educators, scholars, and other professionals in knowledge development and dissemination; and equipping NAFSA members to develop evidenced-based practices. During the last several years, NAFSA has offered a preconference workshop on research and outcomes assessment in education abroad with industry leaders and seasoned researchers as facilitators. The Association of International Education Administrators' Research Committee has also offered valuable and timely conference sessions on research and outcomes assessment. AIEA and NAFSA are members of the Association for Studies in International Education (ASIE), which publishes the *Journal of Studies in International Education*. Both the *Journal of Studies in International Education* and *Frontiers: The Interdisciplinary Journal of Study Abroad* are leading journals in the field.

Studies Focusing on More than One Learning Domain

Engle, Lilli, and John Engle. (2004). *Assessing Language Acquisition and Intercultural Sensitivity Development in Relation to Study Abroad Program Design*, Frontiers: The Interdisciplinary Journal of Study Abroad, 10, 219–236.

This study, based on the assertion that a strong correlation exists between learning of students abroad and the design of the program in which they are studying, measures increases in student learning in second-language acquisition and in intercultural sensitivity. It also explores the extent to which learning in one domain correlates with learning in the other. The study is noteworthy in two respects. First, unlike most education abroad research, which is based on a single academic term or year of data, this study is based on data collected over eight semesters. Second, the program on which it is based—the American University Center of Provence, which the authors developed and continue to run—was engineered in reverse,[7] that is, designed by working backwards, from first identifying the desired learning outcomes, and only then designing the specific courses and activities required of participating students. In measuring the two desired outcomes—significant improvement in

French proficiency across all four skills and meaningful integration into the cultural life of Aix-en-Provence, where the program is based—and in exploring correlations between the two domains, the study offers surprising insights about student learning that point the way to future research.

DiBiasio, David, and Natalie Mello. (2004). *Assessing a Nontraditional Study Abroad Program in the Engineering Disciplines.* Frontiers: The Interdisciplinary Journal of Study Abroad, 10, 237–252.

This study examines another exercise in engineering in reverse, this time involving the curriculum of an entire institution. The authors describe Worcester Polytechnic Institute's (WPI) multilevel assessment of its Global Perspective Program (GPP). WPI provides a good example of an institution that deliberately linked theory and practice. The institution has since 1970 developed its curriculum by first identifying the learning outcomes of its students, and then developing coursework and other academic activities designed to allow students, whether studying on campus or completing group projects in the United States or abroad, to meet those outcomes. The institution relies on a multilevel assessment program that measures the extent to which WPI students are meeting the learning objectives the institution has identified for them. The results of that assessment program indicate, among other things, that WPI students who participate in the GPP, completing group projects abroad, meet their learning goals to a greater extent than students who complete these projects in the United States.

WPI has continued to refine its reverse engineering approach to curricular design, and since 2000 has adapted its academic program to the new, internationally focused ABET standards.

Paige, R. Michael, Andrew D. Cohen, and Rachel L. Shively. (2004). *Assessing the Impact of a Strategies Based Curriculum on Language and Culture Learning Abroad.* Frontiers: The Interdisciplinary Journal of Study Abroad, 10, 253–273.

This study measures the impact, on two learning domains, of a recently published guidebook that students are trained to use while abroad. The guidebook, *Maximizing Study Abroad: A Students' Guide to Language and Culture Strategies and Use* (whose senior authors are Paige and Cohen), is designed to prepare students to improve their second-language and intercultural learning while abroad. The study relies on two instruments to collect an array of demographic information about student participants—a group that studied abroad and another that stayed at the University of Minnesota—and on several other instruments to test students on a pre-and posttest basis: the Intercultural Development Inventory (IDI); E-Journals; the Strategies Inventory for Learning Culture (SILC), an instrument designed as a part of the *Maximizing* guidebook; and the Language Strategy Survey and the Speech Act Measure of Language Gain, both of which were designed specifically for this study.

Vande Berg, Michael J., Al Balkcum, Mark Scheid, and Brian J. Whalen. (2004). *The Georgetown University Consortium Project: A Report from the Halfway Mark.* Frontiers: The Interdisciplinary Journal of Study Abroad, 10, 101–116.

This study investigates study abroad learning outcomes from four diverse institutions: Georgetown University, Rice University, the University of Minnesota, and Dickinson College. The study specifically examines learning outcomes in multiple domains: second-language learning, intercultural learning, and learning within a disciplinary context. It also explores what sort of relationships may exist between or across the three domains. Second-language learning was measured using the Simulated Oral Proficiency Interview (SOPI), with pre- and posttesting of experimental groups composed of students studying abroad and control groups of students on campus. Intercultural learning was measured using the Intercultural Development Inventory (IDI) and was pre-, post- and post-posttested. This study was particularly innovative in attempting to measure learning within a disciplinary context. Working with faculty members in business, the humanities, engineering, and the sciences, the researchers identified four key competencies for learning within a disciplinary context:

1. Ability to function on multicultural teams
2. Understanding of ethical and professional responsibility
3. Understanding of the impact of disciplinary solutions in a global and societal context
4. Ability to apply disciplinary knowledge

An interview protocol was then designed to explore whether students who have participated in programs abroad acquired, enhanced, or developed the four competencies to a greater extent than students who stayed at home.

Sutton, Richard C., and Donald L. Rubin. (2004). *The GLOSSARI Project: Initial Findings from a System-Wide Research Initiative on Study Abroad Learning Outcomes.* Frontiers: The Interdisciplinary Journal of Study Abroad, 10, 65–82.

This unusually comprehensive, six-phase and multiyear University System of Georgia study has collected data from more than 20,000 students during the past five years. It is designed to explore the extent to which students acquire both curricular content knowledge and cognitive understanding while abroad, as compared to students who stay at home.

Phase I, which is now complete, compares the self-reported learning outcomes of study abroad participants and nonparticipants. Phase II, also recently completed, compares pre- and post-departure self-reported learning outcomes. Phase III will compare participants and nonparticipants on course-specific examinations. Phase IV will compare academic performance measures, including graduation rates and licensing examination outcomes, of participants and nonparticipants. Phase V will correlate learning outcomes with program design features, including orientation, length of stay, location, post-return debriefing, and percentage of unstructured time in the host culture. Phase VI will compare self-reported learning outcomes, career paths, and other factors two to five years after graduation. The study relies on a variety of measures, including several designed specifically for the project.

Ingraham, Edward, and Debra Peterson. (2004). *Assessing the Impact of Study Abroad on Student Learning at Michigan State University.* Frontiers: The Interdisciplinary Journal of Study Abroad, 10, 83–100.

This ongoing, multiphase study, which began in 2000, explores the impact of study abroad not only on students, but on faculty, academic departments, and Michigan State University (MSU) as a whole. The study explores the extent to which the university is meeting six objectives through its promotion of study abroad: facilitating students' intellectual growth, contributing to students' professional development, accelerating students' personal growth, developing students' skills for relating to culturally different others, enhancing students' self-awareness and understanding of their own culture, and contributing to the internationalization of the students' home departments, colleges, and the university.

Like the University System of Georgia study, this project is making excellent use of data already being collected at Michigan State University, in addition to relying on a variety of instruments and methods, qualitative and quantitative. These include student self-assessment data collected through pre- and post-program surveys, post-program retrospective questionnaires, journal entries, and student focus groups. MSU has by now collected five years of demographic data about successive student cohorts—data that allows for comparisons of gender, ethnicity, academic discipline, and time to graduation, between students who have and have not studied abroad.

While continuing to solicit student input by means of continually revised instruments, the MSU project has placed increasing emphasis on faculty leaders' observations of how their study abroad programs affect their students and their own professional lives, information provided in end-of-program reports. These faculty reports have strongly confirmed what earlier phases of the study discovered about student learning. These reports also serve as a starting point for the assessment of study abroad's impact on faculty.

The Impact of One or More Variables on Student Learning

While early assessment studies tended to seek evidence that students were in fact learning something useful abroad—and as we have seen, that something was usually a second language—much recent research has focused not only on how much students learn abroad but also on what sorts of specific variables impact their learning. Some of these studies focus on the impact of one variable, while others explore how multiple variables influence learning.

Program Duration

Several studies that measure the impact of one variable, program duration, examine one of the most widely held pieces of conventional wisdom about education abroad: that to be meaningful, a sojourn abroad needs to last at least a semester, if not a year.

Chieffo, Lisa and Lesa Griffiths. (2004). *Large-Scale Assessment of Student Attitudes after Short Term Study Abroad Program.* Frontiers: The Interdisciplinary Journal of Study Abroad, 10, 165–177.

This study explores whether a large sample of students enrolled in courses abroad during five-week University of Delaware January-term programs were as successful as students who stay at home during January term in acquiring "global awareness." The authors developed a survey instrument that allowed them to measure what they suggest are the four essential dimensions of cultural awareness: intercultural awareness, personal growth and development, awareness of global interdependence, and functional knowledge of world geography and language.

Dwyer, Mary. (2004). *More is Better: The Impact of Study Abroad Program Duration. Frontiers:* The Interdisciplinary Journal of Study Abroad, 10, 151–63.

This study, which involved more than 3,700 participants in the Institute for the International Education of Students (IES) programs during the previous 50 years, allowed the authors not only to identify a variety of outcomes that former participants associate with study abroad but also to correlate those outcomes with the duration of programs in which those participants had studied. The study describes the questionnaire used in the longitudinal data-collection exercise and identifies the impact of programs of varying length on five outcomes: student academic choices, career development, personal and social development, foreign language commitment and use, and intercultural competence and intercultural awareness. The correlations between these different outcomes and the duration of IES programs—summer, fall semester, spring semester, and academic year— challenge conventional study abroad wisdom in interesting ways. Six other duration studies are based on an unusually rich retrospective longitudinal research project conducted by IES.[8]

Grading

Trooboff, Steve, Bill Cressey and Susan Monty. (2004). *Does Study Abroad Grading Motivate Students?* Frontiers: The Interdisciplinary Journal of Study Abroad, 10, 201–217.

A recent study focusing on the impact of a single variable examines another piece of conventional wisdom: that home institutional grade reporting policies—whether letter grades or pass/fail notations are used, and whether grades simply appear on transcripts or are calculated into grade point averages—affect the motivation and hence the performance of US students abroad. The authors investigated whether grades earned on Council on International Education Exchange (CIEE) programs correlated with the grading policies of the students' home institutions. The results of their study provide evidence that, once again, challenges conventional study abroad wisdom.

Another group of studies, those that explore the impact of factors in the education abroad environment, have grown out of the simple recognition that research posited on the existence of a sort of generic notion of study abroad could not lead to meaningful conclusions about student learning. Experience with returning students had taught education abroad professionals that the various types of programs abroad provided a range of environments that seemed to allow for very different sorts of learning. While professionals have long appreciated that different programs allow for different sorts of learning, they have frequently held very different views about what sorts of programs provide the most effective learning environments.

Some practitioners have claimed that direct enrollment programs offer the best opportunities for immersion experiences, while others have asserted that faculty-led island programs allow for a degree of academic control notoriously lacking in other approaches, and so on. The debate about the merits of one program type over another, however, has been confined largely to anecdote and conjecture; relatively little research-based evidence has been offered in support of claims about the superiority of one particular program type over others.

That situation changed dramatically at the June 1998 NAFSA conference in Denver, when John and Lilli Engle proposed a very different approach to classifying education abroad programs. Their system provided a breakthrough for research purposes: a testable hypothesis that eight key elements—eight independent variables—significantly impact student learning abroad. The program classification system that education abroad professionals relied on in the past was not a classification system at all. In referring to *island, direct enrollment, faculty-led semester, short-term*, and *experiential* or *service learning* programs, the conventional system referred to program *types* that in practice frequently overlapped. Students enrolled in an *exchange* might be participating in a direct enrollment, a faculty-led, or even a short-term program. An island program might in practice rely on faculty from a local university or enroll students for some part of their courses at that local university, and a faculty-led semester or direct enrollment program might provide opportunities for students to engage in experiential or service learning activities. The term *hybrid program*, which attempted to acknowledge the overlap among program types, offered no help at all for research purposes. The conventional approach was fundamentally flawed. A semester-length direct enrollment program that put students in classrooms and housed them in apartments with other US students provided for very different types of learning than a semester program that included, in addition to the classroom, structured experiential work and housing with a host family.

Engle and Engle's new system, which the Forum on Education Abroad's Outcomes and Research Committee has endorsed for research purposes, classifies programs in a more logical and consistent way than does the conventional approach. In focusing squarely on student learning, this new system is based on a simple proposition: Programs can be compared according to the extent to which they provide students with structured, focused opportunities to integrate culturally. Within this system, an individual program is not described as *short term* or as *semester direct enrollment*, but is instead described with reference to the ways that the program's design responds to the eight predetermined features, each of which presumably influences student learning. This approach, which amounts to deconstructing all study abroad programs into basic, shared elements, allows learning outcomes to be measured through relying on a common basis of comparison across programs. The key program characteristics are:

1. Length of student sojourn
2. Student predeparture second-language competence
3. Required second language use, in class and out (when applicable)
4. Host or home institution faculty teaching students

5. Type of courses students take abroad (with other program students, with other international students in specially organized classes, with host country students in regular university courses, etc.)

6. Presence or absence of mentoring, of guided cultural reflection

7. Whether students are required to participate in experiential learning initiatives

8. Type of student housing

A recent study, The Georgetown University Consortium Project, has based its research design on Engle and Engle's system, using their key program elements as the study's primary independent variables. As we have seen earlier in this chapter, that study documents student learning in three domains—second-language acquisition, intercultural sensitivity, and disciplinary learning—at more than 60 programs abroad. In adopting Engle and Engle's eight key elements as independent variables, the study provides a direct test of the hypothesis that key program characteristics significantly influence student learning, and is measuring the extent to which each variable, as well as groupings of the variables, influence student learning in each of the three domains.

Studies Organized Around Different Learning Domains

Second-language acquisition

Brecht, Richard, Dan Davidson, and Ralph B. Ginsberg. (1993). *Predictors of Foreign Language Gain During Study Abroad.* Washington, DC: National Foreign Language Center and American Council of Teachers of Russian.

Brecht, Richard D. and Jennifer L. Robinson. (1993). *Qualitative Analysis of Second Language Acquisition in Study Abroad: The ACTR/NFLC Project.* Washington, DC: National Foreign Language Center and American Council of Teachers of Russian.

These two related research studies explore the second-language learning that occurs in a study abroad context. Of particular interest is that the researchers explore, from both a quantitative and a qualitative perspective, the second-language learning of students who studied for four months over a four-year period in Russia. In Predictors of Foreign Language Gain during Study Abroad, the authors conducted a large-scale statistical study that analyzed the language gains of 658 students.

The authors examined gains in proficiency-oriented oral language use, listening comprehension, reading, and writing, along with a series of learner variables related to their prior language learning background. The primary finding of this study is that several learner variables are significant predictors of second-language gains, including gender, knowledge of other foreign languages, aptitude as measured by the Modern Language Aptitude Test, and prior proficiency in another foreign language.

In the second article, Qualitative Analysis of Second Language Acquisition in Study Abroad, the authors used qualitative methods, including gathering data from student journals, field observations, interviews, and recordings. The data were used to analyze the students' experiences abroad, their language-learning behaviors, and the students' own perceptions of their language learning. The findings of this research in large measure support and add depth to the findings of the quantitative study.

Segalowitz, Norman, and Freed, Barbara F. (2004). *Context, Contact, and Cognition in Oral Fluency Acquisition: Learning Spanish in At Home and Study Abroad Contexts.* Studies in Second Language Acquisition, 26, 173–199.

In this study, the authors examine the role of context of learning in second-language acquisition. This study compares gains in second-language acquisition for students studying on campus with students studying abroad to determine whether students' second-language acquisition improves through studying abroad. The researchers compared 40 students studying Spanish on their home campus and 40 students studying Spanish on a study abroad program in Spain. They examined several measures of oral performance gains, including temporal and hesitation phenomena and gains in oral proficiency, as measured by the Oral Proficiency Interview (OPI). These oral gains were also related to cognitive measures of speed of word recognition, efficiency of lexical access, and speed and efficiency of attention control that is thought to underlie oral performance. The findings of this research suggest that the students studying Spanish abroad made greater gains in second-language learning than students who studied on campus; however, the role of context was not the only important factor. The nature of the individual student and his or her readiness to take advantage of the opportunity provided by studying abroad were critical as well.

Intercultural competence

Intercultural competence has been defined in a variety of ways over the past 30 years. The first study that documents consensus among leading intercultural experts on a more precise definition was conducted by Darla K. Deardorff in 2004. In this study, intercultural competence is defined through a visual model with the measurable outcome being *communicating and behaving appropriately and effectively in intercultural situations.* Elements in the model detail requisite attitudes, knowledge, and skills as well as internal and external outcomes.[9]

Affective/attitudes

Carlson, Jerry S. and Keith F. Widaman. (1988). *The Effects of Study Abroad During College on Attitudes Toward Other Cultures.* International Journal of Intercultural Relations, 12, 1–17.

This research study assesses changes in attitudes and perceptions toward international understanding by students who studied abroad for an academic year at universities in Sweden, Spain, France, Germany, Italy, and the United Kingdom. This research seeks to assess one of the central assumptions in education abroad, namely that students' attitudes toward other cultures and their own country change as a result of studying abroad. This study surveyed 450 students who studied abroad during their junior year and 800 students who stayed on their home campus. Students were asked a set of questions about areas such as their awareness of global problems, concern for problems of the developing world, desire for international peace, wish to help find solutions to global problems, respect for other cultures, need for closer cooperation among nations, and desire to travel to other countries. The researchers asked the students to reflect on these issues both from the perspective of before their departure for study abroad and after their return from study abroad. Students were also asked to judge the degree of change in their perspectives since before studying abroad to the present on issues such as negative feelings about foreigners, positive feelings about their own country, and critical views of their own country, among others. The researchers used factor analysis to analyze the data. The major findings of the research indicate that the students who studied abroad showed higher levels of international political concern, cross-cultural interest, and cultural cosmopolitanism than the comparison group of students who did not study abroad.

Behavioral/skills

Gurman, Ernest B. (1989). *Travel Abroad: A Way to Increase Creativity?* Educational Research Quarterly, 13, No. 3, 12–16.

This research study examines the relationship between study abroad and creativity. This study uses an interesting experimental design to compare gains in creativity between students who studied abroad and students who did not. The experimental group contained 24 students who participated in an abnormal psychology course as part of a summer study abroad program in London. The control group consisted of 24 students who took the same course taught on the home campus in the United States. The instrument used to measure creativity was the Torrance Test of Creative Thinking, Verbal Forms A and B. The test was administered to each group on the first day of the class and again on the final day of the class. The test looked at three variables: fluency, flexibility, and originality. The results of the analysis indicate that both the experiment and the control groups improved in each of the variables; however, only the results of the experimental groups were statistically significant. The author concluded that the exposure of the experimental group to a foreign culture and a variety of new experiences increased the students' creativity.

Long-term impact

Dwyer, Mary M. (2004). *Charting the Impact of Studying Abroad.* International Educator, 14–20.

In this research study, the Institute for the International Education of Students (IES) has undertaken a large-scale longitudinal survey of its alumni. This study is particularly important because it is the only longitudinal quantitative study of study abroad alumni measuring the impact of study abroad on students' academic, career, and life choices. IES surveyed 17,000 students and received 3,700 responses from students who had studied abroad through IES from 1950 to 1999.

In the area of academic impact, the majority of respondents indicated that studying abroad had a positive impact on their academic careers, particularly in their commitment to foreign language study, and that it enhanced their interest in academic study and influenced their subsequent educational experiences. In regards to career development, the majority of respondents who participated in internships abroad reported that the internship experience influenced their careers. Additionally, over time more respondents reported working for overseas employers. In regards to intercultural development, the majority of respondents indicated that their study abroad experience had a positive impact on their intercultural development as measured in areas such as the following: influenced to seek out a greater diversity of friends, given an ongoing appreciation of the arts, continues to influence perspective on the world, and influenced to explore other cultures. And in the area of personal and social growth, the students' responses were consistently positive and lasting as measured by tolerance of ambiguity, learning something about themselves, maintaining friendships with US friends met abroad, maintaining friendships with host country friends, and sparking an interest in travel.

Pre- and Post-Program Programmatic Interventions

Significant challenges exist in attempting to assess the impact and outcome of pre- and post-program interventions, such as predeparture orientation and reentry support. The first is methodological; it is quite difficult to isolate program interventions' impact from other contributing factors that impinge and impact upon education abroad participants. Opinions regarding the effectiveness of such interventions also may depend to some extent upon the audience in question; for instance, education abroad personnel and international educators may have different criteria regarding the ideal outcomes of these interventions than the actual education abroad participants. Finally, conceptual issues can obfuscate the assessment of programmatic interventions, especially those related to reentry. In fact, several of the international educators who have made the most significant contributions to reentry research have chosen to focus their investigations primarily upon the nature of the reentry experience itself, believing that until the reentry process is more fully understood, it is not possible to design and assess appropriate interventions during this post-study abroad phase of the participant experience.

Pre-Program Interventions

Martin, Judith N. (1989). *Predeparture Orientation: Preparing College Sojourners for Intercultural Interaction.* Communication Education, 38, No. 3, 249–258.

This article describes a predeparture orientation course. It further discusses the difficulties encountered in trying to assess the effectiveness of the course, due to the lack of student outcome data and methodological challenges involved in surveying students after their study abroad experience regarding the impact of the predeparture orientation.

Szabo, Mary. (1996). *Predeparture Orientation for Study Abroad: Perceived Importance of Components.* Master's thesis, University of Alberta.

This research explored the critical components of predeparture orientation as perceived by academics and practitioners, the sponsoring institution, students preparing to study abroad, and past participants of study abroad. Data were acquired using a focus group, interviews, and a questionnaire. The findings show some disparity between what students believed would be most useful and what the international educators actually provided. In general, students claimed to want specific and personalized information during orientation, and they preferred an experiential approach.

Post-Program Interventions

Citron, James L. (1996). *The Cross-Cultural Re-Entry Experiences of Short-term Study Abroad Students from the United States.* PhD diss. University of Pennsylvania.

Citron, James L. *U.S. Students Abroad: Host Culture Integration or Third Culture Formation? (2002). In Rockin in Red Square: Critical Approaches to International Education in the Age of Cyberculture, ed.* Nana Rinehart and Walter Gurnzweig. Munster, Germany: LIT Verlag, distributed in U.S. by Transaction Publishers/Rutgers University Press.

This research focused on a group of undergraduate students attending a semester abroad program in Spain and followed them from preprogram through the program to post-program in order to learn more about their reentry experiences. The research utilized a variety of quantitative and qualitative data collection techniques, including participant observations, researcher-participant interviews, student-participant journals, and student-participant self-report rates. Data were considered both collectively and individually. The focus was upon identifying longitudinal patterns for students' adjustment overseas and during reentry.

Citron's conclusions refute the blanket application of the U-curve/W-curve paradigm to all overseas sojourners. Instead, the author posits that cultural adjustment and reentry does not follow a single common path but varies among participants. Some of the study cohorts did integrate into the host culture and reenter their home cultures having adopted new values, norms, and assumptions; but others developed what he terms a *third culture*, which primarily evolved from the norms and behaviors of the study abroad group itself, rather than the host culture. The nature of the reentry experience was related to whether a student had lived in Spain according to the home culture's norms, the third culture's norms, or the host culture's norms.

These conclusions affect the design of reentry programs as well as the type of program interventions carried out during the course of the study abroad program to encourage student integration vs. third culture retreat.

Henderson, Myer. (1999). *Facilitating Reentry for American Study Abroad Participants.* Master's thesis. The School for International Training.

This study examines the relationship between University of Rhode Island returning study abroad participants' engagement as peer mentors and their reentry experiences. A comparable number of returning students who participated and did not participate in the optional peer mentor program were included as a control group. Both oral interviews and a written instrument were used to obtain data. The findings indicate that the peer mentor program affected the participants positively in several ways, including easing their reentry to the United States and helping them to positively utilize their international experiences on the home campus and in society.

Assessment of Education Abroad Impact upon Host Culture

To date, the international education community has focused primarily on assessing the impact of the education abroad experience upon program participants and, to a lesser extent, the sending universities and colleges. Little attention has been devoted to considering what impact a education abroad program and students might have upon the host culture, in particular those peoples and institutions who have direct contact with the program participants—host families, hosting universities and institutions, participant host country peers, and more. Such impact can be significant in some cases, especially where education abroad programs are operating in cultures and settings that are markedly different than the United States in terms of economic resources, social structures, and/or cultural norms. Hopefully, this important theme will be the focus of greater assessment attention in the future.

Some of the studies that have assessed education abroad impact upon the host culture are:

Burns, Patrick Dean. (1996). *Foreign Students in Japan: A Qualitative Study of Interpersonal Relations Between North American University Exchange Students and their Japanese Hosts.* PhD diss. University of Massachusetts, 1996.

This study examines the problems of interpersonal relationship-building between Japanese hosts and US study abroad students during their one year of study at a Japanese university. These data were obtained via in-depth interviewing and direct behavior observation methods. The conclusion was that the study abroad students evidenced frustration regarding the perceived shallowness of relationship development with their respective host family.

Gorden, Raymond L. (1995). *Living in Latin America: A Case Study in Cross-Cultural Communication.* Chicago: National Textbook Co.

This landmark study examines the communication (and miscommunication) between US students and Peace Corps trainees on one hand and Colombian host families on the other. To date, it is the most extensive and comprehensive research on the interrelations between US study abroad students and host families. It was initially a doctoral dissertation (titled *American Guests in Colombian Houses: A Study in Cross-Cultural Communication*, 1968), and was later published in book format. The author obtained information from 90 Colombian host families and 120 US students and Peace Corps trainees over a three-year period. Several data acquisition methods were utilized, including group discussions, participant observation, questionnaires, and individual interviews. Gorden developed an interviewing methodology in which US researchers interviewed the US students and Colombian researchers interviewed the host families, to avoid getting bogged down in the same cross-cultural misunderstandings that were being studied.

Conclusions focus on nonlinguistic aspects of culture and silent assumptions as the most important in facilitating (or inhibiting) effective cross-cultural dialog and communication. Often in the guest/host family interface, dissonant communication and understanding was attributable not to value differences but to seemingly trivial issues such as mealtime, bath time, location of the television, etc. These findings led the author to argue against orientation programs that draw heavily upon US returnees from abroad to instruct US students about to go to the same country. He argues that this often perpetuates distortions, blind spots, and the dissemination of inaccurate information regarding the hosts, since returnees typically are unaware of their own cross-cultural lacunae.

Iino, Masajazu. (1996). *Excellent Foreigner! Gaijinization of Japanese Language and Culture in Contact Situations: An Ethnographic Study of Dinner Table Conversations between Japanese Host Families and America Students.* PhD diss., University of Pennsylvania.

This study focuses on how language acquisition takes place in the host family setting. It draws upon data gathered from observing and recording dinner conversations between host family members and study abroad students during an eight-week intensive language program in Kyoto, Japan. The author concluded that the Japanese hosts modified both their language use and presentation of culture in their interactions with the study abroad student. The author supplemented the observational and recorded data with questionnaires, interviews, and group discussions.

Levy, Julie A. (2002). *Host Culture Perception of a Study Abroad Program and its Impact on the Community.* Master's thesis, The School for International Training.

This study investigates the perceptions of heads of host families regarding their role and purpose in receiving study abroad students. The research was carried out among a long-term group of host families from a *barrio* in Managua, Nicaragua, using both interviews and questionnaires. Despite the small size of the interview pool (11 completed questionnaires) and the *sui generis* nature of the neighborhood and program, the study results are elucidating and may be applicable to other host family situations and sites. The author concludes that the host family heads consider themselves professionals who play a key role in informing and educating the study abroad students about the host culture and society. Additionally, the host families did not perceive a strong impact of the students upon the local neighborhood and host society.

Stephenson, Skye. (1999). *Study Abroad as a Transformational Experience and Its Effect Upon Study Abroad Students and Host Nationals in Santiago, Chile.* Frontiers: The Interdisciplinary Journal of Study Abroad, 5, 1–30.

This study assesses the impact of a study abroad program in Santiago on the values of the program participants as well as some of the host nationals with whom they interacted. The host nationals included were the host family heads and university professors. Information was acquired via questionnaires (different for each of the three target groups) and follow-up interviews with some of the respondents. In total, 52 students, 56 host families, and 33 professors completed the questionnaires.

The results reveal that the program impacted not only the program participants, but also the host culture members and certain aspects of the host culture. Both the Chilean host families and the university professors experienced certain value transformations/changes as a result of their relationship with the US students, particularly in views of the "other" and US culture and views of Chilean culture, and around issues of racial tolerance, acceptance of differing sexual practices, and a broadening of dialog and discourse. The applicability of these findings to other host cultures is not clear, although it does seem likely that similar patterns would be found in at least some other receiving sites, especially those that do not have a long history of receiving study abroad students.

Stephenson, Skye. *International Educational Flows (IEFs) between the United States and Cuba (1959–2005): Policy Winds and Exchange Flows.* Journal of Cuban Studies, forthcoming.

This study examines the significant role that study abroad and international educational programs have had in the bilateral relationship between the United States and post-Revolutionary Cuba. Based on interviews with policy-makers and international educators in both countries, the assessment draws on oral histories and written records and documents. Its conclusion points to the often unheralded importance of international educational flows in the international, globalized arena.

UNESCO, Ingrid Eide, ed. (1970). *Students as Links Between Cultures. A Cross Cultural Survey Based on UNESCO Studies.* Oslo: UNESCO and the International Peace Research Institute.

This study is not primarily assessment based, nor is its main focus on US study abroad students. However, the issues and concerns that the authors raised in 1970 relate to international education and its impact not only on exchange students but also on host cultures, and these continue to be relevant today. Among the most significant chapter authors who address this topic are Klineberg and Breitenbach; both raise the importance of considering the impact of exchanges on the host country and community and suggest areas for future assessment and study.

Program Assessment in Education Abroad

Education abroad program assessment has long been a common and important practice in international education. Assessing education abroad programs and concern for standards in the field can be traced as far back as the late 1950s. Although education abroad program assessment has become more complex over the past 50 years, much of the early work done in this area continues to lay the foundation of program assessment today.

Comprehensive education abroad program assessment plans should include both formative and summative assessment data. Formative assessment data provides information about specific program areas, such as student learning, and offers insight on improvement. Formative assessment can and should be implemented at any time during an education abroad program. Summative assessment provides a more comprehensive overview of the entire study abroad program and typically occurs upon completion of the program. Summative assessment data is used to evaluate the quality or worth of an entire education abroad program.

Council on Student Travel. (1965). *A Guide to Institutional Self-Study and Evaluation of Educational Programs Abroad.* New York: Council on Student Travel, Inc.

This guide by the Council on Student Travel was one of the first of its kind in the field of study abroad. Despite being 40 years old, if you removed all dates, the price tag of $1.00, some of the historical background on the project, and some of the terminology, you would be unable to tell if the guide was published in 1965 or 2006. This guide identifies many of the same concerns the field has today about the quality of programs and the importance of program evaluation. It is divided into the following four sections:

1. All programs
2. Undergraduate programs abroad
3. Nonacademic programs abroad

4. Overseas programs for secondary school students

Like many higher education and study abroad program assessment guides, this guide does not prescribe a specific set of outcomes for a successful study abroad program. Instead, it provides researchers with general principles they may want to consider and suggestions for questions they may want to ask about the study abroad program being assessed.

Frey, James. Chair. (1979). *Study Abroad Programs: An Evaluation Guide.* Washington, DC: AACRAO/NAFSA Task Force on Study Abroad (ANTFOSA).

This study abroad program evaluation guide, a joint publication of the AACRAO/NAFSA Task Force on Study Abroad (ANTFOSA),[10] identified seven steps to evaluate study abroad programs. This guide was based on systematic analysis of various study abroad program components categorized under the following four headings:

1. Basic information
2. Academic aspects
3. Interaction with host culture
4. Administrative aspects

The guide also provides questions relating to each of the 89 study abroad program components. It remains a useful guide on standards of successful study abroad program evaluation.

Marsh, Harriet L. (1994). *NAFSA Self-Study Guide: The Assessment of Programs and Services for International Educational Exchange at Postsecondary Institutions.* Cranberry Twp., PA: NAFSA: Association of International Educators.

This NAFSA self-study guide is comprehensive in scope and addresses all areas in the field of international education, including study abroad programs. The author provides a helpful history of NAFSA's early attention to self-study efforts in the field. This well-written guide informs readers about self-regulation from the institutional perspective and provides valuable information about self-study as a concept and its definition and purpose. The author also focuses on practical matters such as designing, organizing, and conducting the assessment study and provides sample questions that may be used in the self-study process. An added bonus is the inclusion of "Principles for International Educational Exchange," which provides principles for working with international students in the United

States, English language programs, community services and programs, and US study abroad. Standards for US study abroad addresses advisory services for study abroad, co-sponsoring study-abroad programs administered by other institutions, and the administration of study abroad programs.

Stimpfl, Joseph R., and David Engberg. (1997). *What to Know Before You Go: Creating a Comparison for Research on Study Abroad Programs.* International Education Forum, 17 no. 1, 7–21.

Stimpfl, Joseph R., and David Engberg. (1997). *Comparing Apples to Apples: An Integrated Approach to Study Abroad Program Assessment.* International Education Forum, 17, no. 2, 97–109.

This two-part article begins with an in-depth review of study abroad research literature. It examines several well-known models used to assess cross-cultural learning and critiques many empirical studies on the study abroad experience. Detailed analysis of the main study abroad assessment models and related research studies allows the researchers to identify many of the problems inherent to study abroad research and provide a preliminary concept of a study abroad program classification. The research was structured by conducting in-depth interviews over 18 months with sojourners from the University of Nebraska-Lincoln and using an analytic induction approach to further refine the study abroad classification model. Similar in goal but different in structure to the Engle classification system (previously described), Stimpfl and Engberg's *comparative matrix* is composed of the following four domains/levels:

1. Level of immersion—the ways and degree to which sojourners are immersed in the host culture.

2. Level of synthesis – the formal programmatic (i.e. structured) relationship between curriculum, pedagogy, and environment.

3. Level of difference – the degree to which the elements of the host culture influence the sojourner.

4. Level of personal development—modeled after Milton Bennet's (1986) Developmental Model of Intercultural Sensitivity

The researchers envision that by assigning values to each of the domains/levels, study abroad professionals may be able to predict program success. Although the Stimpfl and Engberg comparative matrix requires further testing on many different types of study abroad programs, it is still a useful tool for comparing and assessing study abroad programs.

Institute for the International Education of Students. (2003). *The IES MAP (Model Assessment Practice) for Study Abroad: Charting a Course for Quality.* Chicago: Institute for the International Education of Students.

Gillespie, Joan., Larry A. Braskamp, and David C. Braskamp. (1999). *Evaluation and Study Abroad: Developing Assessment Criteria and Practices to Promote Excellence.* Frontiers: The Interdisciplinary Journal of Study Abroad, 5, 101–127.

Perhaps the best known study abroad program assessment tool is the IES MAP (Model Assessment Practice). A task force of leaders in international and higher education and assessment developed the IES MAP for the Institute for the International Education of Students (IES) for internal program assessment and development purposes. Now in its third edition, the IES MAP was first published in 1999 after an extensive series of site visits by task force members and significant data analysis. The IES MAP, widely recognized as the industry leader in study abroad program assessment, laid a valuable foundation for The Forum on Education Abroad in the development of the Standards of Good Practice for Education Abroad. Although the Institute for the International Education of Students uses the IES MAP internally, the organization freely shares and distributes this assessment tool to faculty and administrators from US institutions of higher education, study abroad professionals, accrediting organizations, and parents and students. Making the IES MAP available to the greater study abroad community allows practitioners and participants to adapt this tool to their own individual program assessment needs. The IES MAP focuses on four academic areas:

1. Student learning environment
2. Student learning: Assessment and intercultural development
3. Resources for academic and student support
4. Program administration and development

The Gillespie, Braskamp, and Braskamp article in *Frontiers: The Interdisciplinary Journal of Study Abroad* provides insight into the development of the IES MAP by the task force members and consultant to the project.

Forum on Education Abroad. (2005). Standards of Good Practice for Education Abroad. Northampton, MA: The Forum on Education Abroad.

Education abroad program assessment and standards of practice in the field often blend together, as we see above. Therefore the *Standards of Good Practice for*

Education Abroad by the Forum on Education Abroad is included in this section on education abroad program assessment. These standards of good practice have been in development since 2002, with the next round of review and testing already planned. In July 2002 the Forum's Committee on the Standards of Good Practice polled the Forum membership to determine the top five critical issues in the field that need standards of good practice. Analysis of this survey data lead to the online version of the *Draft Standards of Good Practice* in May 2003. In June 2004 the first edition of the *Standards of Good Practice for Education Abroad* was distributed to Forum members for review, critique, and feedback, followed by preliminary testing by the School for International Training (SIT) and the Foundation for International Education in London. The second edition of the *Standards of Good Practice for Education Abroad* was released in November 2005. The Forum has recruited a cross-section of institutions and education abroad program types and is now in the beta testing phase of the project, which consists of self-study followed by an examination team's onsite visitation. The *Standards of Good Practice for Education Abroad* use a queries based approach under the following eight standards:

1. Ethics and integrity
2. Mission, policies, and procedures
3. Academic framework
4. Organizational and program resources
5. Student selection and code of conduct
6. Learning environment
7. Student learning and development
8. Health, safety, and security

The Forum's *Standards of Good Practice for Education Abroad* is a tremendous asset in the field for use as a tool for program evaluation and improvement.

Education abroad professionals have a variety of instruments and resources at their disposal to assess education abroad programs. These resources offer invaluable advice and direction for the professional, institution, or provider new to assessing education abroad programs. These tools and resources also provide seasoned education abroad program assessment professionals and offices with the resources necessary to fine-tune their current assessment methods or ideas and support to restructure current practices.

Institutional Internationalization[11]

As education abroad exists within the context of a US degree program, it is important to assess it as an element of institutional internationalization within US higher education. Generally speaking, one view of education abroad in US higher education is that it has taken a unique path, different from other higher education systems around the world. Understanding that path requires a framework of how US higher education exists and how internationalization fits within that system.

Control, Review, and Approval of US Higher Education

In the United States, formal review and approval of a college or university comes from regional accrediting agencies. These accrediting bodies make decisions about the approval of new higher education institutions. Once an institution is approved, the regional accrediting agencies are responsible for regular review and approval for existing institutions through a self-study and peer review process.

The Council for Higher Education Accreditation provides a good background on the fundamentals. The accreditation process looks closely at issues like library holdings, faculty-student ratios, percentage of tenured versus nontenured faculty, and the academic credentials of the faculty. However, accreditation has provided only a limited focus (if any) on internationalization issues, including study abroad.[12] Even formal review through the accreditation process is limited in its definition of program quality at the highest levels. The process is responsible for confirming a minimum standard and promoting the highest standards for each institution. Because the process is different in each region, and accreditation provides institutions with the ability to implement programs in many different ways, one of the distinguishing factors of US higher education in general is the differences and distinguishing factors of the various colleges and universities across the United States.

If one sees variance in other parts of the operation of US higher education, it is multiplied in internationalization efforts. They are rarely reviewed in depth as a critical component for maintaining institutional accreditation, and state and federal funds are limited in supporting internationalization efforts. Although some of the regional accrediting agencies have put in some time and effort to review education abroad programs, the review and emphasis is limited in scope. The number of formal accreditation visits to the many education abroad programs where more than 205,000 US students study each year, as a percentage basis of all programs and all students, is small at best.[13] As a result, education abroad programs have developed within varying institutional internationalization frameworks and varying models, in terms of how they fit in the institutional hierarchy and how offices are staffed and programs are implemented. At the same time, an increasingly large number of colleges and universities have included internationalization issues into their strategic plans and mission statements, some of which include references to education abroad. The most recent Harvard College Curriculum Review (which takes place only every 30 years) focused significantly on internationalization issues. In November 2005, Goucher College announced that it will require all undergraduate students to study abroad. As noted above, the implementation of internationalization and study abroad efforts takes place on a campus-by-campus basis. While the Harvard Curriculum Review and Goucher College were framing study abroad growth, one of the community colleges with the longest history of providing study abroad closed its district's study abroad office.[14] At the same time as the district office closed, study abroad continued at individual colleges with less central support. Will these study abroad opportunities, whether at Harvard or a community college, be another way for college students to find a party and be of legal drinking age overnight abroad, or will they fit into a student's academic curriculum and be a part of an institutional strategy for internationalization?

The study abroad experience is not always integrated into a college or university curriculum. Many students participate in programs not operated by their home institution. Even when the home institution does operate a program, courses may not even count toward the student's degree, general education, or elective needs. As discussed above, there are currently few graduate degree programs with a focus on the internationalization of US higher education. In fact, many institutions do not even have a study abroad office or full-time study abroad administrator or comprehensive staff.

At the same time, the education abroad field has pushed study abroad forward as a critical international experience that should be part of the college or university academic career of a larger number of our students. At this time, only a small percentage of US college and university students study abroad. The most recent data shows 205,983 US students studying abroad during the 2004–05 academic year, an increase of 8% from the previous year. When compared with the College Board's data on overall US higher education enrollments, the percentage of US higher education students studying abroad in any given year is estimated between 1% and 3%, depending on the College Board's total higher education enrollment figure for that year. Alternatively, a cohort analysis of education abroad participation of students over the course of a four-year degree program suggests that somewhere between 9% and 12% of.US students at four-year undergraduate institutions study abroad at some point before they graduate. Depending on whether the focus is only on four-year institutions, which send the majority of US students abroad, or on all undergraduate institutions, including community colleges, the participation rate can range from 3% to 12%, which is consistent with other analyses conducted outside of the Institute of International Education.[15] Congress named 2006 The Year of Study Abroad,[16] and the Lincoln Commission has suggested in a recently released report that the field should increase participation from less than 200,000 students to over 1 million students studying abroad each year.

As US higher education internationalization and education abroad continue to grow in importance, the international education profession is at a point in its development where the only mechanisms to ensure the quality and purpose of programs for an institution come from the institution itself. In recent years, institutions have increasingly emphasized the importance of education abroad for their students. Trying to understand the purpose of education abroad at US colleges and universities in the broadest sense requires understanding how colleges and universities are international in nature and how education abroad fits into that featured area.

"Study abroad can be one of the most life-changing experiences in a US college or university." This statement is heard regularly from faculty and staff administering education abroad programs and from students who participate in the programs. However, the field has not yet come to a point where the outcomes research and quantitative data demonstrate the impact of study abroad on an individual student or on a college or university. What does the education abroad experience bring back to the institution? Important questions include issues related to the impact of education abroad on the campus community—students, faculty, staff, and the local community outside of campus.

1. How does education abroad change a students' perspective, and how does that impact their institution (curricular aspects: courses, major and minor departments, involvement of students in research, changes in language course enrollments and language learning, etc.)?

2. How does education abroad change faculty members' perspectives based on their participation in or leadership of study abroad programs? Are there improvements in on-campus learning because of returned education abroad students in classes? Are more students who studied abroad taking advanced language classes that would not have been offered otherwise? Are additional opportunities for international learning, research, and travel available to faculty because of on-campus education abroad and international exchange agreements?

3. How does education abroad change staff members' perspectives based on their participation in or leadership of study abroad programs? Do staff members outside of the education abroad office get involved in the study abroad process? Are they able to lead or support programs? Are returning students

impacting cocurricular and extracurricular processes in a way that changes the campus?

4. How does education abroad impact the community? Are returning students getting more involved in outreach and new models of international learning in ways that they would not if education abroad programs were not available? Are returning students bringing back skills for the global marketplace that can enhance the international climate of a local town or city?

Goodwin, Craufurd, D. and Michael Nacht. (1991). *Missing the Boat: The Failure to Internationalize American Higher Education.* Cambridge: Cambridge University Press.

Goodwin and Nacht's research challenged colleges and universities and pointed out weakness in US higher education internationalization related to education abroad as early as 1991. This book reports the results of an investigation into the internationalization of US higher education through the experience of faculty, using impressions and data from extensive campus visits and interviews at 37 institutions nationwide as well as data from four previous studies.

Development and implementation of education abroad mirrors that of running an entire college or university with a smaller number of students in many countries around the world. There is not currently a consistent model of either education abroad program development or administration. As discussed above, nor is there a consistent way to review and approve the institutions that provide education abroad programs based on their administration of programs. Accredited US colleges or universities run some programs. Others are administered onsite through foreign universities. Others are run by education abroad organizations that are a consortium of college and university members. Some programs are run by independent non- and for-profit companies with no academic credentials in the United States or abroad. An increasing number of programs are a hybrid mix of internally developed programs that may be administered by a company abroad that is not a college or university.

To provide a better understanding of the place of education abroad programming at a US college or university and to assess its impact, it is important that faculty, staff, and institution policy-makers look more closely at education abroad administration within US higher education internationalization efforts.

Internationalization on a US College or University Campus

Higher Education Internationalization

The three main areas of focus of US colleges and universities are teaching/learning, research, and community service. Stated simply, "Internationalization at the national, sector, and institutional levels is defined as the process of integrating an international, intercultural, or global dimension into the purpose, functions or delivery of postsecondary education."[17] The following articles by Jane Knight help provide a definition on what internationalization in higher education really means. Gilbert Merkx also provides a useful introduction to these issues, and Philip Altbach and Patti McGill Peterson provide a challenge to the level of internationalization in place.

Knight, Jane. (2004). *Internationalization Remodeled: Definition, Approaches, and Rationales.* Journal of Studies in International Education, 8, no. 1, 5–31.

In higher education. international contexts are becoming increasingly important, complex, and confusing. This article reexamines and updates the conceptual frameworks underpinning the notion of internationalization in light of today's changes and challenges. This article studies internationalization at both the institutional and national/sector level.

Both levels are important. The national/sector level has an important influence on the international dimension through policy, funding, programs, and regulatory frameworks. Yet the real process of internationalization is usually taking place at the institutional level. This article analyses the meaning, definition, rationales, and approaches to internationalization using a bottom-up (institutional) approach and a top-down (national/sector) approach, and examines the dynamic relationship between these two levels. Key policy issues and questions for the future direction of internationalization are identified.

Knight, Jane. (Fall 2003). *Updating the Definition of Internationalization.* Center for International Higher Education Newsletter, no.33, Boston.

Knight calls for revisiting the definition of *internationalization* to ensure that the meaning reflects current changes and challenges; is understood at the national and sector level as well as at the institutional level; and is appropriate for a broad range of contexts and countries of the world. Emerging terms discussed include *transnational education*, *borderless education*, and *cross-border education*. The paper proposes a new working definition of internationalization and looks at the way in which definitions can shape policy and how practice can influence definitions and policy. The author concludes that internationalization is changing the world of education, and globalization is changing the world of internationalization.

Knight, Jane. (Winter 2004). *New Rationales Driving Internationalization.* Center for International Higher Education Newsletter, no.34, Boston.

This article emphasizes the importance of having clearly articulated rationales for internationalization. It describes some important and discernible shifts in the rationales driving internationalization in the last decade, including: n*ational level, human resources development, strategic alliances, commercial trade, nation building, social and cultural development, institutional-level rationales, international profile and reputation, student and staff development, income generation, strategic alliances*, and *research and knowledge production. It argues that* **as** the rationales driving internationalization vary from institution to institution, from stakeholder to stakeholder, and from country to country, a clearer articulation of the values guiding internationalization is becoming increasingly important.

Merkx, Gilbert W. (Winter 2003). *The Two Waves of Internationalization in U.S.* Higher Education. International Educator, 12, no.1, 6–12.

The internationalization of American higher education is a complex process that has led to varied outcomes at the different types of educational institutions. Such diversity of experience is one of the reasons the term *international education* has different meanings to the various communities in higher education that are engaged in international activity. This article contrasts the dimensions of the first wave of internationalization in US higher education with the characteristics of the newer international challenges facing American higher education in the opening decade of the 21st century. Responding to these challenges requires innovation in administration, curriculum, foreign partnerships, and funding.

Altbach, Philip G. and Patti McGill Peterson. (Spring 1998). *Internationalize American Higher Education? Not Exactly.* Boston College Center for International Higher Education, no. 11. Boston.

The authors challenge US higher education institutions to look at whether they are really providing a framework for institutional internationalization and whether institutions themselves are providing a clear strategy for internationalization. The authors challenge higher education to provide learning that reverses existing insularity and promotes the importance of reversing insular practices instead to "study foreign cultures, interact with colleagues in other countries, send our students to study and learn firsthand about the rest of the world, and in the process build up not only expertise, but also goodwill and mutual understanding between the United States and the rest of the world." This article provides a vantage point for looking at one's own institution, in light of the internationalization efforts articulated the article , and those chronicled in publications noted below (published after 1998) that provide greater clarity on internationalization in general, and then on models of internationalization at various US colleges and universities.

Five Important Documents to Start with in Obtaining Appropriate Background and Taking Part in Institutional Assessment of Internationalization in the United States

Five documents are particularly useful in both framing the place of internationalization of US higher education and understanding the roles of those who carry out internationalization on US college and university campuses.

Beyond September 11: A Comprehensive National Policy on International Education: An International Policy Paper. (2002) Washington, DC: American Council on Education.

This policy paper provides a perspective that many US higher education associations endorsed on May 12, 2002. It attempted to raise issues and questions about the place of US higher education and higher education reform to take on a leadership role in developing "citizens with a broad set of international skills and cross-cultural understanding..." and which the administration and Congress could support by "declaring a national policy on international education." Along with the push for the government role in developing policy, the paper reviews many of the components of an effective internationalization strategy. Thirty-three higher education, scholarly, and exchange associations have endorsed this new proposal for a national policy on international education. The report outlines the US need for international and foreign language expertise and citizen awareness, examines the shortages in those areas, and proposes strategies and government policies to meet these needs.

Open Doors: Report on International Educational Exchange, Institute of International Education. New York.

Open Doors, published each year by the Institute for International Education (IIE), reports basic data on student exchange in US higher education. This publication provides the actual numbers of US students studying abroad, international students and faculty in the United States, and English-language program enrollments in US higher education. As one of the central components of US higher education, internationalization is the exchange of students and scholars across borders. It is important to understand the quantitative data provided by IIE. The most current data on education abroad, international students, and English as a second language participants can be found on the IIE website. Some of the more detailed data can only be obtained by IIE members.

Green, Madeleine F. and Christa Olson. (2003). *Internationalizing the Campus: A User's Guide.* Washington DC: American Council on Education.

This guide provides a foundation to understanding the issues behind campus internationalization. It provides a background on how to frame internationalization, a rationale for internationalization, and how to consider whether internationalization will be on the surface or an integrated part of institutional focus and identity. The authors then guide readers through the issues involved in considering ways to internationalize. This background leads to Appendix A: Questions to Guide an Institutional Review. This survey provides a method to review existing internationalization efforts as a self-study process, which can then lead an institution toward a strategy for institutional change. Institutions that are a part of the ACE Internationalization Collaborative use the survey as a starting point to analyze efforts on their campuses.

Bridges to the Future: Strategies for Internationalizing Higher Education. (1992). Ed. Charles B. Klasek. 13: 204–207. Carbondale, IL: Association of International Education Administrators.

Although published in 1992, this volume (published by AIEA, the higher education association that focuses on internationalization issues) provides a good background on some components of US higher education internationalization in terms of the administrative offices and the responsibilities of stakeholders across a campus that support it. In contrast to *A Users Guide*, AIEA's *Bridges to the Future* helps readers look more deeply at the administrative practices that make up the different components of internationalization.

American Council on Education. (2003). *Mapping Internationalization on U.S. Campuses: Final Report*, Washington, DC.

This 2003 report followed surveys conducted in 2001 on internationalization. Through that survey process, ACE created an internationalization index. The six dimensions listed by ACE include:

- Articulated commitment
- Academic offerings
- Organizational infrastructure
- External funding
- Institutional investment in faculty
- International students and student programs

This report examines the internationalization efforts of US colleges and universities with comparisons to previous data, as appropriate and possible. It also looks at the international experiences and attitudes of undergraduate students and faculty. Key questions include: To what extent are institutions internationalizing the undergraduate experience? What practices and policies are in place to support internationalization efforts? Do students graduate with international skills and knowledge? What international experiences and skills do students and faculty possess? Do students and faculty support international education initiatives?

The report concludes that colleges and universities should focus their efforts on the curriculum to ensure broad exposure to international learning; identify and build upon their existing available resources; bridge the disconnect between attitudes and actions; clearly articulate their commitment to internationalization; and create conditions that will increase the level of international learning on campus.

The American Council on Education published four documents focused on measuring internationalization by grouping of institutions at the following levels:

- Research universities
- Comprehensive universities
- Liberal arts colleges
- Community colleges

Measuring Internationalization by Type of Institution

The following ACE reports address how each type of institution is internationalizing its curricula and student experiences, as well as what strategies institutions have typically used to pursue internationalization, by examining the responses given to an institutional survey conducted by ACE in 2001 and funded by the Ford Foundation. The reports expand on the earlier descriptive report's findings. By creating an internationalization index, the data is reexamined to measure internationalization along six key dimensions, distinguishing high-activity institutions from less active institutions. The six dimensions of the internationalization index are articulated commitment, academic offerings, organizational infrastructure, external funding, institutional investment in faculty, and international students and student programs.

Measuring Internationalization at Research Universities. (2005). ACE.

Based on responses given by 144 research universities, a medium-high level of overall internationalization exists for research universities, with 57 percent scoring *medium-high* (4 on a 5-point scale) and 34 percent scoring *medium* (3). The report also provides scores for each dimension of the internationalization index, compares the top two quartiles of research universities (*highly active*) with the bottom three, and outlines activities that are more exclusive to highly active universities.

Measuring Internationalization at Comprehensive Universities. (2005). ACE.

Based on responses given by 188 comprehensive universities, a medium to medium-high level of overall internationalization exists for comprehensive universities, with 55 percent scoring *medium* (3 on a 5-point scale) and 26 percent scoring *medium-high* (4). The report also provides scores for each dimension of the internationalization index, compares the top two quartiles of comprehensive universities (*highly active*) with the bottom three, and outlines activities that are more exclusive to highly active universities.

Measuring Internationalization at Liberal Arts College. (20005). ACE.

Based on responses given by 187 liberal arts colleges, a medium level of overall internationalization exists for liberal arts colleges, with 49 percent scoring *medium* (3 on a 5-point scale). The report also provides scores for each dimension of the internationalization index, compares the top two quartiles of liberal arts colleges (*highly active*) with the bottom three, and outlines activities that are more exclusive to highly active colleges.

Measuring Internationalization at Community Colleges. (2005). ACE.

Based on responses given by 233 community colleges, a low level of overall internationalization exists for community colleges, with 61 percent scoring *low* (2 on a 5-point scale). The report also provides scores for each dimension of the internationalization index, compares the top two quartiles of community colleges (*highly active*) with the bottom three, and outlines activities that are more exclusive to highly active colleges.

Why Models of Internationalization are Important

It remains clear that across the more than 3,000 colleges and universities in the United States, no consistency exists in the way they deal with the issue of how to internationalize, or whether to even focus on internationalization as an issue important enough to be included in the mission statement or strategic plan. At this time, internationalization efforts vary by college or university, by individual departments and schools, and in the interest level of students and their parents. In some ways, understanding how internationalization of higher education takes place at US colleges can best be understood by looking at different models of campus internationalization.

US institutional initiatives can be assessed from a number of different perspectives.

- **National perspective:** Through *US News and World Report* or national organizations that support and review institutions from a national perspective.

- **Regional perspective:** Through accreditation standards as defined by each regional accrediting agency. Many institutions are viewed more as regional than national institutions in terms of many of their strengths.

- **Statewide perspective:** Whether an institution is a part of a public state system of higher education or has as its main focus serving students and programs in the state, it is important to view each institution in terms of how it is placed and serves the state in which it is located.

- **Community perspective:** One of the three primary missions of a US college or university is service to the community. Four-year colleges and universities do this in many ways, but community service often falls below the teaching/learning and research areas of the institutional mission. However, community colleges are clear in prioritizing the connection of teaching/learning and training and how it serves the local community.

- **International perspective:** More difficult is comparing a US college or university perspective to the perspectives of other institutions around the world. A number of US membership organizations include international institutions. However, most, like NAFSA: Association of International Educators, focus most of their energies on issues from the perspective of US colleges and universities. UNESCO and the International Association of Universities include a broadly international perspective, but their relevance for individual US colleges and universities may be limited. The Association of Pacific Rim Universities (APRU) is based on connections between universities from different countries, but their dealings are from the perspective of each different university and its home country, not the creation of an APRU degree-granting authority.

The strongest focus on the study of higher education internationalization around the world comes from a comparative perspective of international higher education systems. In Europe following the formation of the European Union, one could look more closely at the integration efforts of the higher education systems across borders. However, it may be more helpful to look at ways in which individual institutions and systems create collaboration across borders. This could include programs for international students to come to the United States or U.S degree programs that are offered abroad. To understand institutional internationalization, or to look at how academic fields have supported cross-border collaborations, may be as important as looking at a sea change in the internal operations of US colleges and universities.

For those interested in internationalization of higher education, the Comparative International Education Society, the Boston College Center for International Higher Education, and the Australian Education International Research Database provide resources and publications that help introduce issues related to internationalization and international education from a broad perspective, not just from the perspective of US higher education or US education abroad. IIE has also begun collecting international exchange data through the IIE Atlas of Student Mobility, which tracks student mobility around the world. The Atlas of Student Mobility includes data for US students studying abroad for a degree, which is not counted in the IIE Open Doors data.

Faculty and staff in the education abroad field who are interested in the assessment of education abroad programs should consider those programs within the context of their campus and in the context of US higher education. The articles above provide background information as well as a framework for looking at education abroad within the campus context, which can serve to inform administrators and the campus community about higher education internationalization and education abroad.

Conclusion

Research and outcomes assessment on US students abroad is a major and important focus in the field. It is crucial for members and leaders of international education and assessment associations, as well as other interested parties, to maintain an open dialog and collaborative approach to research in the field. Knowing what others are doing and planning will not only prevent overlap and duplication of efforts, but will also lead to the pooling of resources and collaboration. Single-program or single-institution data limit comparability. Collaboration is needed to increase the significance of results. Partnership and dialog on research efforts will better serve our profession, our education abroad programs and, most importantly, our students.

Endnotes

[1] A special note of thanks to Barbara Craig, Ph.D., at Georgetown University for providing ideas and content in the "Resources for Assessment in Higher Education" portion of this chapter and for her review and feedback on the entire chapter.

[2] Both the *9 Principles of Good Practice for Assessing Student Learning* by the former American Association for Higher Education (AAHE) Assessment Forum and the *Ethical Standards of the American Educational Research Association* are available on the Research/Scholarship Network website of the NAFSA: Association of International Educators Teaching, Learning and Scholarship Knowledge Community.

[3] Notification of the Forum on Education Abroad's collaboration with the annual North Carolina State University Undergraduate Assessment Symposium was announced in November 21, 2006 edition of the *Forum News*.

[4] Darla Deardorff will chair the new international education track at the Symposium and will be assisted by Mell Bolen.

[5] Data was compiled from a review of the three main research bibliographies on study abroad (U.S. students). Weaver, Henry D. (Ed.). *Research on U.S. Students Abroad: A Bibliography with Abstracts*. (Council on International Educational Exchange; Education Abroad Program, University of California; Institute of International Education; and National Association of Foreign Student Affairs, 1989); Chao, Maureen. (Ed.) *Research on U.S. Students Abroad, Volume II, A Bibliography with Abstracts 1989–2000*. (NAFSA: Association of International Educators/SECUSSA (Section on U.S. Students Abroad) 2001); and, Comp, David. (Ed.). *Research on U.S. Students Abroad, Volume III, 2001 to 2003 with Updates to the 1989 and Volume II Editions*. (Loyola Marymount University, 2005).

[6] The 2000–2003 total includes research identified through May 2003. A conservative estimate is that by the end of 2009, there may well be over 1,000 research-based articles, reports, books, and presentations on study abroad.

[7] See also concept of backward design in Wiggins, Grant. And Jay McTighe. *Understanding by Design* 2nd ed. Alexandria, VA: Association for Supervision and Curriculum Development, 2005.

[8] Akande, Y., & Slawson, C. A Case Study of 50 years of Study Abroad Alumni. *International Educator*, 9 no. 3 (2000): 12–16.; Dwyer, M. Charting the Impact of

Studying Abroad. *International Educator*, 13 no. 1 (2004): 14–17.; Dwyer, M., & Peters C. The Benefits of Study Abroad. *Transitions Abroad*, 27 no.5 (2004): 56–57.; Ruhter McMillan, A., & Opem, G. Study Abroad: A Lifetime of Benefits. *Abroad View Magazine*, 6 no. 2 (2994): 58 & 60–61.; and Steinberg, M. Involve Me and I Will Understand: Academic Quality in Experiential Programs Abroad. *Frontiers: The Interdisciplinary Journal of Study Abroad*, 8 (2002): 207–227.

[9] Deardorff, Darla K. The Identification and Assessment of Intercultural Competence as a Student Outcome of Internationalization at Institutions of Higher Learning in the United States. PhD diss. North Carolina State University, 2004.

[10] James Frey served as chair of ANTFOSA, and it was his doctoral dissertation, *The Development of a Criterion Instrument for Evaluating Agency-Sponsored Study Abroad Programs* (Indiana University, 1976), that was later tested and refined by ANTFOSA and the Associate Directorate for Educational and Cultural Affairs of the International Communication Agency that shaped their study abroad program evaluation guide.

[11] A special note of thanks to Joe Hoff, Ph.D., at Oregon State University for his assistance in updating the literature review, providing some of the abstracts, as well as feedback on the content in the "Institutional Internationalization" portion of this chapter.

[12] New Middle States Commission on Higher Education (MSCHE) standards 7 & 14, instituted in 2002, focus much more closely on assessment of student learning, and would include study abroad.

[13] Data obtained from Koh Chin, Hey-Kyung (Ed.). *Open Doors 2006: Report on International Educational Exchange*. New York: Institute of International Education, 2006.

[14] One of the community colleges with the longest-standing history of providing study abroad is The Coast Community College District in California. The individual colleges still offer study abroad, but the district office that supported programs is now closed.

[15] Institute of International Education Research & Evaluation division (2006).

[16] On November 10, 2005, the U.S. Senate passed a resolution (S.RES.308) designating 2006 as the Year of Study Abroad. Introduced by Sens. Richard Durbin (D-IL) and Lamar Alexander (R-TN), and co-sponsored by Sens. Larry Craig (R-ID), Norm Coleman (R-MN), Russ Feingold (D-WI), Daniel Akaka (D-HI) and Thad Cochran (R-MS), it passed unanimously.

[17] Knight, Jane. Updating the Definition of Internationalization. *Center for International Higher Education Newsletter*, no.33. Boston. Fall 2003.

Chapter 7

Using Instruments in Education Abroad Outcomes Assessment

R. Michael Paige, Elizabeth M. Stallman

Introduction

This chapter focuses on the use of instruments for outcomes assessment in education abroad. The rapid growth in international educational exchange has been accompanied by an increasing demand for accountability, i.e., for evidence that the investments in education abroad produce the desired individual and institutional outcomes. In this chapter, we examine a set of paper and pencil instruments and inventories that are designed to measure specific traits, qualities, developmental outcomes, and other characteristics relevant to education abroad.

The selected instruments primarily focus on the individual education abroad participant as the unit of analysis, rather than the organization (such as the university or academic department), although we will comment on the latter. Further, the *participant* definition has grown in recent years to include faculty, staff, and alumni in addition to students. Depending upon the program and degree of outreach by education abroad administrators, the instruments that follow may possibly be used in training and assessment for any of these groups. The central purpose of the chapter is to identify and describe instruments that are appropriate for education abroad outcomes assessment, are valid and reliable, and, preferably, have been utilized in education abroad research.

It was a daunting task to identify an appropriate set of instruments from the plethora of inventories that exist. There is an extensive reference literature, some of the best-known publications being *Tests in Print*[1] and the *Mental Measurements Yearbook*,[2] both of which are updated periodically. There are additional texts in a variety of areas such as multicultural assessment[3] and psychology, education, and business.[4] Important contributions from the intercultural literature include the substantive descriptions of seven different instruments[5] that appear in Fowler and Mumford's *Intercultural Sourcebook, vol. II*,[6] along with commentaries about instruments that can be found in works by Gudykunst,[7] Brislin and Yoshida,[8] Reddin,[9] Bhawuk and Triandis,[10] Cushner and Brislin,[11] and Singelis.[12] The most elaborate account to date is Paige's review of 35 "intercultural instruments" that appeared in the *Handbook of Intercultural Training*.[13] This was of particular value to us in helping narrow the field of instruments, identify relevant instruments, and establish categories of instruments.

Finally, we examined the Fall 2004 special research issue of *Frontiers: The Interdisciplinary Journal of Study Abroad*[14] to see which instruments were being used in the latest, state-of-the-art study abroad research. These literature reviews were significant because we could then identify the most commonly used instruments, look at their properties, and determine if they met our criteria for inclusion.

The result of our analysis was the identification of 15 assessment instruments that we determined could be valuable for education abroad outcomes assessment.

The organization of this chapter is as follows. We first discuss in greater detail the purposes for using instruments in education abroad research, assessment, and evaluation. We then discuss the selection criteria we used for selecting these particular assessment instruments. The core of the chapter is the description of the instruments themselves. In this section, we provide an overview of the instrument along with information regarding the key concepts being measured, the item format of the instrument, and reliability and validity data. We conclude the chapter with some closing observations about the limitations, challenges, and opportunities of using these instruments in education abroad assessment.

As the profile of education abroad increases on campuses nationwide, calls for accountability have also been on the increase.[15] Meeting these demands has resulted in the increasing use of (mostly quantitative) instruments. In our view, institutions choose to assess education abroad outcomes for five primary reasons: tracking student learning, charting personal growth, examining participant satisfaction/attitudes, supporting program development, and generating institutional data. Each purpose is briefly described below.

Tracking student learning: The most commonly cited purpose for outcomes assessment of education abroad is to assess student learning. Institutions and departments frequently wish to know the level of culture and language learning that students achieve. Academic performance is assessed to a lesser degree and is generally measured by GPA.[16] Assessment of these learning outcomes addresses the question regarding the degree to which the education abroad program is realizing its learning objectives.

Personal growth: Another purpose of assessment is to quantify the growth that students achieve during a period of education abroad in areas such as leadership, independence, creativity, and maturity.[17]

Participant satisfaction/attitudes:[18] Participant satisfaction has long been one of the most common things to measure at the conclusion of an education abroad program. This is helpful to program providers and administrators for determining where improvements are needed and if they are being well received. Student attitudes regarding such things as their views of the host culture and their perspectives of their own society have also been a focus of education abroad assessment. There is considerable interest in whether education abroad is contributing to a more global perspective.

Program development[19]: An important reason to assess a particular program is to determine what the needs are for program refinement and future development. This is particularly important in light of the institutional investments that are being made today in creating and sustaining education abroad programs.

Institutional data[20]: At the core of evaluation and assessment is the need for institutional data. For example, learning outcomes data collected over time and across diverse student populations can provide the institution with important information about the value and impact of particular programs on certain types of students. Such information can support student advisement, predeparture orientation, on-site programs, and more.

Selection Criteria for Assessment Instruments

We selected the 15 instruments described in this chapter based on four primary criteria. These are presented below in the form of the questions we posed for ourselves in arriving at our decisions.

First, *does the instrument measure human development and learning in a manner relevant to education abroad?* This was our key question, and the answer came from diverse sources, including the key themes we found in the education abroad research literature, the international education literature on desired learning outcomes, our own experiences as professional international educators, and the literature on instruments.

Second, *is there a theoretical foundation for the instrument*? It was important for us to know that the instrument was based on a theory or conceptual model that reasonably links the education abroad experience to the learning outcome. The existence of a theoretical foundation lends legitimacy to the instrument and, more importantly, to the assessment. This was determined by examining the conceptual structure of the instruments.

Third, *is the instrument a valid and reliable measure?* The integrity of the assessment enterprise rests on the quality of the research design and the strength of the research instruments. Validity in general refers to the capacity of the instrument to measure what it is designed to measure. Reliability has to do with consistency of response (as determined by internal consistency reliability and test-retest coefficients). We established validity and reliability by reviewing the relevant literature.

Fourth, *are the administrative and logistical issues involved manageable?* Here we looked at factors such as cost, requirements for using the instrument (such as certification), instrument administration procedures, scoring procedures, and so forth. Some fine instruments, such as the Intercultural Development Inventory,[21] are restricted in use to qualified administrators. We didn't necessarily rule out such instruments, but we wanted the reader to know about these conditions of use. We report on these issues in the next section.

Instrument Profiles

Figure 1 organizes the 15 instruments into three broad categories: language learning, culture learning, and disciplinary learning. These sets of outcomes appear repeatedly in the internationalization literature.[22] The culture learning frame is a broad rubric that subsumes a number of important areas: intercultural development, intercultural communication, culture learning strategies, intercultural adaptation, intercultural sensitivity, and worldmindedness. Below, each instrument is briefly described and the key references are cited.

I. Language/Language Learning/Language Development

1. Oral Proficiency Interview

The Oral Proficiency Interview (OPI)[23] (American Council on the Teaching of Foreign Languages, 1999) is the most widely used of all language proficiency tests. Because it is not language-specific in its structure, it is adaptable and useful for the 47 languages in which raters are currently trained. An example of the OPI used in an education abroad research context is in Brecht, Davidson, and Ginsburg.[24] They conducted a study of 658 Russian language students and, using the OPI, demonstrated that speaking competence improved more for students who spent a study abroad period in a Russian-speaking country compared to students who studied four years of college-level Russian.

The OPI determines where an individual's oral language proficiency lies on a 10-point scale: *Novice-Low, Novice-Mid, Novice-High, Intermediate-Low, Intermediate-Mid, Intermediate-High, Advanced-Low, Advanced-Mid, Advanced-High*, and *Superior*. The test-taker converses in a structured conversation with a trained interviewer, in person or by telephone. The oral proficiency is assessed against specific tasks.

The OPI involves four phases: 1) warm-up: the interviewer relaxes the test-taker and does an initial level assessment; 2) level check: the initial assessment is confirmed or changed; 3) probes: the interviewer tests the level of difficulty to determine the test-taker's limits; and 4) wind-down: relax back to the confirmed level. An interview takes anywhere from 10 to 30 minutes.

The OPI stresses a holistic flow of speech and the verbal and nonverbal interaction between interviewer and test-taker. While specific elements are not tested for, in general proficiency rates are determined on the following five global tasks: function, context, content, accuracy, and discourse.[25]

Although some point to weaknesses with regard to validity of the OPI, specifically referencing the subjectivity of relying on raters and the lack of explicit target abilities,[26] there is a solid research literature on using the OPI, and it is acknowledged as the best available language-general oral testing instrument.[27]

Figure 1. ***A Conceptual Map of Education Abroad Assessment Instruments***

Category and Instrument	Key References
I. Language/Language Learning/ Language Development	
1. Oral Proficiency Interview	ACFTL, 1999
2. Simulated Oral Proficiency Interview	ACTFL, 1999
3. Speech Act Measure	Cohen & Shively, 2003
4. Language Strategies Survey	Cohen & Chi, 2001
II. Culture/Culture Learning/Intercultural Development	
1. Intercultural Development Inventory	Hammer, 1999; Hammer & Bennett, 1998, 2002
2. Intercultural Conflict Style Inventory	Hammer, 2002
3. Strategies Inventory for Learning Culture	Paige, Rong, Zhang, Kappler, Hoff, & Emert, 2003
4. Cross-cultural Adaptability Inventory	Kelley & Myers, 1999
5. Sociocultural Adjustment Scale	Ward & Kennedy, 1999
6. Bicultural Involvement Questionnaire	Szapocznik, Kurintes & Fernandez, 1980
7. Multigroup Ethnic Identity Measure	Phinney, 1992
8. Multi-Index Ethnocultural Identity Scale	Horvath, 1997; Yamada, 1998
9. Cross-Cultural World-Mindedness Scale	Der-Karabetian & Metzer, 1993
III. Learning in the Disciplines	
1. Disciplinary Learning Interview Protocol	Hammer, Malone, & Paige, in press
2. Global Awareness Profile	Corbitt, 1998

2. Simulated Oral Proficiency Interview

The Simulated Oral Proficiency Interview (SOPI) was developed from the OPI. In contrast to that instrument, the SOPI is not a live interview. Instead the test-taker independently listens to taped speech and questions, reads passages, examines pictures, and responds by speaking into a tape recorder. It is meant to be a more cost-effective and efficient way to test language proficiency. Only materials from the Center for Applied Linguistics (the developer and administrator) and a proctor are necessary to take the test. Multiple tests can be administered at the same time.

The SOPI was developed to fill a gap of the OPI—to test less commonly taught languages. The first instruments were designed for Arabic and Chinese; at least nine other languages are currently available. Also, administration of the SOPI is not limited by the schedule of available trained raters. since only materials and a proctor are necessary to take the test. Upon completion, audiotaped responses are given or sent to a trained SOPI rater for evaluation.

The main difference between the SOPI and the OPI is that the SOPI is much more like an exam than a natural conversation. The SOPI is a fixed test that treats all test-takers equally. Two forms of the test have evolved. The first is primarily meant to measure proficiency of lower-level learners (*Novice* and *Intermediate*) and can be used to determine readiness to take the second form. That form is designed for higher-level learners (*Advanced* and *Superior*). This is a change from the original format, where the lowest level tested was *Intermediate-Low*. Kuo and Jiang[28] note that the fixed-topic format may result in artificially high scores if the topic is one that a novice happens to know particularly well.

The SOPI uses the same scale as the OPI: ten levels from *Novice-Low* to *Superior*. There are five parts to the SOPI: warm-up, pictures, topics, situations, and wind-down. The SOPI typically takes 45 minutes to complete.

Stansfield and Kenyon[29] determined that the SOPI is a reliable substitute for the standard OPI. As a test with predetermined topics, the SOPI's reliability and validity may be stronger than the more subjective OPI because its test materials are more precisely measured and controlled. In large research projects, such as the Georgetown University Consortium Project,[30] the SOPI is recommended for its ease of use with larger numbers of subjects.

It should be noted that there is a third generation of the OPI, called the COPI or Computerized Oral Proficiency Instrument. Space prevented us from including an evaluation of it here.

3. Speech Act Measure

The Speech Act Measure (SAM) is a paper and pencil instrument designed to measure multiple rejoinders in the speech acts of requesting and apologizing.[31] It was designed by Cohen and Shively[32] for the Maximizing Study Abroad (MAXSA) research project as an empirical measure of language gain in study abroad. In the SAM, written vignettes of social situations and dialogs with native speakers place examinees in native contexts where they must respond. Three cultural cues—social status, social distance, and degree of severity (apologies) or degree of imposition (requests)—give the examinee crucial contextual information to aid in determining the appropriate speech act.[33]

The SAM is a written instrument meant to mimic spoken language. Two speech acts (apologies and requests) are tested, and 10 or 11 situations are given for each. Contextual information appropriate to the situation and culture are noted. Examinees write what they would say in the given interaction with a native speaker. There are two formats employed in the SAM. The first is a passage followed by a prompt to write the appropriate speech act. The second is a dialog in which the examinee fills in blanks with appropriate speech acts. The SAM has been created for research projects involving learners of French, Japanese, and Spanish (Peninsular and Latin American versions).

The SAM allows efficiency in gathering large amounts of data, as obtaining speech acts in real life may be difficult and time-consuming. Although tests have not yet been performed on the SAM, the controlled structure of the instrument contributes to a higher likelihood of reliability and validity.

4. Language Strategies Survey

The Language Strategies Survey[34] (LSS) is a self-administered instrument in which a language student reports frequency of use of a variety of language learning strategies. It was developed for *Maximizing Study Abroad: The Students' Guide*[35] and revised for the MAXSA research project. The MAXSA research project examined five empirically generated LSS factors: learning structure and vocabulary; speaking; listening; reading; and asking for clarification. In subsequent analyses, these were found to possess sound reliability and validity[36]

In addition to the four main skill areas of language learning (speaking, listening, reading, and writing), the LSS adds vocabulary and translation skills. Statements can be used as insight to strategies currently used as well as new strategies that respondents can try. Respondents can compare their strengths and weaknesses in the various skill areas with their responses to the frequency of strategies they employ in language learning.

The LSS consists of 89 statements. Respondents are asked to rate on a 5-point scale the frequency with which they use the language strategy. The LSS is a self-report examination of the six skill areas in language learning as noted above.

In the MAXSA research project, five factors were evaluated for reliability and validity: learning structure and vocabulary, speaking, listening, reading, and asking for clarification. The LSS was found to be a valid measure of these language-learning strategies ($p < .001$ or .005).[37]

II. Culture/Culture Learning/Intercultural Development

1. Intercultural Development Inventory[38]

The IDI[39] is a 50-item measure of Bennett's[40] Developmental Model of Intercultural Sensitivity. Bennett[41] posits six developmental levels of intercultural sensitivity; these range on a continuum from the three ethnocentric worldviews (Denial, Defense, Minimization) through the three "ethnorelative" levels (Acceptance, Adaptation, Integration). It is the best-known and most frequently used instrument for assessing intercultural development and intercultural competence.

The IDI generates scores for Denial/Defense, Reversal, Minimization, Acceptance/Adaptation, and Encapsulated Marginality, as well as for the Denial, Defense, Acceptance, and Adaptation subscales.

The IDI utilizes a 5-point response set ranging from *agree* to *disagree*. Sample items include:

- People from other cultures like it when you are just yourself.
- I try to understand the values of people from different cultures.

Empirical evidence regarding the reliability and validity of the IDI is reported in Hammer, Bennett, & Wiseman[42] and Paige, Jacobs-Cassuto, Yershova, & DeJaeghere.[43]

2. Intercultural Conflict Style Inventory

The Intercultural Conflict Style Inventory[44] (ICSI) is a self-assessment instrument that measures a person's orientation to conflict in intercultural communication terms. The ICSI is constructed around two continua of communication considered to be central to intercultural interactions in conflict situations: *indirectness* versus *directness* (DI scale) and *emotional expressiveness* versus *emotional restraint* (ER). Four intercultural conflict patterns are generated by the ICSI: *discussion* (direct and emotionally restrained), *engagement* (direct and emotionally expressive), *accommodation* (indirect and emotionally restrained), and *dynamic* (indirect and emotionally expressive).

The ICSI utilizes a paired statement response format in which respondents are presented with two alternative responses to conflict. They are given five points to distribute however they wish between the two alternatives with their stronger preference being given more points. Sample items include:

• In general, when resolving conflict with another party, my preferred approach is to:

A. Fully express my convictions. ____

B. Be cautious in sharing my own wants, goals, and needs. + ____

=5

There is preliminary evidence[45] that the ISCI is a valid and reliable instrument. Hammer's item analysis, based on two separate samples ($n = 487$; $n = 510$), shows that the DI and ER scales have internal consistency reliability coefficients ranging from .71 to .85. In addition, confirmatory factor analysis supports the construct validity of the instrument by finding that the two-factor model of directness-indirectness and emotional expressiveness-restraint represented the best fit with the data.

3. Strategies Inventory for Learning Culture

The Strategies Inventory for Learning Culture[46] (SILC) was originally designed as a self-assessment tool and printed in *Maximizing Study Abroad: A Student's Guide to Strategies for Language and Culture Learning and Use*. It was also revised for use as a research instrument. In this section we highlight the latter instrument.

The main purpose of the SILC is to measure an individual's tendency to use particular culture learning skills when living in another culture. It is framed by nine approaches to culture learning: adapting to culturally different surroundings; culture shock/coping strategies; interpreting culture; communicating across cultures; communication styles; nonverbal communication; interacting with culturally different people; homestay strategies; and reentry strategies.

The 52 items are phrased as statements to which respondents indicate how often they use that particular strategy. The frequency is on a 4-point scale, ranging from *very often* to *seldom*. *Not applicable* is also an option. Sample items include:

- I examine how my own nonverbal communication is influenced by my culture.
- I keep connected with friends that I made in the other culture.

As reported in Paige, Cohen, and Shively,[47] the SILC was subjected to validity and reliability testing. The researchers note internal consistency reliability coefficients ranging from .72 to .86. The validity structure is supported by confirmatory factor analysis. This instrument can be employed to determine to what extent participants use culture-learning strategies during their education abroad experience. This could be accomplished via a pre- and posttest administration. The first administration would be during a predeparture orientation or class to establish a baseline score; the second administration would be after a period of time in the host culture or upon returning to the home culture.

4. Cross-Cultural Adaptability Inventory[48]

The CCAI[49] is a 50-item self-assessment instrument that measures four theoretically posited qualities of cross-cultural adaptability. The four concepts measured by the CCAI are *flexibility and openness* (FO), *personal autonomy* (PA), *emotional resilience* (ER)), and *perceptual acuity* (PAC). The FO items focus on a person's orientation to new ways of thinking and behaving. The PA scale assesses the strength of the respondent's sense of cultural identity, i.e., culturally derived values and beliefs. ER pertains to the stated ability of the person to handle the emotional stresses and the ambiguity known to be associated with living and working in a new cultural environment. The PAC items tap into the capacity of the person to perceive and make sense out of cultural cues, such as nonverbal communication patterns.

The CCAI consists of 50 statements, and respondents select from among six response choices arranged on a continuum from *definitely true* to *definitely not true.* Sample items include:

- I am not good at understanding people who are different from me.
- I can function in situations when things are not clear.

Kelley and Meyers[50] utilized a normative sample ($n = 653$) to establish the validity and reliability of the instrument. The four scales were shown to have internal consistency reliability coefficients ranging from .68 to .82, while the validity of the instrument was established on using an expert panel review and factor analysis of the items. As noted here, the CCAI is meant to determine an individual's ability to adapt to a culture different from one's own; thus the best use of it in education abroad contexts is likely as a predeparture instrument, such as to determine the kind of orientation and training that is appropriate.

5. Sociocultural Adjustment Scale

The SCAS[51] was developed to measure the theoretically and empirically derived cognitive and social aspects of sociocultural adaptation. An extension of Furnham and Bochner's[52] Social Situations Questionnaire, the SCAS consists of 29 items. Sociocultural adaptation refers to the ways in which a person thinks about (the cognitive dimension) and responds to (the behavioral dimension) a new culture. The two dimensions of the construct are *behavioral adaptation* and *cognitive adaptation.*

Respondents analyze the 29 SCAS statements utilizing a format consisting of five alternatives ranging from *no difficulty* to *extreme difficulty*. Sample items include:

- Making yourself understood.
- Understanding jokes and humor.

There is considerable evidence to support the reliability and validity of the SCAS. Ward and Kennedy, summarizing the results from 21 different samples, demonstrate that the instrument has strong internal consistency reliability.[53] Their research also examines the convergent, factorial, and criterion validity of the instrument.

6. Bicultural Involvement Questionnaire[54]

The BIQ is a 33-item instrument that was developed to measure the cultural identity of bicultural persons. The BIQ refers to the American and Hispanic cultures, but the monocultural-multicultural continuum has transferability to other culture groups.

Based on their answers to the 33 items, respondents are assessed in terms of their *Americanism* and *Hispanicism,* placed on a continuum ranging from *biculturalism* to *monoculturalism*, and determined to be *culturally involved* or *culturally marginal.*

For 10 items, respondents indicate how comfortable they are speaking Spanish and English in five situations. Seven cultural activities are then presented, and respondents indicate how much they enjoy these in their Hispanic and American forms (n = 14 items total). The concluding section present nine aspects of cultural life (such as food and music) and asks respondents if these are entirely or mostly Hispanic, entirely or mostly American, or both. The data generate scores for American monoculturalism, Hispanic monoculturalism, biculturalism, and cultural involvement/cultural marginality. Sample items include:

- How comfortable do you feel speaking Spanish in general?
- How comfortable do you feel speaking English in general?

Szapocznik et al.[55] reported on the internal consistency, test-retest reliability, and criterion validity of the instrument. Bicultural teacher ratings served as the external measure.

7. Multigroup Ethnic Identity Measure[56]

The MEIM is similar to the BIQ in that it was designed to measure various dimensions of an individual's ethnic identity. The MEIM, however, focuses on the group-specific identity, i.e., one's sense of belonging to an ethnic group, commitment to it, and willingness to explore ethnicity. There are three dimensions of ethnic identity assessed by the MEIM: *sense of belonging and affirmation*, *ethnic behaviors and practices*, and *ethnic identity achievement*. It also measures *orientation to other groups*. Respondents are asked to indicate their ethnic identity by means of an open-ended item, and they are asked to indicate the ethnicity of their parents.

Items. The items are presented as statements and respondents answer them using a four-choice agree-disagree format. Sample items include:

- I have a lot of pride in my ethnic group and its accomplishments.
- I like meeting and getting to know people from ethnic groups other than my own.

Phinney[57] presents evidence of the MEIM's internal consistency reliability and factorial validity. In education abroad contexts, the MEIM could be quite useful because many students are beginning or continuing to explore their ethnic identity. These contexts include sites for heritage-seeking students; cultures in which Caucasians are not dominant; and programs that include fellow participants of different ethnicities. Regarding the latter, research has shown that the subjects of race and ethnicity surface for American participants when they leave the United States: "Students removed from their typical environment will ask new and/or deeper questions about themselves and their societies."[58]

8. Multi-Index Ethnocultural Identity Scale[59]

The MEIS[60] is a 27-item ethnic identity instrument that is very similar to the MEIM but differs from it with its behavioral rather than attitudinal emphasis. *Ethnocultural identity*, defined by Marsella and Kameoka as "the extent to which an individual endorses and practices a way of life associated with a particular cultural tradition" (as cited in Horvath, 1997, p. 171), is the central concept. The MEIS measures the strength of perceived identification with the respondent's ethnic group and the respondent's degree of participation in 27 different activities associated with the group.

The 27 participation items utilize a five-point response format ranging from *very little* to *very much* and a seven-point response format for assessing strength of identification with one's ethnic group. Sample items include:

- Attend the traditional religious or spiritual services of the group.
- Am active in the political movement or ideology of the group.

There is no mention of reliability or validity in the two major published works on the MEIS by Horvath and Yamada.[61] Depending on what the goal of assessment may be, either the MEIS or the MEIM may be used to introduce discussions of ethnic identity as encountered in education abroad.

9. Cross-Cultural World-Mindedness Scale[62]

The Cross-Cultural World-Mindedness Scale is a newer version of the original world-mindedness scales by Sampson and Smith[63] and Silvernail.[64] World-mindedness scales measure a variety of attitudes and values such as immigration, patriotism, world government, and global economic justice. The key concept being assessed is *worldmindedness*, which is defined by Der-Karabetian as positive attitudes toward these global issues. The scale measures these global orientations.

The CCWMS includes 26 statements and respondents select from among six alternatives ranging from *strongly agree* to *strongly disagree* with the statement.

Sample items include:

- It would be better to be a citizen of the world than of any particular country.
- The rich nations should share their wealth with the less fortunate people of the world.

Der-Karabetian[65] reports internal consistency reliabilities based on data gathered in his 10-nation survey. Der-Karabetian and Metzer[66] provide support for the criterion validity of the scale and provide additional evidence of internal consistency reliability based on two US samples.

III. Learning in the Disciplines

1. Disciplinary Learning Interview Protocol

The Disciplinary Learning Interview Protocol (Hammer, Malone, & Paige, in press) was developed for the learning outcomes study conducted by Georgetown University under the auspices of a US Department of Education International Research and Studies Project Title VI grant. Disciplinary learning is defined in terms of the ability of the person to apply disciplinary knowledge on the job, the person's understanding of the ethical responsibilities one has as a professional, having the capacity to work as a member of a team, and knowing how disciplinary knowledge can both contribute to solving problems in other cultures and what is involved in doing so.

The instrument uses an interview format in which the respondent is applying for a position or for graduate school. Respondents are given three scenarios, organized with increasing levels of cross-cultural complexity, and have to answer why they think they would be a good choice for the position or for admission to graduate school. Interviews are evaluated based on the degree to which the respondents effectively address the issues mentioned above: application of disciplinary knowledge, sense of professional ethics, team orientation, and understanding of cultural context.

This is a brand-new instrument; evidence of its validity and reliability does not yet exist. However, it is important that the dimensions of disciplinary learning were generated by a one-year research process consisting of intensive focus group interviews with faculty members in five disciplines—the humanities, business, engineering, health sciences, and biological sciences. The core areas being measured by the instrument reflect the consensus of the representatives of these disciplines regarding disciplinary learning in the education abroad context.

2. Global Awareness Profile

The Global Awareness Profile (GAP), according to the author,[67] "is designed to measure one's awareness and knowledge of global issues and geography." The GAP evaluates three types of knowledge: *geographic knowledge* of the different regions of the world (e.g., Asia, Africa, and the Middle East), *subject matter knowledge* (e.g., environment, politics, geography), and *knowledge of broad global issues*.

The GAP consists of 115 multiple-choice items. Sample items include:

- Which of these European countries has the largest oil reserves in the region? (a) England (b) Germany (c) Russia (d) Italy

- A common farming technique in South America that leads directly to deforestation is: (a) irrigation (b) cooperative farming (c) commercial farming (d) slash and burn

There is limited evidence regarding validity and reliability. One study by Corbitt[68] reports a satisfactory test-retest reliability coefficient (.83). This study provides evidence of the instrument's validity by showing that the GAP was able to discriminate between individuals who had and had not studied abroad.

Conclusion

We sincerely hope that education abroad administrators will find this chapter both useful and inspiring in determining appropriate instruments for their assessment needs. Although only a few of the above instruments were developed strictly with the education abroad participant in mind, it is our estimation that all serve the various purposes and goals that education abroad professionals are working toward. The main challenge was our knowledge that research is being done in the profession, but we lack documentation of it. A call that resounds in this chapter as well as throughout this volume is the need for more documented research on the uses of assessment instruments in education abroad. The work that our colleagues report can only serve to inform and improve the field as a whole.

Endnotes

[1] L. L. Murphy, B. S. Plake, and J. C. Impara, eds., *Tests in print V: An index to tests, test reviews and the literature on specific tests* (Lincoln, NE: Buros Institute of Mental Measurements of the University of Nebraska, 1999).

2 B. S. Plake, J. C. Impara, and R. A. Spies, eds., *The fifteenth mental measurements yearbook* (Lincoln, NE: Buros Institute of Mental Measurements of the University of Nebraska, 2003).

[3] L. A. Suzuki, J. G. Ponterotto, and P. J. Meller, eds., *Handbook of multicultural assessment: clinical, psychological, and educational applications*, 2nd ed. (San Francisco, CA: Jossey-Bass, 2001).

[4] T. Maddox, ed., *Tests: A comprehensive reference for assessments in psychology, education and business.* (Austin, TX: Pro-Ed, 1997).; and R. C. Sweetland and D. J. Keyser, eds., *Tests: A Comprehensive Reference for Assessments in Psychology, Education, and Business*, 3rd ed. (Austin, TX: Pro-Ed, 1991).

[5] C. Brown and K. Knight, "Introduction to Self-Awareness Inventories," in *Intercultural Sourcebook: Cross-Cultural Training Methods*, ed. S. M. Fowler & M. G. Mumford (Yarmouth, ME: Intercultural Press, 1999).; P. Casse, *Training for the Multicultural Manager* (Washington, DC: The Society for Intercultural Education, Training and Research, 1982).; P. Casse, "The Four-Value Orientation Exercise Using a Self-Awareness Inventory," in *Intercultural Sourcebook: Cross-Cultural Training Methods*, ed. S. M. Fowler and M. G. Mumford (Yarmouth, ME: Intercultural Press, 1999).; M. R. Hammer, "A Measure of Intercultural Sensitivity: The Intercultural Development Inventory," in *Intercultural Sourcebook: Cross-Cultural Training Methods*, ed. S. M. Fowler and M. G. Mumford (Yarmouth, ME: Intercultural Press, 1999).; C. Kelley and J. Meyers, "The Cross-Cultural Adaptability Inventory," in *Intercultural Sourcebook: Cross-Cultural Training Methods*, ed. S. M. Fowler and M. G. Mumford (Yarmouth, ME: Intercultural Press, 1999).; and M. F. Tucker, "Self-Awareness and Development Using the Overseas Assignment Inventory," in *Intercultural Sourcebook: Cross-Cultural Training Methods*, ed. S. M. Fowler and M. G. Mumford (Yarmouth, ME: Intercultural Press, 1999).

[6] S. M. Fowler and M. G. Mumford, eds., *Intercultural sourcebook: cross-cultural training methods*, vol. 2 (Yarmouth, ME: Intercultural Press, 1999).

[7] W. B. Gudykunst, *Bridging Differences: Effective intergroup communication*, 2nd ed. (Thousand Oaks, CA: Sage, 1994).

[8] R. W. Brislin and T. Yoshida, eds., *Improving intercultural interactions: Modules for cross-cultural training programs* (Thousand Oaks, CA: Sage, 1994).

[9] W. J. Reddin, *Using tests to improve training: The complete guide to selecting, developing and using training instruments* (Englewood Cliffs, NJ: Prentice Hall, 1994).

[10] D. P. S. Bhawuk and H. C. Triandis, "The role of culture theory in the study of culture and intercultural training," in *Handbook of intercultural training*, ed. D. Landis and R. S. Bhagat (Thousand Oaks, CA: Sage, 1996).

[11] K. Cushner and Brislin. R. W., *Improving intercultural interactions: modules for cross-cultural training programs*, vol. 2 (Thousand Oaks, CA: Sage, 1997).

[12] T. M. Singelis, ed., *Teaching about culture, ethnicity, & diversity: Exercises and planned activities* (Thousand Oaks, CA: Sage, 1998).

[13] R. M. Paige, "Instrumentation in intercultural training," in *Handbook of intercultural training*, ed. D. Landis, J. M. Bennett, and M. J. Bennett (Thousand Oaks, CA: SAGE, 2004).

[14] Michael Vande Berg, ed., *Frontiers: The Interdisciplinary Journal of Study Abroad*, vol. X (Carlisle, PA: Frontiers Journal, Inc., 2004).

[15] See chapter 1 in this volume for more information regarding accountability in education abroad.

[16] R. C. Sutton and D. L. Rubin, "The GLOSSARI project: initial findings from a system-wide research initiative on study abroad learning outcomes," *Frontiers: The Interdisciplinary Journal of Study Abroad* X (2004).; Michael Vande Berg et al., "The Georgetown University consortium project: A report from the halfway mark," *Frontiers: The Interdisciplinary Journal of Study Abroad* X (2004).; R. M. Paige, A. D. Cohen, and R. L. Shively, "Assessing the impact of a strategies-based curriculum on language and culture learning abroad," *Frontiers: The Interdisciplinary Journal of Study Abroad* X (2004).; and A. Immelman and P. Schneider, "Assessing student learning in study abroad programs: A conceptual framework and methodology for assessing student learning in study abroad programs," *Journal of Studies in International Education* 2, no. 2 (1998).

[17] E. C. Ingraham and D. L. Peterson, "Assessing the impact of study abroad on student learning at Michigan State University," *Frontiers: The Interdisciplinary Journal of Study Abroad* X (2004).

[18] Sutton and Rubin, "The GLOSSARI project: Initial findings from a system-wide research initiative on study abroad learning outcomes."; and L. Chieffo and L. Griffiths, "Large-scale assessment of student attitudes after a short-term study abroad program," *Frontiers: The Interdisciplinary Journal of Study Abroad* X (2004).

[19] L. Engle and J. Engle, "Assessing language acquisition and intercultural sensitivity development in relation to study abroad program design," *Frontiers: The Interdisciplinary Journal of Study Abroad* X (2004).; and D. DiBiasio and N. A. Mello, "Multi-level assessment of program outcomes: Assessing a nontraditional study abroad program in the engineering disciplines," *Frontiers: The Interdisciplinary Journal of Study Abroad* X (2004).

[20] Sutton and Rubin, "The GLOSSARI project: initial findings from a system-wide research initiative on study abroad learning outcomes."

[21] M. R. Hammer and M. J. Bennett, "The Intercultural Development Inventory (IDI) Manual," (Portland, OR: Intercultural Communication Institute, 1998, 2001).

[22] J. M. Mestenhauser and B. J. Ellingboe, *Reforming the higher education curriculum: Internationalizing the campus* (Phoenix, AZ: American Council on Education/The Oryx Press, 1998).; Hans deWit and Jane Knight, eds., *Quality and internationalisation in higher education* (Paris: Organisation for Economic Co-operation and Development, 1999).; Walter Grunzweig and Nana Rinehart, eds., *Rockin' in red square: critical approaches to international education in the age of cyberculture* (Bonn: VG Bild-Kunst, 2002).; and Paul Crowther et al., "Internationalization at home: A position paper," (Amsterdam: European Association for International Education, 2000).

[23] American Council on the Teaching of Foreign Languages, "ACTFL Proficiency Guidelines for Speaking," (Hasting-on-Hudson, NY: ACTFL, 1999).

[24] Richard D. Brecht, Dan E. Davidson, and Ralph B. Ginsberg, "Predictors of foreign language gain during study abroad," in *Second language acquisition in a study abroad context*, ed. Barbara F. Freed (Philadelphia, PA: John Benjamins North America, 1995).

[25] Jane Kuo and Xixiang Jiang, "Assessing the Assessments: The OPI and the SOPI," *Foreign Language Annals* 30, no. 4 (1997).

[26] Rafael Salaberry, "Revising the revised format of the ACTFL Oral Proficiency Interview," *Language Testing* 17, no. 3 (2000).

[27] J. E. Liskin-Gasparro, "The ACTFL proficiency guidelines and the Oral Proficiency Instrument: A brief history and analysis of their survival," *Foreign Language Annals* 36, no. 4 (2003).; E. A. Surface and E. C. Dierdorff, "Reliability and the ACTFL Oral Proficiency Interview: reporting indices of interrater consistency and agreement for 19 languages " *Foreign Language Annals* 36, no. 4 (2003).; and E. Swender, "Oral proficiency testing in the real world: Answers to frequently asked questions " *Foreign Language Annals* 35, no. 4 (2003).

[28] Kuo and Jiang, "Assessing the assessments: The OPI and the SOPI."

[29] C.W. Stansfield and D.M. Kenyon, "Research on the comparability of the oral proficiency interview and the simulated oral proficiency interview," *System* 20 (1992).

[30] Vande Berg et al., "The Georgetown University Consortium Project: A report from the halfway mark."

[31] Paige, Cohen, and Shively, "Assessing the impact of a strategies-based curriculum on language and culture learning abroad."

[32] A. D. Cohen and R. L. Shively, "Speech Act Measure of language gain," (Minneapolis, MN: University of Minnesota, The Center for Advanced Research on Language Acquisition, 2002).

[33] A. D. Cohen et al., "Maximizing study Abroad through language and culture strategies: Research on students, study abroad program professionals, and language instructors," (Minneapolis, MN: University of Minnesota, The Center for Advanced Research on Language Acquisition, 2005).

[34] A. D. Cohen and J. C. Chi, "Language Strategy Use Survey," (Minneapolis, MN: University of Minnesota, The Center for Advanced Research on Language Acquisition, 2001).

[35] R. M. Paige et al., *Maximizing study abroad: A student's guide to strategies for language and culture learning and use* (Minneapolis, MN: University of Minnesota, The Center for Advanced Research on Language Acquisition, 2002).

[36] Cohen et al., "Maximizing study abroad through language and culture strategies: Research on students, study abroad program professionals, and language instructors."

[37] Paige, Cohen, and Shively, "Assessing the impact of a strategies-based curriculum on language and culture learning abroad." (Minneapolis, MN: Center for Advanced Research on Advanced Language Acquisition, University of Minnesota, 2002).

[38] Hammer, "A measure of intercultural sensitivity: The Intercultural Development Inventory." Hammer and Bennett, "The Intercultural Development Inventory (IDI) manual."

[39] Hammer and Bennett, "The Intercultural Development Inventory (IDI) manual."

[40] M. J. Bennett, "Toward ethnorelativism: The developmental model of intercultural sensitivity," in *Education for the Intercultural Experience*, ed. R. M. Paige (Yarmouth, ME: Intercultural Press, 1993).

[41] Ibid.

[42] M. R. Hammer, M. J. Bennett, and R. Wiseman, "Measuring intercultural sensitivity: The Intercultural Development Inventory," *International Journal of Intercultural Relations* 27, no. 4 (2003).

[43] R. M. Paige et al., "Assessing intercultural sensitivity: A psychometric analysis of the Hammer and Bennett Intercultural Development Inventory," *International Journal of Intercultural Relations* 27, no. 4 (2003).

[44] M. R. Hammer, "The Intercultural Conflict Style Inventory [Instrument]," (Ocean Pines, MD: Hammer Consulting, LLC, 2003).

[45] Ibid.

[46] R. M. Paige et al., "Strategies inventory for learning culture," (Minneapolis, MN: Center for Advanced Research on Advanced Language Acquisition, University of Minnesota, 2002).

[47] Paige, Cohen, and Shively, "Assessing the impact of a strategies-based curriculum on language and culture learning abroad."

[48] Kelley and Meyers, "The Cross-Cultural Adaptability Inventory."

[49] C. Kelley and J. Meyers, "The Cross-Cultural Adaptability Inventory: Self-assessment," (Minneapolis, MN: NCS Pearson, 1995a).

[50] C. Kelley and J. Meyers, "The Cross-Cultural Adaptability Inventory: Manual," (Minneapolis, MN: NCS Pearson, 1995b).

[51] W. Searle and C. Ward, "The prediction of psychological and sociocultural adjustment during cross-cultural transitions," *International Journal of Intercultural Relations* 14, no. 4 (1990).; and C. Ward and A. Kennedy, "The measurement of sociocultural adaptation," *International Journal of Intercultural Relations* 23, no. 6 (1999).

[52] A. Furnham and S. Bochner, "Social difficulty in a foreign culture: An empirical analysis of culture shock," in *Cultures in contact: Studies in cross-cultural interaction*, ed. S. Bochner (Oxford: Pergamon Press, 1982).

[53] Ward and Kennedy, "The measurement of sociocultural adaptation."

[54] J. Szapocznik, W. Kurintes, and T. Fernandez, "Bicultural involvement and adjustment in Hispanic-Americans," *International Journal of Intercultural Relations* 4, no. 3 (1980).

[55] Ibid.

[56] J. S. Phinney, "The multigroup ethnic identity measure: A new scale for use with diverse groups," *Journal of Adolescent Research* 7 (1992).

[57] Ibid.

[58] K. Cressy, "A long-term vision for diversity in education abroad," IIE Network, Retrieved March 2, 2006, from http://www.iienetwork.org/page/71207/.

[59] A. M. Horvath, "Ethnocultural identification and the complexities of ethnicity," in *Improving intercultural interactions: Modules for cross-cultural training programs*, ed. K. Cushner and R. Brislin (Thousand Oaks, CA: Sage, 1997).; and A.-M. Yamada, "Multidimensional identification," in *Teaching about culture, ethnicity & diversity: Exercises and planned activities*, ed. T. M. Singelis (Thousand Oaks, CA: Sage, 1998).

[60] A. J. Marsella and A.-M. Horvath, "The Multi-Index Ethnocultural Identity Scale," (University of Hawai'i at Manoa, 1993).

[61] Yamada, "Multidimensional identification"; and Horvath, "Ethnocultural identification and the complexities of ethnicity."

[62] A. Der-Karabetian and J. Metzer, "The cross-cultural world-mindedness sScale and political party affiliation," *Psychological Reports* 72 (1993).

[63] D. Sampson and K.P. Smith, "A scale to measure world-minded attitudes," *Journal of Social Psychology* 45 (1957).

[64] D. L. Silvernail, "The assessment of teachers' future world prospective values," *The Journal of Environmental Studies* 10 (1979).

[65] A. Der-Karabetian, "World-mindedness and the nuclear threat: A multinational study," *Journal of Social Behavior and Personality* 7 (1992).

[66] Der-Karabetian and Metzer, "The cross-cultural world-mindednessscale and political party affiliation."

[67] J. N. Corbitt, *Global awareness profile* (Yarmouth, ME: Intercultural Press, 1998).

[68] J. N. Corbitt, *Global awareness profile.*

References

American Council on the Teaching of Foreign Languages. ACTFL proficiency guidelines for speaking. Hasting-on-Hudson, NY: ACTFL, 1999.

Bennett, M. J. Toward ethnorelativism: The developmental model of intercultural sensitivity. In *Education for the intercultural experience*, edited by R. M. Paige, 21–71. Yarmouth, ME: Intercultural Press, 1993.

Bhawuk, D. P. S., and H. C. Triandis. The role of culture theory in the study of culture and intercultural training. In *Handbook of intercultural training*, edited by D. Landis and R. S. Bhagat, 17–34. Thousand Oaks, CA: Sage, 1996.

Brecht, Richard D., Dan E. Davidson, and Ralph B. Ginsberg. Predictors of foreign language gain during study abroad. In *Second language acquisition in a study abroad context*, edited by Barbara F. Freed, 37–66. Philadelphia, PA: John Benjamins North America, 1995.

Brislin, R. W., and T. Yoshida, eds. *Improving intercultural interactions: Modules for cross-cultural training programs*. Thousand Oaks, CA: Sage, 1994.

Brown, C., and K. Knight. Introduction to self-awareness inventories. In *Intercultural sourcebook: Cross-cultural training methods*, edited by S. M. Fowler & M. G. Mumford, 19–30. Yarmouth, ME: Intercultural Press, 1999.

Casse, P. The four-value orientation exercise using a self-awareness inventory. In *Intercultural sourcebook: Cross-cultural training methods*, edited by S. M. Fowler and M. G. Mumford, 31–44. Yarmouth, ME: Intercultural Press, 1999.

———. *Training for the multicultural manager*. Washington, DC: The Society for Intercultural Education, Training and Research, 1982.

Chieffo, L., and L. Griffiths. Large-scale assessment of student attitudes after a short-term study abroad program. *Frontiers: The Interdisciplinary Journal of Study Abroad* X (2004): 165–78.

Cohen, A. D., and J. C. Chi. Language strategy use survey. Minneapolis, MN: University of Minnesota, The Center for Advanced Research on Language Acquisition, 2001.

Cohen, A. D., R. M. Paige, R. L. Shively, H. Emert, and J. Hoff. Maximizing study abroad through language and culture strategies: Research on students, study abroad program professionals, and language instructors. Minneapolis, MN: University of Minnesota, The Center for Advanced Research on Language Acquisition, 2005.

Cohen, A. D., and R. L. Shively. Speech act measure of language gain. Minneapolis, MN: University of Minnesota, The Center for Advanced Research on Language Acquisition, 2002.

Corbitt, J. N. (1998). *Global awareness profile*. Yarmouth, ME: Intercultural Press.

Cressy, K.A. Long-term vision for diversity in education abroad, IIE Network, Retrieved March 2, 2006, from http://www.iienetwork.org/page/71207/.

Crowther, Paul, Michael Joris, Matthias Otten, Bengt Nilsson, Hanneke Teekens, and Bernd Wächter. Internationalization at home: A position paper. Amsterdam: European Association for International Education, 2000.

Cushner, K., and Brislin. R. W. *Improving intercultural interactions: Modules for cross-cultural training programs*. Vol. 2. Thousand Oaks, CA: Sage, 1997.

Der-Karabetian, A. World-mindedness and the nuclear threat: A Multinational Study. *Journal of Social Behavior and Personality* 7 (1992): 293–308.

Der-Karabetian, A., and J. Metzer. The cross-cultural world-mindedness scale and political party affiliation. *Psychological Reports* 72 (1993): 1069–70.

deWit, Hans, and Jane Knight, eds. *Quality and internationalisation in higher education* Paris: Organisation for Economic Co-operation and Development, 1999.

DiBiasio, D., and N. A. Mello. Multi-level assessment of program outcomes: Assessing a nontraditional study abroad program in the engineering disciplines. *Frontiers: The Interdisciplinary Journal of Study Abroad* X (2004): 237–52.

Engle, L., and J. Engle. Assessing language acquisition and intercultural sensitivity development in relation to study abroad program design. *Frontiers: The Interdisciplinary Journal of Study Abroad* X (2004): 219–36.

Fowler, S. M., and M. G. Mumford, eds. *Intercultural sourcebook: Cross-cultural training methods*. Vol. 2. Yarmouth, ME: Intercultural Press, 1999.

Furnham, A., and S. Bochner. Social difficulty in a foreign culture: An empirical analysis of culture shock. In *Cultures in contact: Studies in cross-cultural interaction*, edited by S. Bochner, 161–98. Oxford: Pergamon Press, 1982.

Grunzweig, Walter, and Nana Rinehart, eds. *Rockin' in red square: critical approaches to international education in the age of cyberculture*. Bonn: VG Bild-Kunst, 2002.

Gudykunst, W. B. *Bridging differences: Effective intergroup communication*. 2nd ed. Thousand Oaks, CA: Sage, 1994.

Hammer, M. R. A measure of intercultural sensitivity: The Intercultural Development Inventory. In *Intercultural sourcebook: Cross-cultural training methods*, edited by S. M. Fowler and M. G. Mumford, 61–72. Yarmouth, ME: Intercultural Press, 1999.

Hammer, M. R. . The Intercultural Conflict Style Inventory [Instrument]. Ocean Pines, MD: Hammer Consulting, LLC, 2003.

Hammer, M. R., and M. J. Bennett. The Intercultural Development Inventory (IDI) Manual. Portland, OR: Intercultural Communication Institute, 1998, 2001.

Hammer, M. R., M. J. Bennett, and R. Wiseman. Measuring intercultural sensitivity: The intercultural development inventory. *International Journal of Intercultural Relations* 27, no. 4 (2003).

Hammer, M. R., Malone, M., and Paige, R. M. (in press). Interview protocol: An instrument for assessing disciplinary learning. Washington, D.C.: Georgetown University.

Horvath, A. M. Ethnocultural identification and the complexities of ethnicity. In *Improving intercultural interactions: Modules for cross-cultural training programs*, edited by K. Cushner and R. Brislin, 165–83. Thousand Oaks, CA: Sage, 1997.

Immelman, A., and P. Schneider. Assessing student learning in study abroad programs: A conceptual framework and methodology for assessing student learning in study abroad programs. *Journal of Studies in International Education* 2, no. 2 (1998): 59–79.

Ingraham, E. C., and D. L. Peterson. Assessing the impact of study abroad on student learning at Michigan State University. *Frontiers: The Interdisciplinary Journal of Study Abroad* X (2004): 83–100.

Kelley, C., and J. Meyers. The cross-cultural adaptability inventory. In *Intercultural sourcebook: Cross-cultural training methods*, edited by S. M. Fowler and M. G. Mumford, 53–60. Yarmouth, ME: Intercultural Press, 1999.

———. The cross-cultural adaptability inventory: Manual. Minneapolis, MN: NCS Pearson, 1995b.

———. The cross-cultural adaptability inventory: self-assessment. Minneapolis, MN: NCS Pearson, 1995a.

Kuo, Jane, and Xixiang Jiang. Assessing the assessments: The OPI and the SOPI. *Foreign Language Annals* 30, no. 4 (1997): 503–12.

Liskin-Gasparro, J. E. The ACTFL proficiency guidelines and the Oral Proficiency Instrument: A brief history and analysis of their survival. *Foreign Language Annals* 36, no. 4 (2003): 483–90.

Maddox, T., ed. *Tests: A comprehensive reference for assessments in psychology, education and business.* Austin, TX: Pro-Ed, 1997.

Marsella, A. J., and A.-M. Horvath. The multiindex ethnocultural identity scale. University of Hawai'i at Manoa, 1993.

Mestenhauser, J. M., and B. J. Ellingboe. *Reforming the higher rducation curriculum: internationalizing the campus.* Phoenix, AZ: American Council on Education/ The Oryx Press, 1998.

Murphy, L. L., B. S. Plake, and J. C. Impara, eds. *Tests in Print V: An index to tests, test reviews and the literature on specific tests.* Lincoln, NE: Buros Institute of Mental Measurements of the University of Nebraska, 1999.

Paige, R. M. Instrumentation in intercultural training. In *Handbook of intercultural training*, edited by D. Landis, J. M. Bennett and M. J. Bennett. Thousand Oaks, CA: SAGE, 2004.

Paige, R. M., A. D. Cohen, J. Lassegard, J. C. Chi, and B. Kappler. *Maximizing study abroad: A student's guide to strategies for language and culture learning and use.* Minneapolis, MN: University of Minnesota, The Center for Advanced Research on Language Acquisition, 2002.

Paige, R. M., A. D. Cohen, and R. L. Shively. Assessing the impact of a strategies-based curriculum on language and culture learning abroad. *Frontiers: The Interdisciplinary Journal of Study Abroad* X (2004): 253–76.

Paige, R. M., M. Jacobs-Cassuto, Y. A. Yershova, and J. DeJaeghere. Assessing intercultural sensitivity: A psychometric analysis of the Hammer and Bennett Intercultural Development Inventory. *International Journal of Intercultural Relations* 27, no. 4 (2003).

Paige, R. M., J. Rong, W. Zhang, B. Kappler, J. Hoff, and H. Emert. Strategies Inventory for Learning Culture. Minneapolis, MN: Center for Advanced Research on Advanced Language Acquisition, University of Minnesota, 2002.

Phinney, J. S. The multigroup ethnic identity measure: A new scale for use with diverse groups. *Journal of Adolescent Research* 7 (1992): 156–76.

Plake, B. S., J. C. Impara, and R. A. Spies, eds. *The fifteenth mental measurements yearbook.* Lincoln, NE: Buros Institute of Mental Measurements of the University of Nebraska, 2003.

Reddin, W. J. *Using tests to improve training: The complete guide to selecting, developing and using training instruments.* Englewood Cliffs, NJ: Prentice Hall, 1994.

Salaberry, Rafael. Revising the revised format of the ACTFL Oral Proficiency Interview. *Language Testing* 17, no. 3 (2000): 289–310.

Sampson, D., and K.P. Smith. A scale to measure world-minded attitudes. *Journal of Social Psychology* 45 (1957): 99–106.

Searle, W., and C. Ward. The prediction of psychological and sociocultural adjustment during cross-cultural transitions. *International Journal of Intercultural Relations* 14, no. 4 (1990): 449–64.

Silvernail, D. L. The assessment of teachers' future world prospective values. *The Journal of Environmental Studies* 10 (1979): 7–11.

Singelis, T. M., ed. *Teaching about a culture, ethnicity, & diversity: Exercises and planned activities.* Thousand Oaks, CA: Sage, 1998.

Stansfield, C.W., and D.M. Kenyon. Research on the comparability of the Oral Proficiency Interview and the Simulated Oral Proficiency Interview. *System* 20 (1992): 347–64.

Surface, E. A., and E. C. Dierdorff. Reliability and the ACTFL Oral Proficiency Interview: Reporting indices of interrater consistency and agreement for 19 languages *Foreign Language Annals* 36, no. 4 (2003): 507–19.

Sutton, R. C., and D. L. Rubin. The GLOSSARI project: Initial findings from a system-wide research initiative on study abroad learning outcomes. *Frontiers: The Interdisciplinary Journal of Study Abroad* X (2004): 65–82.

Suzuki, L. A., J. G. Ponterotto, and P. J. Meller, eds. *Handbook of multicultural assessment: Clinical, psychological, and educational applications.* 2nd ed. San Francisco, CA: Jossey-Bass, 2001.

Sweetland, R. C., and D. J. Keyser, eds. *Tests: A comprehensive reference for assessments in psychology, education, and business.* 3rd ed. Austin, TX: Pro-Ed, 1991.

Swender, E. Oral proficiency testing in the real world: Answers to frequently asked questions *Foreign Language Annals* 35, no. 4 (2003): 520–26.

Szapocznik, J., W. Kurintes, and T. Fernandez. Bicultural involvement and adjustment in Hispanic-Americans. *International Journal of Intercultural Relations* 4, no. 3 (1980): 353–65.

Tucker, M. F. Self-awareness and development using the overseas assignment inventory. In *Intercultural sourcebook: Cross-cultural training methods*, edited by S. M. Fowler and M. G. Mumford, 45–52. Yarmouth, ME: Intercultural Press, 1999.

Vande Berg, Michael, ed. *Frontiers: The Interdisciplinary Journal of Study Abroad.* Edited by Brian Whalen. Vol. X. Carlisle, PA: Frontiers Journal, Inc., 2004.

Vande Berg, Michael, A. Balkcum, M. Scheid, and B. J. Whalen. The Georgetown University consortium project: A report from the halfway mark. *Frontiers: The Interdisciplinary Journal of Study Abroad* X (2004): 101–16.

Ward, C., and A. Kennedy. The measurement of sociocultural adaptation. *International Journal of Intercultural Relations* 23, no. 6 (1999): 659–77.

Yamada, A.-M. Multidimensional identification. In *Teaching about culture, ethnicity & diversity: Exercises and planned activities*, edited by T. M. Singelis, 141–45. Thousand Oaks, CA: Sage, 1998.

Chapter 8

Defining Terms for Use in Designing Outcomes Projects

Chip Peterson, Lilli Engle, Lance Kenney, Kim Kreutzer,
William Nolting, Anthony Ogden

Introduction

Semantic ambiguity has long plagued the education abroad profession. At times this ambiguity borders on anarchy. Several different terms may be used for the same concept, or the same term may have several different meanings. Education abroad professionals have had no agreed-upon set of definitions to which to turn. To illustrate, is *short-term program* a useful term? If so, what exactly does it mean? (Is it defined by time of year? If so, are all summer programs short-term by definition? Or is it defined by length alone? If so, how many days or weeks constitute the cutoff point?) What do we call a study abroad program that places students in regular classes, alongside host-country students, in a foreign university? (Direct enrollment? Integrated study? University study? Integrated university study?) Can we agree on a term for a program run by an external provider but with which an institution has special ties? (An affiliated program? A co-sponsored program? An approved program? An endorsed program? A highlighted program? A featured program?) When we group programs geographically, what countries do we consider to constitute, say, *Western Europe*, *Southern Africa*, or *the Middle East*?

Some of this confusion is inevitable. Different institutions organize their education abroad efforts differently, and a definition that makes sense for one institution may not for another. Moreover, many terms are used widely outside education abroad as well as within, and education abroad professionals are in no position to impose definitions unilaterally. Yet our profession does potentially have the power to reduce semantic ambiguity significantly.

The need for conventions may be mild or acute, depending on the uses to which terms are to be put. For our everyday professional lives, the lack of precision may be only a minor inconvenience. On the other hand, clarity is essential when terms are to be used for, say, data collection—or, more to the immediate point, for effective outcomes assessment. Definition of terms for research purposes constitutes one of the first and essential steps in creating a viable study. Comparability of data across studies also becomes viable if terms have some validity outside one institution's usage.

For more than a year, a Forum task force has been working to develop an education abroad glossary. This task force has searched publications, had numerous conversations with colleagues who are experts in the respective areas, and circulated several drafts to other Forum members and/or committees for comment and feedback. The guide presents the relevant results of this process to date.

As this book goes to press, a first draft of the entire glossary has been completed. Further editing, as well as wider discussion among education abroad professionals, will be needed before it is published. In the meantime, chapter authors have selected entries from the draft glossary that seem especially relevant to the subject of outcomes assessment. In the end, about 52% of the terms appear in this guide. The remainder of this section comprises that subset of the terms and definitions from the draft glossary. Entries in the glossary will attempt whenever feasible to standardize meanings, and when not, at least to identify competing usages explicitly. Sections of the glossary have been omitted entirely when they were felt to be less immediately relevant to outcomes assessment as discussed in the guide. However, section titles, and the original section and subsection number of its placement in the full glossary. have been retained to give researchers an idea of the categories of terms they may need to define in conducting studies.

To facilitate discussion, the full glossary will be posted at the Forum on Education Abroad website (http://www.forumea.org), as a WIKI. This allows members and others to comment on the definitions and suggest alternatives. In the Forum conferences in 2007 and 2008 there will be conversations about the definitions in an effort to fine-tune the draft and come to initial agreement as a field on working definitions.

In developing the glossary, several decisions needed to be taken concerning scope and audience:

- The focus is on education abroad for US college and university students. No attempt has been made to define terms concerned mainly with students from other countries who study in the United States or elsewhere, or with education abroad for primary or secondary school students or for adult learners who are not students.

- The primary audience is education abroad professionals and faculty, both in the United States and in destination countries, who work with such students.

- The glossary covers not only what has been traditionally been defined as study abroad but also other forms of education abroad, including work, internships, volunteering, service-learning, and educational travel.

- Some entries attempt to distill for the education abroad profession current usage, especially when the term comes from outside the field. Others propose conventions for use in the field.
- Definitions reflect (or in some cases recommend) US usages. A similar glossary for the UK or another Anglophone country would contain many differences. Here and there, for the sake of clarity, there is some information on contrasting usages in other Anglophone countries, but no attempt has been made at comprehensiveness.

Those involved in outcomes assessment projects and anyone who contemplates doing such work should take the time to participate in this discussion. Shared terminology will allow us to compare data across programs, institutions, and research studies. They make the data presented more understandable to professionals in the field. Most importantly, shared terms allow for the increased acceptance of international education as an intellectual domain that scholars can pursue for serious research purposes. If international educators wish to encourage such a process, participation in the discussion of definitions constitutes and important step in promoting it.

I. Understanding the US Educational System

This section has been heavily edited for this Guide as many of the terms are familiar to our audiences and have widely shared meaning across the US educational sectors. For the full list, see the Forum website listed above or in the references.

Although some of the following definitions may be useful to professionals working in the United States, this section is designed especially for overseas staff and faculty who work with US students. A comprehensive list would be many times as long; nonetheless, this short list is designed to include many of the terms that host-country nationals working with US students are most likely to encounter.

I-A. Levels of Education and Types of Institutions

The definitions in this cluster are based on US usages. Some of the terms have rather different meanings in other Anglophone countries.

1. K-12 EDUCATION — Term used widely in the US to describe collectively primary and secondary education. ("K" refers to kindergarten; "12" refers to twelfth grade, normally the last year in a high school education.)
2. POST-SECONDARY EDUCATION — Education beyond the high school level.

3. VOCATIONAL/TECHNICAL EDUCATION — A subcategory of post-secondary education focused on preparation for a specific profession and not leading to or toward a university degree. Examples include beauty schools, electronics schools, or secretarial schools. Credits earned at vocational or technical institutions are typically not accepted for transfer by institutions of higher education

4. HIGHER EDUCATION — A subcategory of post-secondary education that leads to or toward a university degree.

5. CARNEGIE CLASSIFICATION — A categorization of US higher education institutions maintained by the Carnegie Foundation for the Advancement of Teaching and widely used within US academia. Basic categories include: Associate's Colleges; Doctorate Granting Universities; Master's Colleges and Universities; Baccalaureate Colleges; Special Focus Institutions; and Tribal Colleges. Categories were updated in 2005. and the full explanation can be viewed at: http://www.carnegiefoundation.org/classifications/index.asp?key=791

I-B. Degrees and Educational Levels

Although many terms in this cluster have fairly standard meanings from one country to another, others tend to be little-used in most countries outside the United States.

1. DEGREE — Awarded by an institution to a student who successfully completes of a program of studies.

2. DEGREE-SEEKING STUDENT (or MATRICULATING STUDENT) — A student who has been admitted to and is enrolled in an educational institution in a status designed to lead to a degree.

3. NON-DEGREE STUDENT — A student who is enrolled in classes but has not been admitted to the institution in a degree-seeking status. Degree-granting institutions that permit students from other institutions to participate in their study abroad programs typically chose to place visiting students in non-degree status.

4. TRANSFER STUDENT — A student at one institution who has previously pursued study at the same level (e.g., undergraduate) at one or more other institutions of higher education. The term applies regardless of whether the current institution awards any degree credit from the previous institution(s).

5. CLASS STANDING — A student's year in school or status based on how far the student has progressed toward finishing degree requirements.

6. TIME TO GRADUATION — Number of semesters or years it takes a student to finish his/her degree requirements.

7. RETENTION — The ability of an institution to avoid losing students before they obtain the intended degree.

8. RETENTION RATE — 1) Percentage of students who remain enrolled (or who earn a degree) at the end of a defined period of time. 2) In the field of education abroad, there are two additional usages of the term: a) the number of students who participate in an education abroad program as a percentage of those who originally inquired about it or who applied or who were accepted for participation; or b) the percentage of students who remain at their home institution and complete their degree after their education abroad experience. Sometimes used to mean the number of students who participate in an education abroad program as a percentage of those who originally inquired about it or who applied or who were accepted for participation.

9. STOP OUT — To drop out of school for one or more terms, then resume studies.

I-C. Credit and Instruction

This cluster includes terms that relate to the administrative aspects of offering coursework on education abroad programs.

1. ACCREDITED — Meeting quality standards in higher education as determined through evaluation by recognized accrediting agencies (in the US) or the Ministry of Education (in many other countries). (For more detail on the US accrediting process, see the Council for Higher Education Accreditation website, http://www.chea.org.)

2. NON-ACCREDITED — Either not evaluated by a recognized higher education accrediting agency or not meeting an agency's standards (see the definition for accredited).

3. ACADEMIC CREDIT — A defined measure of academic accomplishment that is used to determine a student's progress toward a degree, a certificate, or other formal academic recognition. In the US, credit is most commonly counted

as CREDIT HOURS (or CREDITS or UNITS at some institutions) that are assigned to each course. Some institutions count courses rather than credit.

4. RESIDENT CREDIT — Academic credit earned at an institution by a student who is in a degree program at that institution. An institution may designate credit earned on their approved study abroad programs to be resident credit. Grades earned often count in the student's grade point average (GPA, see below), although institutional policies vary in this respect.

5. TRANSFER CREDIT — Academic credit earned at another institution but accepted in lieu of resident credit toward the degree at a student's home institution. Grades earned usually do not count in the student's GPA.

6. UNDERGRADUATE CREDIT — Academic credit that will apply toward a degree, certificate, or other formal academic recognition for a student completing a program that is at the baccalaureate level or lower.

7. GRADUATE CREDIT — Academic credit that is potentially applicable to a graduate-level degree.

8. CREDIT BY EVALUATION — Academic credit assessed and awarded for students' experiences (academic, life experiences, or other). May be used at some institutions to award credit for learning achieved on non-accredited study abroad programs, or other overseas living experiences, for which the home institution will not grant transfer credit.

9. CREDIT BY EXAM — Credit awarded by an institution on the basis of an exam that evaluates a student's proficiency in the subject matter (e.g., language proficiency). Some institutions allow students to use this mechanism to earn credit for learning on non-accredited study abroad programs.

10. NON-CREDIT — Coursework or co-curricular activities for which students do not earn academic credit.

11. INDEPENDENT STUDY — Although meanings vary, this term most typically is used to refer to an individualized course, most often in the form of a research project, which a student undertakes under direct faculty supervision. Normally contact hours for such courses take the form of individual consultation between student and faculty. Some institutions use the term DIRECTED STUDY instead.

12. DISTANCE LEARNING — An option for completing courses away from the campus and its faculty through such means as television, Internet, correspondence courses, CD-ROMs, etc.

13. SYLLABUS — A detailed summary of the content and requirements of an academic course (typically includes lecture or discussion topics, assigned and optional readings, assignments, and evaluation criteria).

14. CURRICULUM — A set of expectations and requirements, and the overall program of study and/or collection of course offerings for a specific academic course or for a program of study (such as a degree program or a study abroad program).

15. TRANSCRIPT — Document produced by an educational institution showing the courses, credits, grades, and degrees earned by a student at that institution. Most institutions issue both OFFICIAL transcripts (produced on special paper and/or with official seals, and often mailed directly to another institution) and UNOFFICIAL transcripts (often issued directly to the student on ordinary paper).

16. GRADE REPORT — Document produced by an educational institution or agency showing the courses, credits, and grades earned by a student at that institution/agency, usually for a brief period of study such as a quarter or semester. It may be a semi-official document, but it is only for the personal use of the student and/or internal use at an institution of higher education. The only truly official academic record at a college or university is the transcript. Some institutions do award resident credit for study abroad on an affiliated program based on a transcript from the provider, however.

17. A-F GRADING — The most common US grading scale in which A is the highest grade and F is a failing grade. Some institutions add +'s and –'s to the grades of A, B, C, D, and/or F, and a few grant intermediate grades (e.g., AB to indicate a grade half way between A and B).

18. PASS-FAIL GRADING (or PASS-NO PASS or S/N for SATISFACTORY/ NOT SATISFACTORY) — This grading scale simply notes whether a student passed the course or failed it. Generally no other levels of evaluation exist, although some institutions might have additional grades, such as "high pass" or "no credit." The awarding body determines the meaning of "pass" grades. They may connote that the student earned the equivalent of a C or better or a D or better. The way the pass-fail grades are handled by an

institution varies by institution. Some fully count the credit and others put limits on how it can be used.

19. INCOMPLETE — Grade indicating that the student has not completed requirements for a course but still has a chance to do so. Usually indicated on a transcript as a grade of I. At some institutions an I automatically becomes an F after a specified period of time if the student does not complete the missing coursework.

20. WITHDRAWAL — Grade indicating that the student officially dropped the course and will earn no credit. Usually indicated on a transcript as a W. Does not affect the student's GPA.

21. GRADE CONVERSION — The process by which an institution translates a grade earned abroad, or at another US institution with a different grading system, to an equivalent grade of its own.

22. GPA (GRADE POINT AVERAGE) — A value given to the average grade a student achieved for a particular period of time (e.g., term, degree program). The most typical system of calculating GPA in the US uses a four-point scale in which 4, 3, 2, 1, and 0 points are assigned to each credit of A, B, C, D, and F respectively. Those institutions that permit faculty to give more nuanced grades using pluses or minuses (e.g., A+ or B-) generally assign intermediate values to grades carrying a plus or a minus (e.g., 3.67 for an A-, 3.33 for a B+). Some institutions, although a distinct minority, use other scales for calculating a student's GPA, and a handful use narrative grades and do not calculate a GPA at all.

23. CREDIT CONVERSION — The process of determining the number of credits an institution should award a student for courses taken abroad or at another US institution with a different credit system. This can involve either: 1) determining how many credits a student should receive for courses that do not earn credits abroad or 2) converting the number of credits earned to the home university's system.

24. COURSE LOAD — The number of courses for which a student is registered during a specified period of time. At some US institutions all courses have the same weight, and a student's load is measured by courses rather than credits.

25. CREDIT LOAD — The number of credits for which a student is registered in a given term.

26. FULL LOAD — 1) The average load a student must take in order to graduate within the expected number of years (four years in most undergraduate programs). In the most common credit-based semester systems, a full load is about 15 credits per semester. 2) The minimum load a student must carry in order to be eligible for full financial aid and other benefits allowed only to full-time students. At many institutions a full load for financial aid purposes is smaller (typically 12 credits per semester) than a full load by the first definition (typically 15 credits).

I-D. Classes and Courses

Like Cluster I-A, this cluster fleshes out terms that have multiple meanings in multiple countries. It is meant to provide guidance to overseas professionals working with US undergraduates.

1. CLASS — 1) In US higher education, the regularly scheduled appointed time when students are taught by college/university faculty around a specific subject. Successful completion of the class—based on faculty assessment—results in the awarding of credits toward a student's graduation. 2) The totality of a student population that completed degree requirements simultaneously (e.g., "the Class of 2007").

2. COURSE — 1) Individual classes (per the first definition above, e.g., "I need five courses in history to graduate"). This is the most common use of the term in the US system. 2) The degree-seeking process as a whole (e.g., "My course of study was History"). This usage is secondary in the US but primary in a number of other Anglophone countries.

3. CONTACT HOUR — An hour of scheduled instruction given to students. In many systems of accounting, a contact hour actually consists of 50 minutes. In typical US systems, a semester credit involves about 15 contact hours; and a quarter credit, 10 hours.

4. HOUR OF STUDENT EFFORT — An hour spent by a student on work designed to fulfill course requirements. Hours of student effort include not only contact hours but also hours spent on such activities as course-related reading, research and writing for term papers, field work, field trips, studying for exams, etc. In typical US systems, faculty are urged to design their courses so that an average student puts in about 45 hours of effort per semester credit (normally consisting of 15 contact hours plus 30 hours out of class), or 30 hours per quarter credit (10 and 20, respectively).

5. DISCIPLINE — An area of academic study or branch of knowledge that constitutes a field unto itself. Examples include accounting, agronomy, art history, electrical engineering, political science, social work, etc. Disciplines in turn are often grouped into clusters such as business, engineering, fine arts, humanities, natural sciences, social sciences, etc.

6. SUBJECT — Used interchangeably with either major ("Her subject at college was history") or discipline ("The subject of the class was history").

I-E. Academic Calendars

There is no national academic calendar in the United States. Most often individual institutions determine their own calendars, and sometimes even individual campuses of the same public university. The following are the calendar systems most commonly used in US higher education institutions.

1. SEMESTER SYSTEM — Academic calendar consisting of two terms, typically 14 to 16 weeks each in duration. Usually fall semester begins in late August or early September and finishes in mid- December or later; spring semester typically begins in early to mid-January and ends in late April to mid-May. There may also be one or more summer sessions, which usually are optional. Students typically must complete eight semesters of full-time study or its equivalent to obtain a four-year undergraduate degree in the US. This is the most common academic calendar among US institutions of higher education.

2. QUARTER SYSTEM — Academic calendar consisting of three terms during the regular academic year, each typically 10 to 11 weeks in duration, plus one or more summer terms that typically are optional and operate with reduced enrollments. In the most common variant, fall quarter runs from late September to mid-December; winter quarter from early January to mid-March; and spring quarter from late March to mid-June. Students normally must complete twelve quarters of full-time study or equivalent to obtain a four-year undergraduate degree in the US. This system is most widespread on the West Coast.

3. TRIMESTER SYSTEM — Similar to a quarter system except that typically there is not a summer session.

4. 4-1-4 SYSTEM — Semester system that includes a 3- to 5-week January term (J-term or Interterm), so that spring semester begins later than in a typical semester system. In some 4-1-4 systems, the J-term is required for graduation; in others, it is optional or is required only for some years.

5. 4-4-1 SYSTEM — Semester system similar to the 4-1-4 system except that the 3- to 5-week term comes after spring semester, typically in May.

6. MODULAR SYSTEM (or BLOCK SYSTEM) — A few institutions have calendars in which students take just one course at a time. One term in such systems usually lasts three or four weeks.

7. SUMMER SESSION — A period of study during the summer that is shorter than a semester and is not considered part of the regular academic year. This definition excludes the third term of an institution operating on a trimester system or the fourth of an institution operating on a quarter system. Some institutions have two or more summer sessions

I-F. Cognition and Skill Development

In education abroad programs, student learning occurs both inside and outside the classroom. The terms in this cluster provide general parameters for addressing that learning and how it might be facilitated.

1. LEARNING OUTCOMES — 1) The knowledge, skills, and abilities an individual student possesses and can demonstrate upon completion of a learning experience or sequence of learning experiences (e.g., course, degree, education abroad program). In an education abroad context, learning outcomes may include language acquisition, cross-cultural competence, discipline-specific knowledge, research skills, etc. 2) Advance statements about what students ought to understand or be able to do as a result of a learning experience.

2. HARD PROFICIENCIES/SKILLS — Knowledge or abilities that a student acquires within a particular academic discipline or technical field that are directly related to the information base of that discipline or field (e.g. understanding the grammatical elements of a second language and being able to use them correctly).

3. SOFT PROFICIENCIES/SKILLS — Knowledge or abilities that a student acquires that are less discipline- or technically based and more perceptive and behavioral (e.g., ability to adjust to the different personal space boundaries that exist in different cultures). In a career context, soft skills have been defined as a cluster of personal habits and social skills that make someone a successful employee. Soft skills typically are developed outside of traditional classroom learning environments.

4. CRITICAL THINKING — An analytical approach to studies where students must apply reasoning and evaluation to cognitive problems.

5. COGNITIVE DEVELOPMENT — Growth in a student's ability to reason, acquire knowledge, and think critically about knowledge.

6. CULTURAL INTELLIGENCE — In organizational and managerial theory, the ability to cope with, make sense of, and integrated oneself into foreign cultures, be they national, ethnic, corporate, vocational, etc. Cultural intelligence (or CQ) has cognitive, behavioral, and affective dimensions.

II. International Education and Education Abroad

In some ways, education abroad is like any other profession: it changes and evolves in its structures and standards; its paradigmatic language shifts over time, and basic terms change in meaning; it is subject to the socio-political forces of its time. However, it is distinct in that as a profession, education abroad is positioned between some very distinct (and sometimes contradictory) binaries: academic/administrative, scholastic learning/student development, global knowledge/local immersion. The clusters in this section outline broadly what education abroad is, and perhaps show how that definition has shifted since the field's inception.

II-A. Delineating the Profession

"International education" as a term is often applied to a myriad of professions, activities, and disciplines. The following definitions attempt to position education abroad within those activities and highlight those terms that are sometimes used interchangeably with "education abroad."

1. INTERNATIONAL EDUCATION — 1) As a profession, collectively the myriad jobs associated with migration of students and scholars across geopolitical borders. Includes, but is not limited to, (on US campuses) support for matriculating and exchange students from countries outside the United States; teaching English as a second language; international student recruiting; assessment of non-US higher education credentials; student services for postgraduate research students and fellows; facilitating education abroad for US students; and (outside the US) any job that provides similar forms of support and services for visiting US students. 2) The knowledge and skills resulting from integrating some component to one's formal education through spending time outside of one's home culture. As a more general term, this definition applies to any international activity occurring through the K-12, undergraduate, graduate, or postgraduate experiences.

2. INTERNATIONAL STUDIES — Overarching term often used by those offices at US institutions of higher education that are responsible for multiple facets of international education. Sometimes used interchangeably for the academic discipline "international relations" (see below) or interchangeably with any on-campus coursework with international content.

3. INTERNATIONAL RELATIONS — An interdisciplinary field of study (usually considered an extension of political science) that studies foreign affairs, relations among state and non-state actors, and other transnational social phenomena (globalization, terrorism, environmental policy, etc.).

4. INTERNATIONAL PROGRAMS — As a term, generally used on US campuses to indicate any outside-the-classroom activity (international student orientation, non-credit-bearing study tour, etc.) with an international dimension. Some campuses use it in addition to, or instead of, study abroad programs.

5. INTERNATIONAL EXPERIENCE — Broad, sweeping term for any opportunity undertaken by a US student that takes place outside the United States. Because of the all-encompassing nature of this term (may include really any kind of international travel), it should not be used interchangeably with education abroad or study abroad.

6. INTERNATIONAL EDUCATIONAL EXCHANGE — Blanket term referring to the migration of students (secondary, undergraduate, graduate, postgraduate) among educational institutions. A narrower usage, covered in IV-B, refers to those reciprocal agreements that allow students, faculty, or staff to spend a period of time (usually a semester or longer) at an institution partnered with their own home institution.

7. INTERNATIONALIZING THE CURRICULUM — A movement to incorporate international content throughout an educational institution's curriculum.

8. CURRICULUM INTEGRATION — Incorporating coursework taken abroad into the academic context of the home campus. It weaves study abroad into the fabric of the on-campus curriculum, including course matching, academic advising, departmental and collegiate informational and promotional materials, and the structure of degree requirements.

II-B. Learning Outside the Home Campus

Education abroad is a subset of a wider universe of study outside the home campus that also includes a variety of educational experiences within the United States. This cluster helps place education abroad in that broader context.

1. OFF-CAMPUS EDUCATION (or OFF-CAMPUS LEARNING) — Activities/programs outside the confines of the participant's home campus whose objectives are educational. Off-campus education embraces not only off-campus study but also a variety of activities that do not result in academic credit or fulfillment of degree requirements. Such experiences as internships, service-learning, and alternative break travel programs all qualify as education abroad when driven to a significant degree by learning goals.

2. OFF-CAMPUS STUDY — Education outside the confines of a college campus resulting in progress toward an academic degree at a student's home institution.

3. DOMESTIC OFF-CAMPUS STUDY — Off-campus study that occurs within the same country as the student's home institution, whether within the community where that institution is located or in another part of the same country. Includes not only domestic exchanges and off-campus study programs parallel to many international student exchanges and study abroad programs, but also such activities as field research projects, biology field campus, internships, or course-embedded service learning.

4. OVERSEAS/ABROAD/FOREIGN — As adjectives, terms used to describe the country or culture that hosts the US student during their international educational experience. Each term has strengths and weaknesses, e.g., US students in Canada are not technically "overseas"; study abroad programs based at Native American reservations are not actually "abroad"; "foreign" often has pejorative usage in popular press, etc.

5. STUDY ABROAD (synonymous with, and preferred to, OVERSEAS STUDY or FOREIGN STUDY) — Education abroad that results in progress toward an academic degree at a student's home institution. Although most often this progress means the earning of credit that will be accepted by the home institution, other goals can include satisfaction of a language requirement or completion of a senior thesis. Optional overseas add-ons to on-campus courses do not qualify unless they carry additional credit. Ironically, this somewhat narrow meaning—which has become standard among international educators in the United States—excludes pursuit of a full academic

degree at a foreign institution, which is the most common meaning of the term study abroad as used in many other countries.

6. EDUCATION ABROAD — Off-campus education that occurs outside the participant's home country. Besides study abroad, examples include such international experiences as internships, work, volunteering, and directed travel, so long as they are driven to a significant degree by learning goals.

7. JUNIOR YEAR ABROAD — Term once used widely in some circles as nearly synonymous with *study abroad*. Was never accurate for many institutions where study abroad for shorter periods of time was the norm, or where many students studied abroad in the sophomore or senior year. Because of the decline of full-year study abroad, and in many cases also the diversification of class standing of the study abroad participants, the term has gradually fallen out of favor even at many institutions where it was once appropriate.

8. INDEPENDENT STUDY ABROAD — 1) A research project or other individualized project that a student pursues overseas; it may be offered as part of the curriculum on an overseas program or the student may be doing the project completely independently. 2) Study abroad programs undertaken by students that are not part of their home university's officially approved study abroad offerings. (This phenomenon goes by various other names as well, such as study on an outside program or study on a nonaffiliated program. Institutions have different policies about this and different terminology.)

III. Culture, Diversity, Student Engagement

Education abroad offers not only an academically focused endeavor but also a holistic, transformative learning opportunity. Living and learning alongside people in other cultures promotes cultural self-awareness, effective intercultural communication, and intercultural competency development. Similarly, students encounter a significant range of attitudes regarding multicultural diversity while abroad. While certainly not comprehensive, this section attempts to pull together the most relevant terms from the fields of intercultural communication and multicultural awareness and presents definitions from the perspective of education abroad.

III-A. Understanding Culture

Although culture has been defined in many ways, often with controversy, most would agree that culture is an integrated system of learned behavior patterns that are characteristic of the members of any given society. The following are terms often used in understanding culture and cultural references.

1. CULTURE — The "set of distinctive spiritual, material, intellectual, and emotional features of society or a social group, and that it encompasses, in addition to art and literature, lifestyles, ways of living together, value systems, traditions, and beliefs." (UNESCO)

2. CULTURE-GENERAL — Those general characteristics that can be found in any culture such as communication style, values, etc. Often used also to refer to an approach in intercultural training that endeavors to help participants understand broad intercultural perspectives, as opposed to focusing on specific cultures. By teaching culture-general learning skills, participants learn intercultural strategies applicable to many cross-cultural situations.

3. CULTURE-SPECIFIC — The distinctive qualities of a particular culture. Often used to refer to an approach in intercultural training that attempts to impart extensive information and knowledge of perceptions and behaviors that are unique to specific cultures. Training provided during onsite orientation tends to be culture-specific.

4. ICEBERG METAPHOR — Probably the most commonly used metaphor for culture. Just as nine-tenths of an iceberg is out of sight below the surface of the water, so is a large proportion of culture out of conscious awareness. One's initial impressions of a culture are based on what one sees, hears, feels, tastes, and smells. This is primary awareness, the level of awareness tourists usually experience, or the tip of the iceberg. In-depth awareness is developed over time, as one scans the environment and gains a deeper understanding of the host culture. A solid in-depth awareness is achieved when one can suspend one's own values, beliefs, and assumptions, seek alternative viewpoints, and understand host country's behavioral norms relative to that culture.

5. OBJECTIVE CULTURE — The institutions of culture, such as literature, food, language, and music—the kinds of things that usually are included in area studies or what a tourist might experience during a brief encounter with a new culture (see ICEBERG METAPHOR).

6. SUBJECTIVE CULTURE (or DEEP CULTURE) — The less obvious aspects of culture or the learned and shared patterns of beliefs, behaviors, and values of groups of interacting people (see ICEBERG METAPHOR).

7. EMIC — A description of behaviors, concepts, and interpretations in terms meaningful to an insider view. Understanding *emic* concepts of a culture can help one to see through the insider's lenses.

8. ETIC — Behaviors, concepts, and interpretations in terms familiar to the observer, the outsider's view. Understanding *etic* concepts is essential to building intercultural understanding on a general level.

9. VALUES — The patterns of goodness and badness people assign to ways of being in the world. Each individual has a core of underlying values that contribute to that individual's system of beliefs, ideas, and/or opinions. A "value system" is in essence the ordering and prioritization of values that an individual or society recognizes as important.

10. ASSUMPTION — Refers to the existence of phenomena rather than the assignment of value to them. An individual employs assumptions to pattern the world, and these are usually felt by the individual to be an aspect of the world itself and not simply his or her perception of it (e.g., an individual can change or improve). Cultural assumptions provide a person with a sense of reality—what is true for the individual.

11. BELIEF — An assertion, claim, or expectation about reality that is presumed to be either true or false, even if this cannot be practically determined, such as a belief in the existence of a particular deity.

12. PERCEPTION — The internal process by which an individual acquires, selects, evaluates, and organizes stimuli from the external environment. People behave as they do because of the ways in which they perceive the world, and behaviors are learned as part of their cultural experience.

13. MORAL (or MORALITY) — A system of principles and judgments, sometimes grounded in religious or philosophical concepts and beliefs, by which humans determine whether given actions are right or wrong. These concepts and beliefs are often generalized and codified by a culture or group and thus serve to regulate the behavior of its members.

14. ETHICS — A branch of philosophy that attempts to understand the nature of morality (see MORAL) and to define that which is right as distinguished from that which is wrong. Ethics seeks to address questions such as what ought to be done or what ought not to be done in a specific situation.

15. NORM (or SOCIAL NORM) — Unwritten and often unstated rules that are socially enforced. Social sanctioning is what distinguishes norms from other cultural products such as meaning and values. Norms are most evident when they are not followed or are broken. This often occurs when an individual finds him/herself in a foreign country, dealing with a new culture where the norms are different.

16. CUSTOM — A common practice among a group of people who have a shared heritage such as a common country, culture, or religion.

17. RITUAL — A formalized, predetermined set of symbolic actions generally performed in a particular environment at a regular, recurring interval. Rituals can have a basic sociological function in expressing, inculcating, and reinforcing the shared values and beliefs of a society.

III-B. Cultural Identity

Understanding the role of culture in the formation of one's own values, beliefs, and patterns of behavior is fundamental to developing intercultural competency. The following terms are often associated with understanding cultural identity and identity development.

1. CULTURAL IDENTITY — The (feeling of) identity of a group or culture, or of an individual as far as s/he is influenced by her/his belonging to a group or culture. Common characteristics and ideas may be clear markers of a shared cultural identity, but essentially that identity is determined by difference: We feel we belong to a culture, and a group defines itself as a culture by noticing and highlighting difference with other cultures. People who feel they belong to the same culture have this ideal because they rely partially on a common set of norms, but the awareness of such common codes is possible only via the confrontation with their absence, namely, with other cultures.

2. CULTURAL SELF-AWARENESS — Understanding the role of culture in the formation of one's own values, beliefs, patterns of behavior, problem-solving orientation, and the like, as well as an awareness of those aspects of oneself that are unique and not shaped by prevailing cultural norms.

3. BELL CURVE — The graph of normal distribution is often called the bell curve or the bell-shaped curve. Bell curve grading is a common method of grading examinations. Applied to culture, the bell curve represents the normal distribution of members of a culture along a specific continuum, with

most being grouped in the middle. The behavior of those members at the extremes, called CULTURAL MARGINALS, deviates somewhat from the norm, either adhering more rigorously to cultural norms or less so.

4. **GLOBAL NOMAD** (or **THIRD CULTURE KID**) — A person who has lived abroad before adulthood because of a parent's occupational choice (with for, example, the diplomatic corps, religious or non-governmental missions, international business) or whose parents were/are abroad independently for career purposes. Those who have spent a significant portion of their childhood outside of their own country belong to a separate "third" culture distinct from that of their home or host countries. Elements from each culture are assimilated into the person's life experience, without having the sense of belonging or full ownership in any.

5. **BICULTURAL** — Belonging to, containing, having, combining, or referring to two distinct cultures. A person who is bicultural has the ability to function effectively and appropriately, and can select appropriate behaviors, and attitudes within either culture.

6. **MULTICULTURAL** (or **MULTICULTURALISM**) — A term often used to describe societies (especially nations) that have many distinct cultural groups, usually as a result of immigration. Multiculturalism has been described as preserving a "cultural mosaic" of separate ethnic groups, and is contrasted to a "melting pot" that mixes them.

7. **SUBCULTURE** — A racial, ethnic, regional, economic, or social community exhibiting characteristic patterns of behavior sufficient to distinguish it from others within an embracing culture or society (e.g., gay and lesbian subculture, youth subculture, religious subculture).

8. **GENERALIZATION** — The categorization of the predominant tendencies in a cultural group. Generalizing recognizes that there may be a tendency for the majority of people to hold certain values and beliefs and engage in certain patterns of behavior. Failure to recognize that not every person in the group will conform to the generalization leads to stereotyping (see **STEREOTYPE**).

9. **STEREOTYPE** — The application of information (whether accurate or inaccurate) that we have about a country or culture group, both positive and negative, to every individual in it. Stereotypes are often used in a negative or prejudicial sense and are frequently used to justify discriminatory behaviors. This allows powerful social groups to legitimize and protect their dominant

position. Stereotypes are seen by many as undesirable beliefs that can be altered through education and/or familiarization.

10. HOST NATIONAL — An individual of the population that is host to the education abroad participant.

11. INTERNATIONAL — Between or among nations or encompassing several nations. In the United States, the term is commonly used incorrectly to denote "outside of the United States."

III-C. Intercultural Awareness

In-depth, intercultural awareness is achieved when one can suspend his/her own values, beliefs and assumptions, seek alternative viewpoints, and understand the behavioral norms relative to a new culture. The following terms are often associated with understanding intercultural awareness and sensitivity to difference.

1. ADAPTATION — The additive process of acquiring new behaviors to one's personal repertoire that are necessary for effective behavior in other cultures. With regard to Milton Bennett's *Developmental Model of Intercultural Sensitivity*, adaptation refers to the ethnorelative stage in which learners use empathy and shift cultural frames of reference to understand and be understood across cultural boundaries (see EMPATHY).

2. ACCULTURATION — The adjustment of an individual to a foreign culture. Applies to the process, from the acculturating recipient's point of view, of having a foreign culture added and mixed with that of his or her already existing one acquired since birth. (Conversely, ENCULTURATION denotes the total activity of learning one's own culture.)

3. INTEGRATION — In the most general sense, the degree and frequency with which education abroad students are immersed in the host culture and society (see CULTURAL IMMERSION). With regard to Milton Bennett's *Developmental Model of Intercultural Sensitivity*, integration refers to the ethnorelative stage in which learners internalize bicultural or multicultural frames of reference, maintaining a definition of identity that is "marginal" to any particular culture and see oneself as "in process."

4. CULTURAL ASSIMILATION — An intense process of consistent integration whereby one is absorbed into an established culture. This presumes a loss of all or many characteristics that have made the newcomer different. A region or society where assimilation is occurring is sometimes referred to as a "melting pot."

5. ETHNOCENTRIC (or ETHNOCENTRISM) — The natural tendency to look at the world primarily from the perspective of one's own culture and to evaluate all other groups from that viewpoint. People tend to use their own verbal and non-verbal codes, their own assumptions and rules to evaluate others. Many claim that ethnocentrism occurs in every society; ironically, ethnocentrism may be something that all cultures have in common.

6. ETHNORELATIVE — Characterizes the developmental stage in which one no longer views their own culture as a center from which others should be judged, but rather as a state of mind in which cultures are respected, compared, and contrasted according to the values and perspective of the cultures involved.

7. CULTURAL RELATIVISM — The principle that practices and customs of another culture should be understood only in terms of its own context and its own standards. All customs are relative to a particular cultural context and should be understood only in terms of that context.

8. DUALISM (or DUALISM) — Thinking along a dichotomy where decisions have a right/wrong quality to them. The world thus consists essentially of two boxes, rights and wrongs, and there is generally little trouble in distinguishing one from the other. When stressed one often returns to a dichotomous way of thinking (see MULTIPLICITY, CONTEXTUAL RELATIVISM).

9. MULTIPLICITY — A developmental stage where learners have moved beyond dualism, where decisions are based on a simple either/or way of thinking, to a stage that acknowledges uncertainty in the world. Instead of two boxes or categories, right and wrong, there are now three: right, wrong, and "not yet known." This acceptance of uncertainty as legitimate, albeit temporary, is a profound departure from the dualistic perspective, and for many students an exciting one (see DUALISM, CONTEXTUAL RELATIVISM).

10. CONTEXTUAL RELATIVISM — A developmental stage where learners have moved beyond a vision of the world as essentially dualistic, with a growing number of exceptions to the rule in specific situations, to a vision of a world as essentially relativistic and context-bound with a few right/wrong exceptions. Learners assess the cultural context before developing a position, taking care to be appropriate in the relevant cultural system (see DUALISM, MULTIPLICITY).

III-D. Intercultural Adjustment

The intercultural adjustment process consists of a series of ups and downs usually experienced in any transition but intensified due to its intercultural nature. Although the process is similar for anyone living in a different culture, the depth and height of the ups and downs varies. The following terms are often associated with the intercultural adjustment process.

1. CULTURAL IMMERSION — The extent to which a sojourner is immersed in the host culture, i.e., interacts extensively with host culture members. Most education abroad students have to work hard to break out of the comfortable enclave where peers share a common language and where familiar customs and mores prevail.

2. CULTURAL ADJUSTMENT (or STAGES OF ADJUSTMENT) — A series of emotional ups and downs that accompany the entry into a new culture. Such feelings are commonly experienced in any transition but are intensified when crossing cultural boundaries. Many researchers have conceptualized the adjustment process as stages or phases that a sojourner experiences. Most researchers include at least a honeymoon phase, a culture shock phase, and recovery phase. When and how each person goes through these stages depends largely on the individual, degree of cultural difference, and other situational factors.

3. HONEYMOON — The initial phase after arrival into a new culture, which is characterized by an emotionally positive period of discovery and exploration. As everything is new, exciting, different, and fascinating, one responds by being on a cultural high and feeling that the new culture is absolutely wonderful.

4. CULTURE SHOCK (or TRANSITION SHOCK) — The anxiety and feelings (of surprise, disorientation, confusion, etc.) felt by an individual coming into contact with an entirely different social environment, such as a different country. It often relates to the temporary inability to assimilate the new culture, causing difficulty in knowing what is appropriate and what is not.

5. REVERSE (or REENTRY) CULTURE SHOCK — Similar to culture shock but refers to the difficult and often unexpected transition process through which one progresses upon return to the home culture after an extensive sojourn in a different culture (see CULTURE SHOCK).

6. THIRD CULTURE FORMATION (or THIRD CULTURE RETREAT) — The adoption of a pattern of behaviors that are neither strictly representative of one's own culture nor strictly those of the host culture, but are instead an

adaptation of a group's own cultural patterns of behavior to the context of the host environment. When a group of foreigners find themselves abroad without a trusted adviser or mentor who can help them make sense of the host culture, they can misinterpret cultural behaviors, become alienated from the host culture, and seek refuge in a third culture of their peers.

III-E. Intercultural Communication

The manner of conveying a message can vary according to the amount of meaning contained implicitly in the situation or explicitly in the actual words. Effective intercultural communication requires knowing where to look for meaning. The following terms are often associated with communication across cultures.

1. INTERCULTURAL COMMUNICATION (or CROSS-CULTURAL COMMUNICATION) — 1) How people from differing cultural backgrounds behave, communicate, and perceive the world around them. 2) The field of study that tries to establish and understand how people from different cultures communicate with each other and emphasizes the development of intercultural communication competence.

2. INTERCULTURAL COMPETENCE — Ability to communicate and behave effectively and appropriately in intercultural situations.

3. INTERCULTURAL COMMUNICATIVE COMPETENCE — Ability to communicate effectively and appropriately across cultures, including non-verbal and sociolinguistic dimensions. Adaptability is key.

4. COMPETENCY — The cluster of skills, abilities, habits, character traits, and knowledge a person must have in order to perform effectively within a certain environment. Competencies are demonstrated through behaviors and can be developed though training and individual effort.

5. EMPATHY — The recognition and understanding of other's states of mind, (including beliefs, desires, and particularly emotions), without injecting one's own. The concept is often characterized as the ability to "put oneself into another's shoes," or to identify with the feelings of the other person on that person's terms. Empathy relies on the ability to set aside temporarily one's own perception of the world and assume an alternative perspective.

6. HIGH-CONTEXT — Adjective used to describe societies or groups where people have had close connections over a long period of time. Many aspects of cultural behavior are not made explicit, because most members know what

to do and what to think from years of interaction with each other. **HIGH-CONTEXT COMMUNICATION** refers to communication in which most of the information is already in the person, whereas very little is in the coded, explicitly transmitted part of the message.

7. LOW-CONTEXT — Used to describe societies where people tend to have many connections but of shorter duration or for some specific reason. In these societies, cultural behavior and beliefs may need to be spelled out explicitly, so that those coming into the cultural environment know how to behave. **LOW-CONTEXT COMMUNICATION** refers to communication where the mass of information is vested in the explicit code. A low-context message primarily uses words for the core of the message and is often directly stated.

8. NONVERBAL COMMUNICATION — Includes all behavior that modifies, adds to, or substitutes for spoken or written language. Nonverbal behavior includes: paralanguage (paralinguistics); body language (kinesics); eye language (oculesics); space language (proxemics); touch language (haptics); and timing in conversations (regulators).

9. CONTACT ZONE — The social spaces where disparate cultures meet, clash, and grapple with each other. The term invokes the spatial and temporal co-presence of subjects previously separated by geographic and historical disjunctures, and whose trajectories now intersect.

10. TOLERANCE FOR AMBIGUITY — The ability to be in an unscripted situation and patiently determine what is appropriate. Those with a low tolerance for ambiguity seek information to support their own beliefs. Those with a high tolerance for ambiguity seek objective information from others to gain an understanding of the situation and to predict accurately the behavior of others.

III-F. Participant Demographics and Diversity

Education abroad professionals are committed to increasing the diversity of students who are sent abroad and the diversity of destinations to which students are sent. Here are some of the terms used when talking about diversity.

1. CITIZENSHIP — Usually relates to membership of a nation state, or political community, and carries with it rights to political participation; a person having such membership is a citizen. It is largely conterminous with nationality (see NATIONALITY), although it is possible to have a nationality without being a citizen (i.e., be legally subject to a state and entitled to its protection without having rights of political participation in it).

2. NATIONALITY — Refers to the legal relationship between a person and a country. The nationals of a country generally possess the right of abode in the country whose nationality they hold. Nationality is distinguished from citizenship (see CITIZENSHIP), as citizens have the rights to participate in the political life of the state of which they are a citizen, such as by voting or standing for election, while nationals need not have these rights, though normally they do.

3. ETHNICITY — An aspect of an individual's identity that is based on that individual's heritage where the individual shares common physical, national, linguistic, and/or religious traits with others who are from the same heritage. (ETHNIC GROUPS are composed of members sharing a common ethnicity.)

4. RACE — A socially defined concept used to categorize people based on a combination of physical characteristics and genetic heritage. While biologists have searched for scientific measures of race, they have not been able to conclusively define racial boundaries. As a result of the lack of scientific basis for the term, it is falling out of favor.

5. MINORITY STUDENT — A student who does not belong to the majority Caucasian population in the US. The term has largely been replaced by the term STUDENT OF COLOR, in part because in some settings, "minority" students actually constitute a majority.

6. STUDENT OF COLOR — A student who does not belong to the majority Caucasian population in the US.

7. HERITAGE STUDENT — A student who studies abroad in a location that is linked in some way (e.g., linguistically, culturally, historically) to his/her ethnic or cultural background.

8. DISABILITY — The US Department of Justice, the administrator of the Americans with Disabilities Act, defines a disability as a physical or mental impairment that substantially limits one or more major life activities.

9. STUDENTS WITH DISABILITIES — Students with mental or physical conditions that prevent them from easily carrying out activities that people in the wider population are able to do.

10. DIVERSITY — A wide variety of personal, social, demographic, or geographic qualities that exist within a larger group. (This term can be used in reference to the student population that studies abroad, professionals in the

field of education abroad, faculty at home and abroad, and characteristics of education abroad programs.)

11. UNDERREPRESENTED GROUPS — Categories of students who study abroad in fewer numbers than they represent in a larger population, such as the US, their home state, or their home institution.

12. UNDERREPRESENTED DISCIPLINES — Academic areas that are not commonly pursued by US students while studying abroad at any one point of time in history.

13. UNDERREPRESENTED OR LESS TRADITIONAL DESTINATION — Study abroad destinations that host only small numbers of US study abroad students. (These low participation rates can be the result of a number of factors, such as lack of student interest, lack of home university support, safety or security issues, or lack of host country infrastructure.)

14. WHOLE-WORLD STUDY — A term coined by education abroad professionals to refer to a goal of greater student participation in overseas education programs based in underrepresented destinations (definition above).

IV. Education Abroad Program Features and Types

Although education abroad professionals probably are unanimous in believing that different kinds of experiences abroad have different educational impacts on their participants, semantic anarchy has impeded systematic discussion of, and research on, those differences. This section attempts a first step toward standardizing usages in the field.

IV-A. Orientation

At its best, orientation programming in study abroad is ongoing and designed to support students throughout the study abroad experience, highlighting ways in which to transform experiences into future personal and professional growth. The following are terms commonly associated with orientation programming.

1. PRE-DEPARTURE ORIENTATION — Orientation programming intended to help prepare students for a meaningful and successful educational experience abroad. Pre-departure orientation addresses everything from practical concerns with passports and student visas, health and safety, and academics to cultural adjustment, intercultural learning, and diversity awareness.

Orientation may consist of written materials, in-person meetings, virtual meetings, email correspondence, or, most typically, some combination of these.

2. PRE-SESSION — In-country programming offered in the weeks between the beginning of an education abroad experience and the beginning of regular classes. Usually pre-sessions are used in university-based programs and are designed to provide intensive preparation for coursework in the host university system. These sessions may involve intensive language or discipline-specific study. Successful completion may be a required provision for participation in the education abroad experience. Academic credit often is awarded.

3. ONSITE ORIENTATION — Orientation programming that is facilitated immediately or shortly after arrival abroad. Onsite orientation usually includes presentations on the academic program, housing, regional geography, health and safety issues, rules of conduct, and other general issues of getting started and living successfully in the new culture. Onsite orientation may include follow-up workshops on housing, cultural adjustment, career preparation, pre-reentry, etc. In contrast to a pre-session, an on site orientation usually does not yield academic credit.

4. ONGOING ORIENTATION — The continuous and unified process of providing orientation during all major phases of the education abroad experience: pre-departure, onsite participation, and re-entry.

5. RE-ENTRY ORIENTATION — Orientation programming intended to support students with their readjustment to their home culture and campus. This orientation encourages students to reflect upon what they learned abroad and articulate their experiences to themselves and others so that they might further build their new skills and perspectives. Re-entry orientation may be built into the in-country program and/or given on the home campus after students' return.

IV-B. Program Descriptors

The terms in this cluster are frequently used in characterizing study abroad formats/models/types.

1. PROGRAM CHARACTERISTICS — Descriptors of an education abroad program on any of a wide variety of dimensions, such as location, length, sponsorship, eligibility, content, format, and pedagogical approach.

2. PROGRAM MODEL — A combination of characteristics that provide a shorthand description of an education abroad program. Examples: short-term, faculty-led study tour; summer intensive language program; geology field research program; integrated program in a Spanish-speaking university; student exchange program in business studies; work abroad program; internship program in environmental studies.

3. PROGRAM TYPE — A grouping of program models into a handful of broad categories (see cluster IV-E).

4. PROGRAM DESIGN — The basic structure of an education abroad program. Combines such considerations as length, timing, level, phases (e.g., 1-week orientation followed by 14 weeks of classroom study), and pedagogical model (e.g., role of field study, role of integrated university courses), etc.

5. SOJOURN — A period of time spent living in a cultural setting different from one's own.

6. DURATION — Length of a sojourn or of an education abroad program. Does not include pre-departure preparation or post-return activities.

7. DIRECT ENROLLMENT — Study in an overseas university without going through a provider other than the student's home institution. Not to be confused with integrated university study, for which it is sometimes used as a synonym.

8. INTEGRATED UNIVERSITY STUDY — Study in regular classes at a host-country university alongside students from that country. May be either via direct enrollment or through a provider.

9. STUDY ABROAD CENTER — An in-country institution whose primary mission is to provide special classes for American students or for a broader range of non-native students. Normally involves permanent staff and office facilities. Centers may be operated independently; may be special units within a host-country university; or may be sponsored by a college or university in another country or by a study abroad provider. They may or may not be accredited.

10. FACULTY-LED PROGRAM — A study abroad program directed by a faculty member from the home campus who accompanies the students abroad.

11. COURSE-EMBEDDED STUDY ABROAD — A short study abroad experience that forms an integral part of, or an optional add-on to, a course given on the home campus. Most commonly the study abroad portion of the course takes place during a mid-semester break or after the end of the on-campus term. Typically the study abroad cannot overlap significantly with the dates of the on-campus term because participants are enrolled in other classes as well.

12. LANGUAGE INSTITUTE — A study abroad center whose primary mission is language instruction. Some language institutes also provide foreign language instruction to students from the host country. Most are non-accredited.

13. FIELD STUDY — Study outside the classroom. Includes such experiences as internships, service-learning projects, field trips and excursions, nature observation and research, small-team field assignments, and individual research projects.

14. MULTI-SITE PROGRAM — A program, typically faculty-led but occasionally center-based, whose students spend a significant amount of time studying in each of two or more locations.

15. STUDY TOUR — An academic program built around relatively continuous travel.

16. ISLAND PROGRAM — An informal term, sometimes used pejoratively, for a center-based or faculty-led program whose format promotes little cultural immersion. In the extreme case of an island program, American students live together and study together in a strictly classroom setting.

17. PENINSULAR PROGRAM — An informal term for a center-based or faculty-led program whose format promotes a significant degree of cultural experience through such things as housing arrangements, use of host-country faculty, field study opportunities, or access to certain integrated classroom study options.

18. IMMERSION PROGRAM — An informal term for a program that integrates students into the host culture to a substantial degree. Includes integrated programs and some varieties of field study programs.

19. EXCHANGE — A program involving a two-way movement of participants—whether faculty, students, staff, or community members—between institutions or countries.

20. STUDENT EXCHANGE — An exchange whose participants are students. Most typically when at the post-secondary level, student exchanges are facilitated on a person-to-person basis (e.g., one US student spends time at an overseas university while a student from that university is enrolled at the US university); or some mathematical variation (e.g., one US student for two incoming international students). These exchanges often involve some system of "banking" tuition (and sometimes other fees) collected from the outgoing student for use by the incoming student. The term "student exchange" is sometimes mistakenly used as a synonym for study abroad.

21. BILATERAL STUDENT EXCHANGE — A student exchange between two institutions.

22. MULTILATERAL STUDENT EXCHANGE — An exchange among three or more participating institutions. Typically in such exchanges the rough balancing of numbers occurs across the system, so that an outgoing student need not go the same institution, or even the same country, as the incoming counterpart (examples: ISEP, the International Student Exchange Program; and NSE, the National Student Exchange).

23. CUSTOM/CUSTOMIZED PROGRAM — A study abroad program administered on contract according to specifications of the contractor (examples: a college or university contracting with a provider, or an academic department contracting with its institution's study abroad office).

24. DEPARTMENTAL PROGRAM — A study abroad program operated by an academic department (or by a college within a university) with little or no participation by the institution's study abroad office.

IV-C. Program Duration

Although many of the terms in this cluster are used quite universally—for example, semester or academic year—definitions are often imprecise. For example, does "semester" refer to the actual amount of time abroad, the period of the year during which the student goes, or the period of registration on the home campus? This cluster represents an attempt to standardize meanings strictly in terms of length of time students are on site in an education abroad program. If such a scheme were eventually to be applied to data gathering, it would first require widespread discussion in the field. Among other things, it would modify the approach that has been taken in Open Doors data gathering by separating the question of length from the question of timing (next section).

1. LONG-TERM — Lasting 60 weeks or more.
2. FULL YEAR — Lasting 40 to 59 weeks.
3. ACADEMIC YEAR — Lasting 25-39 weeks.
4. TWO QUARTERS — Lasting 18-24 weeks, regardless of whether the institution is on a quarter system or not.
5. SEMESTER — Lasting 12-17 weeks and occurring entirely or mostly during the academic year.
6. QUARTER — Lasting 8-11 weeks.
7. SHORT-TERM — Lasting 4-7 weeks.
8. MICRO-TERM — Lasting 3 weeks or less.

IV-D. Program Timing

The definitions in this cluster represent a first step toward standardizing meanings. Lots of discussion in the field will be necessary before this cluster is ready to be applied to data gathering. Definitions need to be easy and unambiguous to apply, and the categorization scheme needs to be useful to education abroad professionals. Remember, these terms are based on researching US students abroad and have that experience as a frame of reference.

1. MORE THAN A YEAR — 60 or more weeks in duration.
2. YEAR — 25-59 weeks roughly aligned with northern hemisphere academic year (usually beginning sometime between July and October).
3. REVERSE YEAR — 25-59 weeks roughly aligned with southern hemisphere academic year (usually beginning sometime between December and March).
4. FALL — Occurring mostly or entirely between September and mid-December. Includes fall semester programs, fall quarter programs, two-quarter fall/winter programs, and summer/fall combinations.
5. WINTER — Occurring mostly or entirely between mid-December and the end of February. Includes winter break programs, J-term programs, and winter quarter programs but not spring semester programs.
6. SPRING — Occurring mostly between January and May. Includes spring semester programs, spring quarter programs, May term programs, two-

quarter winter/spring programs, spring break programs, and combination spring/summer programs. Does not include winter quarter, winter break, or J-term programs.

7. SUMMER — Occurring mostly between June and August.

IV-E. Study Abroad Program Types

This cluster is perhaps the most tentative—and potentially most controversial—in the glossary. It attempts to synthesize various program characteristics into a small number of idealized models. Following considerable discussion and modification, such a classification scheme might eventually be employed in data reporting on study abroad participation. Before that could happen, a consensus would need to be reached in the field, not only about which categories to include but also on how to define their boundaries concretely enough to minimize ambiguity. This particular cluster, then, is meant to be the opening salvo in a long conversation rather than a standard for the field.

1. INTEGRATED UNIVERSITY STUDY — A study abroad program type in which the predominant study format is participation in regular courses alongside degree-seeking students from the host university

2. CLASSROOM STUDY ABROAD PROGRAM — A study abroad program type in which the predominant study format consists of classroom-based courses designed for non-native students. May include a variety of subtypes such as language institutes, area studies programs, institutes for foreigners at host-country universities, and faculty-led programs.

3. FIELD STUDY PROGRAM — A study abroad program type in which field study is a required and pedagogically central component.

4. OVERSEAS CAMPUS — A separate campus of a college or university whose main campus is located in a different country. Formal accreditation is typically that of the country where the main campus is located, and academic structure typically mirrors that of that country. Unlike most study abroad programs, overseas campuses offer degrees (sometimes only a two-year degree, more typically a full undergraduate degree, and sometimes graduate degrees as well). They may be aimed primarily at host-country students or at students from the country of the sponsoring institution. Many are also open to study abroad students pursuing a degree elsewhere; such students—but only such students—are included in conventional statistics on study abroad by US students.

5. STUDY TOUR — A study abroad program type that revolves around travel, whether within a country or among a number of different countries. Synonyms include traveling program or travel seminar. Examples include a shipboard education program, a European cultural studies tour, or a faculty-led travel seminar. Not to be confused with *field trips* or *excursions* within other program types/subtypes.

6. HYBRID (or MIXED) PROGRAM — A study abroad program type that combines two or more of the preceding types to a significant degree. For example, a classroom study abroad program might permit students to take some courses just for study abroad participants but also to enroll in host university courses and to do a credit-bearing internship. The hybrid category is a useful reminder that program types do not fit into neat boxes but represent tendencies on a series of continua. On the other hand, if the education abroad profession were eventually to attempt to gather participation data by program types, the hybrid category might be difficult to delimit in a useful way.

IV-F. Study Abroad Program Subtypes

The following are common terms to describe types of programs. Most are subtypes within categories in the previous cluster. These terms are useful for conceptualizing different types of study abroad experience but are not designed for use in data reporting.

1. LANGUAGE PROGRAM — A subtype of classroom study program whose primary purpose is language instruction. May be center-based or faculty-led.

2. AREA STUDIES PROGRAM — A subtype of classroom study program whose primary focus is the study of the host country or region, from the perspectives of a variety of disciplines. If the host country is not Anglophone, the curriculum usually includes language instruction. May be center-based or faculty-led.

3. THEME PROGRAM — A subtype of classroom study program focused on a particular theme (e.g., the European Union, environmental studies, gender and development). May be center-based or faculty-led.

4. RESEARCH PROGRAM — A subtype of field study program in which the main focus is research by participating students.

5. ACADEMIC INTERNSHIP PROGRAM — A subtype of field study program in which the focal activity is an internship. See also *internship* and *internship program,* both of which are broader because they do not necessarily result in progress toward a degree.

6. SERVICE-LEARNING PROGRAM — A subtype of field study program in which the focal activity is a service-learning placement.

IV-G. Work, Internships, Volunteering, Service-learning

The terms in this cluster focus on education abroad through structured experiences outside the classroom, whether within a credit-bearing or a co-curricular framework.

1. EXPERIENTIAL EDUCATION — The term *experiential education*, which traces its origins to the works of John Dewey, essentially means learning by doing. It encompasses a vast array of approaches to learning outside the classroom, sometimes complementing classroom-based instruction. These approaches may include research, field trips or seminars, and field work or observation as well as immersion in workplace settings such as internships, volunteering, teaching, and paid jobs. Giving structure to the learning experience through means such as observation and reflection is often seen as an essential element of experiential education. Experiential education may be curricular (for credit) or co-curricular (not-for-credit).

2. FIELD STUDY (FIELD-BASED RESEARCH, OBSERVATION, WORK) — Methodology for learning in a non-classroom environment. For example, the School for International Training describes its "Field Study Seminar" as incorporating "cross-cultural adaptation and skills building: project selection and refinement; appropriate methodologies; field study ethics; developing contacts and finding resources; developing skills in observation and interviewing; gathering, organizing and communicating data; and maintaining a work journal."

3. INTERNSHIP ABROAD (or INTERNATIONAL INTERNSHIP) — A work abroad placement in an apprenticeship capacity, usually connoting working with professionals. Essentially synonymous with the terms **PRACTICUM** and **PRACTICAL TRAINING** (though the latter term also describes a status for international students pursuing an internship in the US, e.g., "optional" or "curricular" P.T.). An internship program may be offered for the experience in its own right, or it may be combined with coursework and offered within the context of a study abroad program for academic credit. An internship may be paid or unpaid.

4. SERVICE-LEARNING ABROAD (or INTERNATIONAL SERVICE-LEARNING) — A volunteer work placement combined with academic coursework, within the context of a study abroad program, and with the learning experience given structure through the principles of experiential education.

5. VOLUNTEERING ABROAD (or INTERNATIONAL VOLUNTEERING) — A non-credit work abroad placement involving service, connoting helping the underprivileged and powerless. Most volunteer organizations today see their role as one of solidarity and social justice, helping those they serve to achieve their own goals. Many programs combine the volunteering with structured learning. Most volunteering is unpaid, although some programs provide a living stipend. Roughly synonymous with INTERNATIONAL COMMUNITY SERVICE.

6. TEACHING ABROAD — A work abroad placement as a teacher or teacher's assistant. Varieties of teaching abroad programs include student teaching (in partial fulfillment of a teaching certificate); teaching English as a second or foreign language; and professional teaching in a K-12 or university environment.

7. WORK ABROAD — As used by international educators, the term *work abroad* (in contrast to *study abroad*) means immersion in an international work environment with the educational value of the experience itself as the primary purpose, whether for academic credit or not, usually through a formally structured program. Depending on the focus of the experience, it may be designated as interning, volunteering, service-learning, teaching, or just working abroad. Work abroad is sometimes used more narrowly to mean working for pay. By design, work abroad programs are temporary, lasting anywhere from a few weeks to two or three years, and they may or may not be related to specific career goals. Educational work abroad is to be distinguished from career-related overseas assignments, permanent jobs abroad, and migration for gainful employment.

V. Program Management

Education abroad offices have been described as "universities within universities." They often have the same management functions that a university has. They need to be concerned with admissions, course registration, fee collection, financial aid, housing, health and safety, program evaluation, and more. All education abroad offices, whether at a college or university, a nonprofit organization, or a for-profit company, will use these terms on a daily basis as they manage their programs.

V-A. Sponsorship and Sponsor Relations

Education abroad programs have primary administrative and academic homes. They also are often shared among partners. This cluster addresses terms used to define the various types of ownerships and partnerships that exist within education abroad.

1. HOME SCHOOL/INSTITUTION — The educational institution in the US where an education abroad student is a continuing student, usually working toward the completion of a degree.

2. HOST SCHOOL/INSTITUTION — The institution that the education abroad student is attending while abroad.

3. SCHOOL OF RECORD — The first institution of higher education in the US that issues a transcript for academic work done on a study abroad program.

V-C. Program Oversight

All programs should periodically be evaluated against quality standards and to determine if they are meeting their goals. Evaluations and assessments can take many forms. Here are some of the terms used in the context of program evaluation and oversight.

1. STANDARDS — Used in reference to standards of good practice, standards refer to minimal quality requirements for various elements of education abroad programming.

2. OVERSIGHT COMMITTEE/BOARD — A group of professionals who make decisions and set policy for an education abroad entity, such as an education abroad office at a university or a non-profit or for-profit education abroad independent provider.

3. ADVISORY COMMITTEE/BOARD — A group of professionals who provide guidance and advice for an education abroad entity, such as an education abroad office at a university or a non-profit or for-profit education abroad independent provider.

4. ASSESSMENT — The process of evaluating and judging a product or a situation based on a review by experts. In the context of education abroad, the following types of assessment are common:(a) the assessment of a student's academic work in a particular course ending in the determination of the student's grade for the course.; (b) the assessment or evaluation of a particular program (see PROGRAM REVIEW). While the terms assessment and evaluation have often been used as synonyms, NAFSA's Guide to Education Abroad (2005) makes the distinction that assessment measures progress by looking at defined variables, while evaluation is in interpretation or judgment relating to quality; (c) the assessment of the outcomes achieved by education abroad programs. (Assessment typically measures a program's growth or progress along particular parameters.)

5. FOCUS GROUP — A group of people who have experience or expertise in an area that a researcher is studying. Focus groups give researchers qualitative feedback on the topics chosen for discussion. Real-time interaction between group members and the researcher/moderator allows for clarification of ideas and the development of thoughts. However, because the data collected is not quantitative data collected from a random sample of individuals, focus group data, as such, cannot be extrapolated to reflect the thoughts of the larger group being studied.

6. EVALUATION — The process of critically examining an overseas program, a host institution, or a US study abroad office to review its effectiveness and the quality of its offerings.

7. PROGRAM REVIEW — The comprehensive evaluation of a program based on a critical look at its component parts. Ideally program reviews are conducted on a periodic basis. The professionals conducting the review may be from inside the organization (internal review) or from outside of the organization (external review). In the context of education abroad, "program review" can refer to two different kinds of programs: (a) reviews of individual education abroad programs that may or may not include an onsite component; (b) reviews of education abroad offices (campus-based or organizationally based).

8. SITE REVIEW — An evaluation of an overseas program that is at least partially conducted onsite. Site reviews can be comprehensive or can focus on one or a few specific issues.

9. SITE VISIT — A trip by US-based study abroad professionals or home campus faculty to an overseas program where one has a relationship (or might have a relationship in the future). Site visits are driven by goals such as the following: to meet with colleagues and/or gather information for program development, to evaluate the program, to learn more about the program, or for other special needs (such as problem-solving).

10. FAMILIARIZATION TOUR (or FAMILIARIZATION VISIT) — A tour of a study abroad provider's overseas program site(s) that is designed for education study abroad professionals and/or faculty. The tour introduces the participants to the academic and co-curricular elements of the provider's programs and to the cultural/social/political context in which they operate.

V-E Participant Status

Accurately identifying participant status is important as it denotes a participant's stage within the study abroad process. Because these terms may be defined differently across institutions, it is essential to seek clarification when working with external organizations to limit confusion and avoid negatively impacting the services participants receive.

1. APPLICANT — Would-be participant who has completed or is completing the necessary paperwork to be considered for admission into an education abroad program.

2. PARTICIPANT — Status referring to one who is taking part or will take part in an education abroad program.

3. ACCEPTED — Status indicating an applicant has been admitted as a participant into an education abroad program. In some cases, full acceptance into the selected education abroad program may be contingent upon receipt of approval from the host institution and/or an external or third party provider (see PARTICIPANT).

4. PROVISIONAL ACCEPTANCE — Status indicating that acceptance into an education abroad is conditional upon the successful completion of provisions outlined at the time of notification. These provisions may take the form of completion of course prerequisites, attainment of a minimum GPA required for participation in the selected program, or other tasks/assignments as deemed necessary by the education abroad office, the faculty or college representative who reviews the applications, the program provider, or the host institution.

5. CONFIRMED — Status of an accepted student who has subsequently submitted additional materials (often including a non-refundable confirmation deposit) to secure his/her spot in the program.

6. REJECTED — Status indicating that an application has been denied participation in the selected education abroad program. The reason is often shared with the applicant at the time of notification.

7. WITHDRAWN — Status of a student who has applied for a program and subsequently notified the sponsor that s/he does not intend to participate. Withdrawal may occur before acceptance or before or after confirmation.

8. CANCELLED — Status of a student whose program was suspended by the sponsor (e.g., because of safety issues or insufficient enrollment).

9. LEAVE OF ABSENCE — A hiatus from a student's home university that allows the student to return after a prescribed period of time without reapplying to the university.

10. RETURNEE — An education abroad participant who has returned to the home institution.

11. ALUMNA/ALUMNUS/ALUMNI — An *alumnus* (masculine) or *alumna* (feminine) is a graduate of a college, university or school. *Alumni* is used for men and mixed groups and *alumnae* for women. Recently, the definition has expanded to include people who have exited from any kind of organization or process. An education abroad program alumnus/a is a student who successfully completed the program.

V-F. Fee Structures

Education abroad professionals use the following terms in budgeting and fiscal management of education abroad offices and programs. (Omitted section)

V-G. Financial Aid

In and of itself, financial aid is a complete field in US higher education. Here are some terms that are commonly used by education abroad practitioners when working with financial aid for education abroad students. (Heavily edited section, see full glossary.)

1. FINANCIAL AID — Monetary assistance provided to a student to cover in whole or in part the costs of participating in an academic program. The aid may be in the form of grants, scholarships, loans, or work-study awards. From http://www.secussa.nafsa.org/financialaid.html: Financial aid can be broadly defined as any help that does not originate with the student or his or her family. Financial aid comes from federal and state governments, institutions of higher education, foundations, ethnic groups and clubs, religious groups and associations, and private and public corporations.

V-H. Student Accommodation

Seemingly as diverse as program type, accommodation offered to study abroad participants varies, ranging from independent housing to full immersion with a local family. An individual study abroad program may offer one or a combination of housing options. These comprise important outcomes variables, as type of housing may indicate important aspects of the type of cultural contact participants have.

1. **APARTMENT** (or **FLAT**) — A self-contained residential unit that occupies only part of a building. Apartments for education abroad participants are usually furnished, and students share cleaning and cooking responsibilities with their apartment mates. In some cases, these apartment mates may be host nationals enrolled in local universities.

2. **LANDLORD** (or **LANDLADY**) — The owner of a room, house, apartment, or land that is rented or leased to an individual or business. In general, the landlord is responsible for repairs and maintenance, and the tenant is responsible for keeping the property clean and safe.

3. **RESIDENCE HALL** (or **DORMITORY**) — Used to describe an entire building for the purpose of housing students. In the US, the term *dormitory* is often controversial at best among residence life professionals, who prefer the term *residence hall*. These buildings are composed of just a few to hundreds of rooms, single and multiple occupancy. Most often, bathrooms with shower, toilet, and sink facilities are provided for a group of rooms. Major factors education abroad students consider when choosing to live in a residence hall include convenience to classrooms and the opportunity to live with local students.

4. **RESIDENTIAL COLLEGE** — A housing system that often physically resembles a residence hall (see **RESIDENCE HALL**) but is more like a living community in spirit. A residential college combines elements of living and academic aspects of the university in one location. Residential colleges encourage participation in a variety of social clubs and offer a tutorial system to all students. They most often have a central theme, such as an academic focus or common interest (e.g., multiculturalism or internationalism). Members of a residential college may be expected to eat their meals together as a unified body. The term is rarely used in the US but common in the UK, Ireland, Australia, and New Zealand.

5. **HOMESTAY** — Private housing hosted by a local family, which often includes a private bedroom, meals, laundry, etc. Homestay experiences usually provide the greatest immersion in the host language and culture, giving students first-hand knowledge of what family life is like in the host culture and the opportunity to use the language in an informal setting. In most cases, the host family welcomes the student like one of the family, getting to know the student and offering a support network to him/her.

6. HOMESTAY VISIT — A short-term homestay for a student otherwise in another type of housing such as a residence hall or an apartment. May be as little as a weekend. Best considered a strategy for cultural enrichment rather than a type of accommodation.

7. BOARDING HOUSE — A house (often a family home) in which students rent one or more rooms for an extended period of time, usually for the duration of the education abroad program. In recent years, it has become common for each room to have its own washing and toilet facilities. For the purposes of education abroad, boarding houses are run by landlords (see LANDLORD). In contrast to a homestay, residents of a boarding house are received as short-term lodgers and are seldom invited to participate in the landlord's family life.

8. HOSTEL (or YOUTH HOSTEL) — Provides short-term accommodation to travelers, particularly encouraging outdoor activities and cultural exchange. In a hostel, students generally rent a bed and share a common bathroom, kitchen and lounge rooms, and often barracks-style bedrooms. The main benefits of a hostel for students are their low cost, informality, and the environment where they can meet other travelers from all over the world. They are generally less formal and expensive than hotels.

9. PENSION — A family-operated guesthouse for short-term travelers. The term is commonly used in Europe and other countries throughout the world as a synonym for inexpensive hostel, where travelers can usually get a room with a shared bathroom. Lodging in pensions is frequently utilized during short-term education abroad experiences.

10. INDEPENDENT HOUSING — Housing arranged by a participant outside of the accommodation provided by the education abroad program. In some cases, students who opt for independent housing may be eligible for a housing allocation deduction from their program fee.

11. HOUSING AND MEALS (or ROOM AND BOARD) — Terms used to describe student accommodation and meals and that are usually explained with documentation of cost, room type, and a description of meal plans. The extent to which housing and meals are provided, if at all, varies across programs. In some programs, students may be independently responsible for securing their own housing and meals, whereas in others, students might choose to live in residence halls and cook with their roommates in common kitchens.

Chapter 9

Securing Funding for Assessment

Veronique Dozier, Maia Stierankova, Kevin Gormley, Mary Schmiedel

Proposal Preparation and Writing

The previous chapters in this book describe the need for assessment and models for doing so. This section describes the types of funding opportunities available for such efforts and the process necessary to acquire these resources. Preparing a competitive funding proposal requires a significant time investment to provide the sophisticated analysis needed for success. Assessment projects are particularly large and complex and thus require substantial support. Therefore, one should begin planning and writing a funding proposal at least a year in advance of the project's start date. It is also unlikely, but not impossible, that one might self-fund a project. This chapter focuses on those projects where outside funding, particularly grant funding, will be necessary to run the project.

Strategic Vision

When seeking funds, the first priority is to have a strategic vision for the future of the project. At the most recent International Collaborative Annual Meeting held by the American Council on Education, Dr. Betty Siegel closed her plenary speech with the simple statement, "resources follow vision, not vice versa."[1] This salient point can be interpreted with two interdependent meanings:

- One who has a vision (and respective passion) for an issue will find the resources, whatever it takes.
- One must first develop an idea that includes a clear and convincing vision before expecting investors to open their wallets.

This is sound advice for those seeking resources for assessment of education abroad. This vision will provide a blueprint as one conducts research, and it will serve as the outline around which one writes the grant proposal. When searching for funding opportunities, the initial step in the research process is to formulate the idea and determine if the project is of interest to private, corporate, or government sponsors.

Having a strategic vision sets the stage for action planning and implementation of the project. A vision provides a comprehensive picture of how the goals will be achieved and establishes the direction and meaning of the project. Ultimately, it serves as a strategy that will be used to address issues that come up throughout the project, while providing manageable goals to achieve the anticipated end results.

Implementation Stage

Once a vision is clearly defined, one can then more confidently move to the implementation plan. The simplest way to begin formulating a plan is to answer the *5 Ws*: who, what, where, when, and why. One should identify why the project is important and what it is one is trying to achieve; how and when one aims to obtain one's objectives; and what and who will need to help in one's efforts to achieve the objectives. If the project requires collaboration with other institutions, one needs to think about the contributions of these researchers vis-à-vis one's own, and determine if they would be listed as consultants or contributors to the project.

While one may have considered the importance and value of undertaking a research project, one will want to consider views of peers in the field who might be contributors to the research or who might sit on a review panel. (Some grants require review panels that help funding agencies decide who will receive funds from the federal government.)[2]

Finally, one should consider whether the project could make an important addition to the existing literature in the field. Chapter 6 of this guide offers help in starting a literature review. Noting these items in the research plan will help one to effectively write a proposal.

Timing

In addition to being strategic, one must be realistic about the time it will take to complete the project. If one is seeking funding for a large assessment project, one must consider how long it is likely to take to reach the project goal. Can the project be completed during the course of an academic year while one is working at a full-time job? Clearly defining a pilot phase, the beginning, and end dates of the project will help one to sketch out a timeline that breaks down the project into discrete segments and allocates the appropriate time and money for each segment. Additionally, one should consider the space that one will need to work on the project, and establish whether one will need conference rooms, computer labs, and office space for additional staff.

Project Cost

How much a project will cost depends invariably on what one is trying to achieve and how one aims to fulfill these objectives. An often neglected item in a research plan is administrative help. It is important to determine what type of administrative help is needed, particularly if a project is large and involves a large number of people, conference planning, coordinating between different research institutions, and significant paperwork. In addition to administrative staff, one may need graduate and/or undergraduate research assistants. Employing students is an economical measure that saves money while financially supporting students and providing them with training. Therefore, one will need to determine whether funding source provide funding for work-study.

Researching Funding Opportunities

Once a concrete plan for the project is in place, the next step is to research funding opportunities and identify funding agencies that might support the project's mission and vision. More information on how to identify funding sources can be found in the second part of this chapter. However, to get started, one may need to collaborate with other units within one's institution, such as the Office of Sponsored Programs (OSP), Office of Research Administration (ORA), or Office of Corporate and Foundation Relations, or similarly named office. In most academic institutions, this office is available to provide necessary support and a variety of expertise to those wishing to pursue external funding. These services include grant consultation, electronic access to computerized databases containing sources of research funding, and direct links to websites of a number of public and private grant-making institutions. Moreover, these offices should be able to answer questions relating to the budget preparation process as well as negotiate the indirect cost (IDC) rate on behalf of the principal investigator and the institution.

If one does not work at an institution that provides such support, one may find resources from professional grant writing services that will work with an institution to help obtain external funding. These services pair a person or an institution with appropriate funding agencies and assist with grant proposal writing for a fee.[3] Alternatively one may know of colleagues who have gone through the grant proposal writing process, and they may be a good source of information about where to go for assistance. One should also feel free to contact program officers at the funding agency to clarify any questions. When doing so, however, one should be certain to prepare specific questions in advance so that one appears organized and efficient. Finally, one may also consider subscribing to various sources online.. The most concise and comprehensive compilation of funding sources can be found on the Community of Science (COS) database, with more than 22,000 records of funding opportunities worldwide worth $33 billion[4].International education grants open up the possibility of working in collaboration with international institutions, which can expand funding sources.. Many countries have reciprocal agreements that allow non-profit, educational organizations to be eligible for funding opportunities across borders. One's institution may be eligible to apply for grant funding within the country where one will lead the project and within the country or countries where the assessment takes place. Information on this can be found by searching non-profit organizational status online or by checking tax treaties between countries. In general, however, having a local partner institution submit the proposal jointly with yours may increase your chances of receiving funding.

Once one determines which grant(s) one would like to pursue, one should order the application guidelines. It is a good idea to start looking at samples of funded proposals that can be used as a model. If a sample proposal is not available from the funding agency, one should contact the OSP or grants office; they have copies of funded proposals from past years. The OSP should be able to provide tips on the type of grant for which one is applying and the agency to which one intends to submit a proposal. If an institutions does not have an OSP, one might request a successful proposal from another institution or individuals. Most agencies publicize the names of their awardees, and one can usually obtain copies of grant proposals from these agencies although these proposals rarely include budget information. One might also ask colleagues who have been successful in winning grants if they would be willing to share their proposals.

Probably the most important thing one should do before beginning to write a proposal is to contact a program officer at the funding agency to which one will be applying. Program officers are the most underutilized and potentially valuable resource available to one in one's efforts to secure grants and fellowships. They should be consulted frequently through all phases of proposal writing, and it is a good idea to try to visit them personally at least once. Developing a relationship with the program officer may greatly increase an applicant's chances of winning a grant.

Unless one has requested the assistance of a grant writer, one will be spending a good deal of time writing the grant proposal. The research plan is therefore very valuable, since it contains the basic facts and figures that one needs to cover in the proposal. The Social Science Research Council provides excellent information that is useful for proposal writing. It has published, among other articles, the *Art of Writing Proposals*, which can be found on its website at http://www.ssrc.org/. Most granting agencies provide guidelines that must be followed in writing a proposal. But for cases where there are no guidelines, a generic format has been provided at the end of this chapter.

Some granting agencies require that a preliminary proposal be submitted. Whether it is required or not, sending an initial report to the program officer well ahead of the final deadline is a good idea. This report could be very rough or very refined, depending upon the amount of time one has devoted to it and the feedback one has gotten on it to date. If one has worked closely with the program officer all along, a preliminary proposal will look very similar to the final proposal, and the comments one receives about it will enable one to fine-tune it. If one has worked without consultation with the program officer, the comments one receives on the preliminary proposal will indicate whether or not one is going in a direction that appeals to the granting agency.

Grant Proposal Budget

Most research institutions rely on the OSP staff for assistance to develop a budget, a task that can be laborious and complex and one that requires a great deal of information that one may not have at one's fingertips, such as: salaries and fringe benefit rates; student assistant salaries and fee remission figures; travel and per diem allowances; indirect cost rates negotiated with federal agencies, etc. For those at other types of institutions, requesting help from a financial expert such as the organization's Chief Financial Officer or an accountant can at least provide basic advice on budgetary concepts and formats. In the end, regardless of one's level of support in the process, one will need to prepare a budget and provide a complete list of all items that one wishes to have funded by the granting agency. These items may include:

- Indirect costs: these are costs that are incurred by the university due to the project. They include costs such as departmental accounting and clerical support, network support, equipment, building and facilities operation and maintenance, library, or sponsored projects administration. These costs are budgeted and charged as a percentage of some of the direct cost elements.

- If one plans to submit a proposal to an agency that pays indirect costs (normally all federal agencies and a few foundations pay indirect costs), one should discuss how to fund the portion of the money needed to cover up front costs. If one works at a research university, one should discuss with one's department and OSP about the availability of divisional seed funds. One can request seed funds from the indirect cost to be set aside to cover any costs associated with preparing a proposal—including travel costs to consult with the program officer or co-PI, funds for services of a grant writer (if needed), and additional funds to help meet the university cost-sharing requirement. Seed funds are commonly contributed toward this required cost-share amount.

- Most often, researchers forget to calculate overhead and indirect costs into the budget plan, leading to inaccurate budget requests. It is important to understand what one's institution asks for in applicable indirect costs. For instance, some universities negotiate a rate of 25-50% on all research projects to be completed on campus.

- Salaries. What salaries, if any, are to be covered by the grant? Will a salary enable someone to take a sabbatical to work on the assessment project? Willa co-PI also receive compensation? Will there be salaries for staff and/or student assistants?

- Fringe benefits. Faculty who request salary payments from a granting agency must also request fringe benefits for the period of time their salary is covered by the grant. The OSP uses set formulas to determine benefits costs.

- Travel and per diem. Will the project require any personnel to travel? If so, one should request, in addition to airfare, ground transportation to and from the airport; car rental; train, bus, or subway fare, etc. Per diem rates may be set by the project institution or by the funding agency. Most universities have charts that give the per diem rates for most of the major cities worldwide. Also, many U.S. funding agencies will accept the U.S. Department of State travel expense guidelines found at http://www.state.gov/m/a/als/prdm/.

- Supplies and expenses. Consider charging supplies that are directly linked to the research, such as duplicating, telephones, faxes, postage, computer disks or software, audio or videotapes, etc.

- Equipment and services. In addition to supplies, one should consider any technology that will be needed for the project. Will computers or other equipment be needed? What type? What about technical support such as computing services and assistance? Will software be needed for data processing and analysis?

- Space. Will there be a need to rent campus/off-campus space such as conference or seminar rooms? If so, how much do they cost? Will there be a need for a language or computer lab to administer tests to research subjects?

- Consultants. Personnel who act as consultants on projects are normally paid stipends or honoraria rather than salaries; therefore, their tasks and salaries should be listed.

When drawing up a budget, tone should ask the OSP or the granting program officer whether the grant mandates a *cost-share*. Some granting agencies require recipients to contribute a certain portion of the total cost of the project, either from organization funds or from funds donated by other external funding agencies. This may include donating the cost of the time one's department contributes to the project, any project-related phone calls and faxes, and a percentage of uncompensated time that one will contribute toward the project. For instance, the U.S. Department of Education typically requires that grant recipients' institutions contribute 15% to 20% of the total cost of the project. One may be able to offset these costs by using divisional seed funds to meet the required cost-share amount.

Submitting the Proposal

If work with a grant writer, she or he is responsible for ensuring that all grant deadlines are met and all requirements fulfilled. However, if one is writing a proposal on one's own, there is much more to remember than just the final deadline for submitting the proposal to the funding agency. As mentioned earlier, one needs to work with the Office of Sponsored Programs to ensure that all the necessary documents are ready to be submitted.

If the project involves the use of human subjects, one needs to request permission from the Institutional Review Board (IRB) and fill out necessary forms. The IRB's role is to safeguard the rights and welfare of all human subjects who participate in research projects. In compliance with federal law and most institutional policy, the IRB must review and approve research projects involving human subjects or human material. All biomedical, social, and behavioral research projects are also subject to the policies and procedures of the IRB. The overall criteria for IRB approval typically include:

- The risks to subjects are minimized as much as possible.
- The risks to subjects are reasonable in relation to anticipated benefits.
- The informed consent is adequate.
- Where appropriate, the research plan makes provisions for the safety of the subjects during the data collection process.
- Where appropriate, there are adequate provisions to protect the privacy of subjects and maintain confidentiality of data.
- Appropriate safeguards are included within the study to protect the rights and welfare of the vulnerable subjects.

It is important to check the specific IRB requirements of one's institution and also to pay close attention to the funding agencies' guidelines.

If an institution has an OSP, the final proposal and budget should be sent to this office at least one month before the final agency deadline. OSP will review the proposal for any final revisions and tie up any loose ends prior to submission. Once it has been reviewed by OSP, it is important to make copies of the final document and send it to the funding agencies either via United Parcel Service, Federal Express, or any postal agency with mail tracking devices.

Finding Funding Resources

Four main kinds of sources are available to find funding support for outcomes assessment research. Each has its peculiarities in the application process and administration requirements, as well as possible suitability for the project's needs. This section gives a general introduction to the four types of funding, followed by a closer look at the unique aspects of each of them.

1. Commercial Off-the-Shelf Systems

A number of organizations offer subscription services whereby institutions can gain access to a Funding Opportunities Database and an Expertise Profiling System. The primary examples are Community of Science and InfoEd, although a variety of others are on the market. These organizations tend to be led by scientists or former university research administrators who understand the nature of university and non-profit research and the type of service that must be delivered. Most relevant for this discussion are the Funding Opportunity Database and the Expertise Profiling System.

The Funding Opportunities Database lists foundation, corporate, and federal government opportunities in all areas of teaching, research, and service. It includes opportunities for student and faculty fellowships, graduate student training, and travel. The Funding Opportunities Database often has the capability to send weekly emails of funding opportunities entered into the database in the preceding week. A person or institution can create funding alerts by designing and saving a search report. This report targets key words describing the interests and areas of expertise for which funding is sought and requests weekly alerts to all new entries in relevant fields.

The Expertise Profiling System is composed of first-person, searchable profiles entered by faculty or staff at participating universities and organizations. This system can be used best to publicize the experience of faculty members and is useful in searching for peer reviewers, collaborators, and general information concerning funding received by faculty in a particular area of expertise.

2. Open Access Opportunities

Foundations and corporations' websites frequently publicize information on the areas in which they wish to fund grants or gifts. Their websites contain program announcements or general information concerning their interests and the process for submitting applications. Note that processes differ significantly across private funders. Whereas some require only a letter of interest, others have a complex application process. Private funders typically describe in great detail the types of expenses that they will and will not fund.

The U.S. government recently launched its Grants.gov initiative, which is a federal government-wide portal for organizations to interact with the 26 government grant-making agencies through one entry point. Grants.gov is the official site for all agency funding opportunities that will result in grants or cooperative agreements. The funding opportunities are being phased in and, as of June 2006, the site contained 75% of all federal government grant and cooperative agreement funding opportunities. The program announcements will also contain the electronic application packages, which will contain much of the pre-populated information relevant to the announcements. Each federal agency also publicizes its funding interests on the agency website. Individuals searching for contract opportunities should check the Commerce Business Daily for those announcements.

The Interagency Working Group on U.S. Government-Sponsored International Exchanges and Training (IAWG) was created in 1997 "to make recommendations to the President for improving the coordination, efficiency, and effectiveness of United States Government-sponsored international exchanges and training."[5] While not necessarily a direct resource for finding funding for assessment of education abroad, this organization provides an annual list of all funding activities sponsored by the U.S. government related to international exchanges and training at http://www.iawg.gov under Annual Report.

In addition to the Grants.gov initiative, each federal agency also publicizes its funding interests on its agency website. Individuals searching for contract opportunities should check the Commerce Business Daily for those announcements.

As part of growing collaborations with governments and non-governmental organizations, different countries have formed partnerships that build greater awareness among key stakeholders and provide funding to projects. For instance, the European Union has partnered with the United States, Australia, Asia, and Africa to provide funding. These initiatives are open to institutions of higher education, consortia of institutions, non-profit organizations, other organizations, and/or agencies.

One specific example is the European Union-United States Atlantis Program grant that promotes student-centered transatlantic aspects in higher education and training. This fund is conducted cooperatively with the U.S. Department of Education's Fund for the Improvement of Postsecondary Education (FIPSE) and the European Commission's Directorate General Education and Culture (DG EAC)[6]. The Australian Department of Education Science and Training (DEST) has also partnered with several countries to form the Australian Education International (AEI) initiative, which integrates the development of international education relations and provides funding to promote Australian education interests abroad. ResearchResearch.com database contains available Australian and international funding opportunities[7].

Various consulting firms specialize in fund raising and providing sources for funding opportunities, including:

- SRA International Grants Web Resources http://www.srainternational.org/newweb/grantsweb/index.cfm
- Custom Development Solutions, Inc. (CDS) http://www.cdsfunds.com/international_foundations.html
- The Grantsmanship Training Program http://www.tgci.com/intl/index.asp
- Fundsnet Services Online http://www.fundsnetservices.com/searchresult.php?sbcat_id=30
- International Grant Makers http://www.lib.msu.edu/harris23/grants/privint.htm

3. Institutional Resources and Funding

There are often extraordinary untapped institutional resources that may be consulted to assist with the search for funding. The Office of Sponsored Programs most likely has detailed websites with a variety of useful information about funding possibilities. An institution's development office is another excellent source of information concerning the trends and the interests of private funders. Development officers may also be able to consult private donors who are interested in giving gifts or endowments in particular project areas. The federal relations office is often well versed in opportunities available at the federal funding agencies as well as extremely helpful in garnering interest on Capitol Hill for large projects that have national impact. Faculty and staff also frequently have their own track record with and contacts at funding agencies.

Institutional funding may be the primary and largest resource for supporting assessment of education abroad. There are numerous examples of institutions that have decided to prioritize internationalization, and as a result, fund assessment of their activities in relation to certain anticipated outcomes. At institutions such as

Georgetown University, Dickinson College, Rice University, the University of Minnesota–Twin Cities, Worchester Polytechnic University, and Michigan State University, assessment activities for education abroad have functioned as stand-alone efforts supported by the institution and have been components that add to a larger effort to internationalize the campus. Accreditation proceedings are often looked on as a necessary evil for most institutions and program administrators. But for education abroad assessors, such events can serve as the impetus for locating resources to bring attention to an institution's strengths through showcasing assessment results.

Within the broad range of institutional funding, assessment activities are conducted by larger education abroad programs, professional associations, or other non-governmental organizations that rely on internal resources and generate them to conduct assessment. The American Association of Colleges and Universities (AAC&U), a professional association, funded a learning outcomes study of U.S. students abroad, including factors of interest to international educators: tolerance and respect for people of other backgrounds, races, ethnicities, and lifestyles; and expanding cultural global awareness and sensitivity.[8] This study provides an example of how assessment of education abroad can be included in studies that examine a broader question funded by a professional association.

Another example in this category is IES Abroad in Chicago, which includes in its fees a small amount dedicated to assess the outcomes of its programs by examining the behavioral and attitudinal changes that occur in students who participate in their education abroad programs. Another variation is the University System of Georgia, which is conducting assessment of all of its international education initiatives, including those related to education abroad, for all its 34 institutions throughout the state. In this case, it may be argued that system-wide sources should be categorized under "state government" rather than institutional. In any case, state systems may provide an additional avenue through which assessment resources can be accessed.

The list below provides a number of specific strategies that have been used to locate resources within an institution to conduct assessment on education abroad:

- Lobby within an organization: In this time of emphasis on internationalization, advocates for assessment of education abroad are in a position to command resources from within their organization or institution.
- Rely on institutional accreditation or program review proceedings to marshal resources to conduct assessment on education abroad.
- Incorporate assessment components into plans and goals for more comprehensive institutional internationalization.

- Integrate assessment for education abroad into evaluation activities that are not necessarily labeled as such.
- Create a line item for assessment in education abroad wherever one can.
- Explore assistance from internal expertise. Some institutions have a department of assessment and evaluation that are dedicated to helping other components of the organization to develop assessment plans.

The most significant conclusion that can be derived from this list is that those interested in locating internal resources may need to network and collaborate in a manner that has not been explored previously.

4. Government Agency Resources

It is true that the U.S. government does have resources directly available for assessment of education abroad. Nevertheless, the resources are limited, and competition is considerable. The majority of funds can be found within the Department of Education, with some also available through the Department of State and the Department of Defense.

Within the Department of Education, the Office of Postsecondary Education has two programs that provide resources available through competitive grants for conducting assessment of education abroad. First is the Fund for the Improvement of Postsecondary Education (FIPSE) Comprehensive Program, which provides grants "to support innovation reform projects that hold promise as models for the resolution of important issues and problems in postsecondary education."[9] In other words, this grant source is available to support any good idea that solves a problem related to higher education. One such grant was awarded to Bryn Mawr College to assess the impact of FIPSE-funded initiatives, including its consortium programs between U.S. colleges and universities and those in the European Union, Canada, Mexico, and Brazil. This is an attractive source due to the breadth of topics this program is willing to address. Second, the International Education Program, host of the distinguished grants for Title VI National Resource Centers, is able to support grants on assessment of education abroad through its program titled International Research and Studies (IRS).[10]

Georgetown University partnered with the University of Minnesota, Dickinson College, and Rice University in a three-year, consortial research project that identified and measured a wide range of student learning outcomes abroad. This comprehensive assessment drew on students from the four participating institutions who were enrolled in a variety of study abroad program types, and gathered data from three learning domains: foreign-language proficiency, intercultural proficiency, and discipline-specific knowledge and skills. These institutions are finalizing a report that will provide valuable data about the role that various study abroad program models play in learning across these three domains.

The Department of State funds possibly the most comprehensive study abroad assessment project in the United States through its Bureau of Educational and Cultural Affairs. In partnership through a grant to the Institute of International Education (IIE), "*Open Doors* is a comprehensive statistical portrait of international students and scholars in the United States, U.S. students studying abroad, and intensive English language program activity in the U.S. IIE has gathered these statistics for over 55 years, and published the findings as *Open Doors* since 1954. The Bureau of Educational and Cultural Affairs has provided funding for this effort since the 1970s."[11]

Furthermore, there are embedded assessment activities within the Department of Education, grants for Title VI National Resource Centers and Language Resource Centers, and Department of Defense, National Security Education Program (NSEP) grants to U.S. universities for the National Flagship Language Initiative (NFLI).

5. State Funding

Compared to federal resources, there is little funding for assessment of education abroad accessible at the state level. However, it is worth mentioning that funding secured for public colleges, universities, and higher educational systems to conduct direct or imbedded education abroad assessment is often drawn from state resources. Nevertheless, access to such funds is through the institution or system, and not the state, which is why this funding source is listed elsewhere. For the purpose of thoroughness, it is noteworthy to mention that one can find occasional international education programs supported by the state (some with a K-12 focus) that include assessment components.

6. Philanthropic Organizations

A history of generosity from philanthropic organizations is well documented within the field of international education. The Ford Foundation provided the American Council on Education (ACE) with a grant to conduct research on internationalization of U.S. campuses. Through funding from Lilly Endowment, Inc., the Center for Women's Intercultural Leadership at St. Mary's College in Notre Dame, Indiana, conducts regular assessment of its education abroad programs. Other examples of such funding can be seen in grants from the Andrew W. Mellon Foundation, the William and Flora Hewlett Foundation, and many others.

In previous years, foundation and philanthropic resources have been accessed through print-based products such as the *Guide to Funding for International and Foreign Programs.*[12] Nevertheless, hardcopy documents like this have become somewhat obsolete. Databases are now available that include detailed lists of information about foundations, including program officers and their contract information, foundation priorities, and application procedures. Furthermore, it is possible to search for funded activities by key words to see which organizations have funded education abroad assessment projects in the past. An example is the Foundation Directory Online, a web-based, searchable database available through subscription at http://fconline.fdncenter.org.[13] The majority of the resources are competitive grants.

7. Other Sources of Funding

In addition to philanthropic agencies, institutions may receive funding from individuals with the means to finance a project. Some examples include:

- A full-time professional choosing to conduct research within his or her existing position with no additional support;
- A faculty member adding a non-funded item to a research agenda;
- A student examining issues for a master's thesis or doctoral dissertation.

For some, these efforts may lead to developing a later request for support. For others, there may be no interest in external support. It is likely that a number of the references from chapter 5 in this guide were developed through self-funding. While not necessarily the method of choice, self-funding remains one way that individuals choose to engage in the assessment of education abroad.

Conclusion

In short, funding sources are numerous and varied in their mission and essence. It takes time and effort to develop the vision and then seek support to fund the project. There is no magic wand to short-circuit the funding process and produce the money instantly. However, when one has a compelling vision, the time spent looking for funds is well worth it. If the goals are not worth this time investment, it is perhaps better to move on to another project worthy of such effort.

Securing funds for a project is as much a process as a means to an end. During the research phase, one will need to assess constantly where one is and if the goals are attainable. The vision or goals might change during the process; however, how successful one will be in winning the funds can be at least partially attributed to the amount of planning and research that one does. On the other hand, even after careful preparation, one might not secure funds with the first application to a funding agency. Rather than despairing. One can use this as a learning experience to regroup and redefine the project goals. Discussing with the program officer the reason for the proposal's rejection might also lead to important ways that it might be improved for resubmission.

Once funds are secured, it is important to realize that working on a research project will be a process in and of itself, with many stages involving different stakeholders and participants. It is important to begin to think about how to begin incorporating the goals into the project and plan how to maintain the project's various stages. Keys to the success of the project are patience and constant evaluation of one's vision.

Summary of a Proposal Form

1. Title Page: Most agencies require a front page that identifies the project title, project period, and amount of funds being requested.

2. Table of Contents: Many reviewers appreciate a table of contents to provide guidance in going through a proposal.

3. Abstract: Because reviewers often judge a proposal based upon the first few pages they read, a persuasive abstract is critical. Although it will appear first, the abstract is best written after the text is finished.

4. Project Description: This section should consist of the following.

5. Introduction: Discuss the problem to be addressed and its significance. Define the scope and intent of the project.

6. Literature Review: Provide a critical review of relevant literature and discuss gaps to be filled. This review establishes the project director's familiarity with the subject area and illustrates how the proposed approach replicates or differs from previous work.

7. Rationale: Clearly state the problem in terms of current unmet needs. Note the long-term importance of the project to the discipline and other fields.

8. Objectives and Expected Outcomes: Identify specific anticipated outcomes by which the success of your project can be evaluated.

9. Methodology: Clearly describe what will be done and how it will be accomplished.

10. Project Schedule: Identify project milestones and project completion dates.

11. Evaluation: Describe the mechanisms for measuring outcome objectives and other indicators of project success.

12. Bibliography: Cite the reference sources used.
13. Budget: Estimate project costs fairly. Do not overstate or underestimate expenses.
14. Appendices: Attach as an appendix materials that add important data yet would impede smooth reading of the text.
15. Required Forms and Assurances: If required, the sponsor usually provides these.

Endnotes

[1] B. Siegel, president, Kennesaw State University. Global Trends and the Changing Context of Higher Education. International Collaborative Annual Meeting, American Council on Education. Feb. 3, 2006. Washington, DC.

[2] Each year, the federal government gives out hundreds of billions of dollars through about 1,500 grant programs. To help agencies decide which groups will receive funds, how much they will get, and what they can do with the money, the government asks citizens to participate on expert grant review panels.

[3] Finding a good professional writer requires a lot of research and patience. You can find information online or at your library, but the best source would be talking with people who have used these services, as you would have a first-hand evaluation on the services.

[4] http://fundingopps.cos.com/

[5] Accessed Feb. 6, 2006 at http://www.iawg.gov/public_index.html.

[6] http://www.ed.gov/programs/fipseec/index.html

[7] Other funding opportunities can be found at http://www.fundsnetservices.com/internat.htm

[8] D. Humphreys & A. Davenport. What Really Matters in College. (Summer/Fall 2005). *Liberal Education 91*, 36-43.

[9] See http://www.ed.gov/programs/fipsecomp/index.html (accessed Feb. 3, 2006).

[10] See http://www.ed.gov/programs/iegpsirs/index.html (accessed Feb. 3, 2006).

[11] Accessed Feb. 6, 2006 at http://www.iiebooks.org/50yearofopdo.html.

[12] *Guide to Funding for International and Foreign Programs.* (2002). Sixth Edition, ed. J.L. Santiago. New York: The Foundation Center.

[13] Accessed Feb. 3, 2006.

Chapter 10

How and Why to Use Results of Outcomes Assessment

Darla K. Deardorff

Outcomes assessment becomes valuable only when international education professionals and others use and effectively communicate the results of the assessment. This chapter explores how and why to use outcomes results.

First, it is important to understand to what end assessment is desired. Why are the data being collected? Who needs to know the results of the outcomes assessment? If one doesn't know how the information will be used and communicated, then it most likely should not be collected. And if we collect information and do nothing with it beyond putting it in a file or on a shelf, there is no need for us to collect such information. It is important to be very clear on why assessment methods and tools are being implemented, and how the collected data will specifically be used and disseminated. This all becomes part of an ongoing assessment plan in which there is clear articulation of the specific goals and outcomes; of how data are collected, analyzed and reported; how results are disseminated, both internally and externally; and how the data will be used to increase student learning, improve the program, and help the institution meet its goals. When an assessment plan has been fully implemented and becomes interwoven into the program, the assessment data become integral to continued program improvement and increased student learning.

Using Results

The primary reason for engaging in student learning outcomes assessment is to increase student learning and development. In this case, how can the education abroad experience be improved to increase the student learning that occurs? Outcomes assessment helps identify gaps between articulated objectives and what students actually learn during their experience abroad. To that end, the data can be analyzed both at the student level (in providing feedback) as well as at the programmatic level.

Providing feedback to students, both during and after their education abroad experience is critical to increasing student learning. In fact, such individual feedback to students has been shown to engender greater student enthusiasm and support for assessment programs (Lopez, 2004). In providing feedback, it is important to consider the following questions:

- Are students clear on the intended outcomes being assessed and the purpose of the assessment?
- Are students clear on the assessment process of *how* their outcomes are being measured?
- Are students clear on how the achievement of these intended outcomes will benefit them in the future?
- Are students clear on who is assessing them?
- When possible, are such assessments connected to professional standards of the profession students have chosen?
- Have the students' learning needs been considered in the assessment process and in providing feedback?
- Is the feedback provided to students both during and after their education abroad experience (based on formative and summative assessment)?
- How can the feedback to students promote their learning instead of merely give an indication of the monitoring of their learning?
- How can the feedback help students redirect their learning to achieve the intended goals and objectives, if those were not achieved?
- Is feedback mutual, allowing students opportunities for sharing information and reflecting on the experience?

Rubrics become an important tool in documenting student learning and in giving precise feedback to students. Rubrics provide specificity in learning/performance targets, including levels or degrees of success. They become excellent tools in promoting learning and in helping students, parents, and administrators understand the degree to which students are performing/learning. One example of a rubric is the University of Nebraska–Kearney's rubric for assessing international studies portfolios.[1]

Feedback would ideally be provided through dialog with the student throughout the program and not solely at the end of a program. As with general counseling principles, it is helpful to focus on behaviors instead of the person, and on specifics instead of generalities. It is also useful to guide the students through questions that help them reflect on the learning process and on themselves as learners. The overall goal in providing feedback is to help students gain insights that will help them become better learners and understand where they currently are relative to where they want to be. It is important to recognize that specific training or modeling may need to be provided for those who will be giving feedback to students.

What do students learn during their education abroad experience? This becomes a fundamental question for parents, who are another key group with whom to share outcomes assessment results. Communicating results to parents includes helping them understand not only the skills and knowledge that their children gained while abroad, but the impact of such skills and knowledge on their children's future. The rubrics used for student feedback can often be helpful in providing feedback to parents. In addition to understanding more clearly their own child's learning achievements while abroad, outcomes assessment can also give parents a snapshot of the learning that occurs at the program level. In communicating effectively with parents, here are some questions to consider:

- Are parents clear on the intended outcomes being assessed and on the outcomes actually achieved? In other words, what did their children learn while abroad?
- Are parents clear on how achievement of these intended outcomes will benefit their children in the future?
- What evidence can be given to demonstrate how students' language skills and cross-cultural skills improved as a result of the education abroad experience?
- What evidence can be given to demonstrate students' further acquisition of life skills?
- What are the trends in student learning across the program?
- How is the program being modified in the future to increase student learning?

Outcomes assessment data greatly aid in improving an education abroad program or course, which provides another key reason for collecting outcomes data. Viewing the data in aggregate can help identify areas of needed improvement to further enhance student learning, to provide resources/personnel that would augment student learning, and to aid faculty and administrators in their responsibilities. In addressing how to use data at the program and institutional levels, it is wise to focus on the most important goals of the program, instead of trying to address a broad range of goals. Programmatic changes are of course based on the feasibility of implementation. Nonetheless, the data provide documentation, beyond anecdotes, of needed changes, thus providing a more compelling argument.

In utilizing the results for programmatic change, here are questions to consider:

- What program changes (procedural, personnel, experiential/curricular, services, etc.) are needed based on the data?
- How can the data be used to revise the current goals and objectives of the program?
- Where are students doing well, and what areas need strengthening to improve their learning in those areas?
- How will the assessment plan/process itself be evaluated and what needs to be improved about the outcomes assessment process itself?
- What support is in place to train faculty and staff responsible for assessment activities? How can this be improved?

In some cases, researchers create a task force of representatives of the key stakeholders and cross-disciplinary team members to analyze and process the outcomes data. The task force carefully reviews the assessment results, using questions similar to those above, and then writes an improvement plan that includes final recommendations. The improvement plan prioritizes deficiencies and ways to address those deficiencies, including an accurate estimate of needed resources, possible constraints, and action steps needed to implement the recommended changes. If no changes need to be made, the assessment effort was essentially wasted. On the other hand, too many changes should not be made at once; prioritize and address the areas deemed of highest priority to improving student learning.

Institutionally, it is important to determine how outcomes assessment collected through education abroad experiences fit with overall institutional goals and values. Two key areas to address institutionally are whether assessment results are being used to inform decision-making at all levels; and the degree to which needed resources are linked to long-term planning and budgeting processes [2] The task force can create short, clear summaries with the most relevant findings to that particular institutional audience prominently presented. Follow-up feedback should be actively solicited. In sharing results' summaries with key stakeholder groups within the institution itself, what additional insights/feedback can be obtained about necessary changes? Such feedback is often helpful to incorporate into the assessment process.

As noted above, a primary way in which you may effectively use outcomes assessment results institutionally is to advocate for and demonstrate the need for further resources. Once you can demonstrate with carefully collected data that programs bring about results expressed as goals in the institutional mission statements, such data can be used to advocate for resources. For instance, many university mission statements include such items as, "The University's mission is to serve the community, the nation, and the world by educating and preparing students to discharge the offices of life with usefulness and reputation."3 If you can tie your results to helping students "serve the world," you can make a stronger argument for a share of institutional resources. Institutionally, such results can be used for strategic planning, fund raising (i.e., study abroad scholarships, external funding for specific programs, etc.), recruitment of potential students to the institution, and retention of current students. Benchmarking performance with peer institutions is yet another way in which assessment results can be used institutionally.

Results can also be used to encourage faculty to participate in education abroad efforts. Proving to doubting faculty in the *lingua franca* of faculty (e.g., research results) that in fact students do learn during international education programs, and do not just become extended-stay tourists, allows for powerful arguments to be made that encourage faculty support for such programming. Faculty may see the advantages in curricular integration of education abroad experiences. Deans and department heads may become more willing to recognize and release faculty for directing such programs. Faculty may recommend more wholeheartedly to their students that they study abroad, and on programs that you run. They may also support the use of resources to create new programs and link such programs to their departmental reputation and standing.

In communicating with faculty, you might possibly need to use statistical terms in reporting data from quantitative methods/instruments. As one assessment expert stated, "Avoiding the use of statistical procedures when they are needed is amateurish but also suggests incompetence. Statistical procedures lend credibility and professionalism to your final report... In some instances, the use of statistical procedures may help defuse hostility by removing an element of subjectivity"[4] (Royse & Thyer, 1996. p. 262). If you feel uncomfortable engaging in statistical procedures or terminology, be sure to enlist the support of assessment experts on your campus or externally to assist you.

Another key way in which results are used institutionally is in the accreditation process. While regional monitoring bodies have traditionally focused on inputs and outputs of institutional programs and services, the trend is for regional accrediting agencies to now emphasize specific outcome measures—both institutional outcomes and student learning outcomes (Santiago, 2004). To that end, numerous institutions have actually built education abroad outcomes assessment into the accreditation process. For example, Wake Forest University included the development and implementation of a comprehensive intercultural competence program for study abroad students into its Quality Enhancement Plan, with intentional assessment built into the entire program. Other institutions have similarly incorporated education abroad outcomes into the accreditation process.

Outcomes data can be used beyond the individual, programmatic, and institutional levels to help persuade those in government—at the state, federal and international level—as to the value of education abroad experiences. Communicating outcomes assessment data to the appropriate government officials can play a role in informing the national discussion on international education and in determining funding for federal programs, grants, and initiatives as well as student funding and scholarship levels. The following section on disseminating results provides more detail on advocacy.

Throughout the data analysis and interpretation process, it is important to stay connected to and be guided by the overall assessment plan, tying the results back to the assessment cycle; that is, identifying outcomes, gathering evidence, interpreting the evidence, and implementing change that includes identifying new outcomes. Below is an example of how the outcomes data portion can be operationalized. It is crucial to make a strong commitment to outcomes assessment that ensures the ongoing assessment process instead of sporadic data collection that does not fit into a cohesive, intentional, and coordinated assessment plan.

Interpret How Results Will Be Used (i.e., Teaching/Learning, Academic Legitimacy/Program Improvement, Decision-making/Political Advocacy)

For example:

- Design more effect student pre-departure orientation.
- Describe expected outcomes more effectively.
- Convince legislators to increase funding for education abroad.

Determine How and With Whom You Will Share Interpretations and/or Results

For example:

- Students: through portfolio review day.
- Senior-level administrators: through periodic reports.
- Government officials: through professional organizations and constituent letters

(Adapted from Maki, 2004)

Disseminating Results

The results of outcomes assessment can be disseminated in numerous ways. In communicating results of the outcomes assessment, it is important to understand the different audiences, purposes, and the anticipated goal(s) of sharing the data, some of which was discussed previously in this chapter. Anticipation of audience questions/needs will greatly improve the reporting process. Clear, concise, and contextualized communication of results is key, regardless of the audience. Potential audiences include key stakeholder groups, colleagues, government officials, funders, the general public, and so on.

Key stakeholder groups could be given a summary of the results of any outcomes assessment implemented through the education abroad programs. We hope that students, as a key stakeholder group, would already receive individual feedback so they can improve their own learning. Parents can receive information during talks at Parents Weekends, from parent relations offices, and via other regular communication that organizations may have with parents. Because of the Federal Educational Right to Privacy Act (FERPA), students' results should be communicated in aggregate data, not in relation to a particular student unless the students have given appropriate permission. Other stakeholder groups include program directors, academic advisors, faculty, alumni, advisory groups, and possible funders/funding agencies. Internal reports would be distributed to senior-level administrators. Admissions offices and public relations offices at institutions welcome such results in their recruitment and marketing efforts. Articles in alumni magazines and other institutional publications can help disseminate the results to other possible stakeholders.

Websites can often be quite instrumental in the distribution of outcomes assessment results. Summaries, reports, rubrics, documentation models, data, etc. can all be placed on the website, so assessment plans, practices, and procedures can be shared with other institutions and programs as well as with the general public. As an example, the 21st Century Learning Outcomes Project, supported by The Pew Charitable Trusts, involved 16 participating institutions, many of which continue to maintain public websites on their assessment work.[5] Such assessment materials can be studied and adapted to meet specific programs and local needs. Website information on outcomes assessment in education abroad programs can also help students or prospective students see the value of assessment. This sets expectations of the importance of engaging in outcomes assessment, thus generating more student support for such endeavors.

Beyond institutional dissemination, it is important to make the time to submit articles to such journals as the *Journal of Studies in International Education* and *Frontiers*, as well as to periodicals such as *International Educator* and *IIENetworker*. Publication in such professional periodicals helps move the field forward and strengthens the efforts of other professionals engaged in outcomes assessment of education abroad. Communicated through professional publications or directly to professional associations, these outcomes assessment results can be used to hone existing professional development opportunities for education abroad administrators and to develop new opportunities that would increase their effectiveness in the field.

Professional conferences are yet another excellent way to disseminate the results to others in the field to increase their own learning in this area. A number of different conferences are worth considering, including conferences organized by NAFSA, The Forum, Council on International Education Exchange, Association of International Education Administrators, and so on. Through the dissemination of outcomes assessment results in professional publications and presentations, the research agenda for the future becomes redefined. Furthermore, such efforts help shape standards of best practice in the education abroad field and beyond.

In addition to communicating outcomes assessment results internally and professionally, it is important that such data be communicated clearly and concisely to those in local, state, and federal government. Institutions can issue public statements in support of education abroad, citing the data as evidence of successful student learning. Institution administrators can meet with local and state officials to discuss the importance and relevancy of education abroad and again, cite the outcomes data to encourage the officials to develop, promote, and support local and state initiatives that promote cultural exchanges as well as education abroad as a way to enhance the region's economic competitiveness. More than half of states currently have international education policies; outcomes assessment data can be used to help spur other states to create such policies and/or revise their current policies. Further details on advocacy efforts for education abroad can be found on The Forum's website (www.forumea.org) or at NAFSA website (www.nafsa.org/act).

Institutional government relations staff generally maintains lists of appropriate contacts to disseminate research study results. They can also be useful in helping to write text that communicates the message in formats acceptable to the intended audiences, whether these are specific government committee members, newspapers, or the general public. If your organization does not have government relations staff, you can still utilize experts by contacting professional organizations' government relations staff. Organizations such as the Alliance for International Education[6] and NAFSA's Public Policy group[7] can provide both advice and potential vehicles for disseminating results.

In addition to communicating results to appropriate government officials, such results can also be taken to the general public. Alerting local newspapers, as well as larger newspapers, to outcomes assessment results can be useful in promoting general public awareness of the importance and value of education abroad. Special interest stories can certainly be enhanced by outcomes data. For example, such stories and letters to the editor can help generate public support and goodwill for education abroad funding.

As the discussion above illustrates, there are numerous ways to disseminate outcomes data on education abroad. The key in disseminating the data is understanding the needs and interests of each audience and then communicating the data in language that can be clearly understood.

Conclusion

Outcomes assessment is crucial to the field of education abroad and to the broader field of international education. However, it is only effective if the results of such assessment are used and disseminated, both internally and externally. The results of outcomes assessment have the potential to not only transform education abroad but to change higher education itself. First, though, it is incumbent upon education abroad administrators to utilize and share the results of outcomes assessment.

Endnotes

[1] http://webcms.unk.edu/academicaffairs/assessment. For additional information on developing rubrics, consult such resources as *Introduction to Rubrics: An Assessment Tool to Save Grading Time, Convey Effective Feedback and Promote Student Learning* edited by D. D. Stevens and A. J. Levi, 2004 or *Learner-centered Assessment on College Campuses: Shifting the Focus from Teaching to Learning* by M.E. Huba and J.E. Freed, 2000.

[2] P. Hernon (2004). Preparing for the future: A view of institutional effectiveness. In *Outcomes assessment in higher education: Views and perspectives*, P. Hernon and R.E. Dugan, eds. Westport, CT: Libraries Unlimited.

[3] http://www.brown.edu/web/about/facts/ (November 28, 2006) University Mission Statement.

[4] Royse, D. and Thyer, B.A. (1996). *Program evaluation*. Chicago; Nelson-Hall Publishers.

[5] (Miles & Wilson, 2004, p. 88)

[6] http://www.intedalliance.org/browse.asp?catID=1774 (November 28, 2006) home page

[7] http://www.nafsa.org/public_policy.sec (November 28, 2006) public policy page

References

Hernon, P. (2004). Preparing for the future: A view of institutional effectiveness. In *Outcomes assessment in higher education: Views and perspectives*, P. Hernon and R.E. Dugan, eds. Westport, CT: Libraries Unlimited.

Lopez, C.L. (2004) A decade of assessing student learning: What we have learned, and what is next. In *Outcomes assessment in higher education: Views and perspectives*, P. Hernon and R.E. Dugan, eds. Westport, CT: Libraries Unlimited.

Maki, P.L. (2004) Developing an assessment plan to learn about student learning. In *Outcomes assessment in higher education: Views and perspectives*, P. Hernon and R.E. Dugan, eds. Westport, CT: Libraries Unlimited.

Miles, C.L. and Wilson, C. (2004). Learning outcomes for the twenty-first century: Cultivating student success for college and the knowledge economy. In *Developing and implementing assessment of student learning outcomes, no 126, summer 2004.*

Royse, D. and Thyer, B.A. (1996). *Program evaluation.* Chicago; Nelson-Hall Publishers.

Santiago, G. (2004) Toward excellence in outcomes assessment: The Middle States approach. In *Hallmarks of effective outcomes assessment*, T.W. Banta, ed. San Francisco: Jossey-Bass.

Contributors

Mell Bolen is President of Brethren Colleges Abroad. Formerly Director of International Programs at Brown University, she has worked in international education for over 18 years in a variety of roles. Her special interests lie in financial management, program development and developing international education research studies. Mell has served on the Forum's Advisory Council and currently chairs the Committee on Research and Outcomes Assessment. She holds an M.A. in Intercultural Relations from Lesley College, and is currently completing her dissertation with a Fellowship from the Department of American Civilization at Brown University, on "American Women in Study Abroad, 1860–1914."

David Comp currently works as an Adviser in The College and serves as the Fulbright Program Adviser at The University of Chicago. He was a founding Co-Chair of the SECUSSA Research Committee, the SECUSSA representative to the NAFSA Task Force on Research, served on the NAFSA Teaching, Learning and Scholarship Task Force and currently serves on the Committee on Outcomes Assessment of the Forum on Education Abroad and as the Research and Scholarship Network Manager within NAFSA's Teaching, Learning and Scholarship knowledge community. He has also consulted on several international education projects for a variety of institutions and organizations of higher education. He received his B.A. in Spanish and Latin American Studies from the University of Wisconsin-Eau Claire, his M.S. in Family Science from the University of Nebraska-Lincoln and is currently a Doctoral student in Comparative and International Education at Loyola University Chicago.

Barbara Craig, Ph.D., is Director of Assessment & Diversity at the Center for New Designs in Learning & Scholarship (CNDLS) at Georgetown University, where she provides leadership on curriculum assessment strategies and services at the course and program levels. Barbara has over 15 years experience as an international educator, having taught linguistics, English as a foreign language, and intercultural communication, including five years as a full-time university faculty member in Taiwan before returning to Georgetown. In her current position, she also plans and facilitates the annual week-long Faculty Seminar on Inclusive Teaching & Learning, and works with departments and other academic units to support and extend Georgetown's work in diversity awareness on campus.

Darla K. Deardorff is Executive Director of the Association of International Education Administrators, a national professional organization headquartered at Duke University, where she also teaches cross-cultural courses. She has held several national leadership positions within NAFSA: Association of International Educators and The Forum and has presented at national and international conferences over the past decade. She has worked in the international education field for over fifteen years and previously held positions at North Carolina State University and the University of North Carolina at Chapel Hill. Dr. Deardorff has authored numerous publications on international education assessment and intercultural competence and serves as a consultant in these areas to universities and non-profit organizations.

Duane L. Deardorff is a physics professor at the University of North Carolina at Chapel Hill where he specializes in assessing students' understanding of physics. He has presented numerous talks on assessment and is a recognized expert in measurement uncertainty. His doctoral research on measurement was conducted through a National Science Foundation grant to Japan and Korea. Dr. Deardorff has held a national leadership position in the American Association of Physics Teachers and has worked to internationalize physics education.

Veronique Dozier is a Computational Linguist at the Department of Defense where her work focuses on applications of machine learning and statistical modeling to natural-language processing. She previously was an Advisor for Short-Term Study Abroad Programs and Assistant Project Director for Department of Education Title VI Grant in Georgetown University's Office of International Programs Veronique also held positions as a Program Manager for the African Studies Program in the School of Foreign Service at Georgetown University; Researcher for the Environmental Policy Center Europe (Belgium); and as a Stagiere for the European Union (Belgium).

Lilli Engle is Co-Founder and on-site Director of the American University Center of Provence in Aix-en-Provence. She has taught at UCLA, Illinois Wesleyan University and the *Université de Provence*. She has published numerous articles on study abroad programs and recently founded a study abroad program in Marseilles devoted to the understanding of Islam.

Joy Evans, M.S.W., is Assistant Director of Scholarship and Research for the Center for Women's InterCultural Leadership at Saint Mary's College, Notre Dame, Indiana. She was trained at the University of Michigan in a variety of research methods, including program evaluation, qualitative research, feminist methods, and collaborative/action research. Her areas of interests are reflexive research processes, education for social justice, the development of intercultural competence, and women's agency. She has worked for non-profit organizations, foundations and within higher education to evaluate program quality and impacts, to consult on programmatic strategic planning and to assess student and organizational outcomes of curricular and co-curricular programs.

Sophie Gladding is a program director at the Learning Abroad Center at the University of Minnesota, Twin Cities. She has been involved in the university's internationalization efforts through study abroad curriculum integration and has been responsible for working with faculty in the science disciplines. She is also a Ph.D. student in the Educational Policy and Administration department specializing in evaluation and assessment.

Kevin Gormley is the Program Officer with the National Security Education Program (NSEP), and holds a Ph.D. in International Development Education (University of Minnesota). His international experience includes many years of experience in community development activities and related research in Latin America, Southeast Asia, and in various regions of the US. His responsibilities with NSEP include directing the English Language for Heritage Speakers (ELHS) program, overseeing all strategic communication initiatives, and serving as a member of the principle leadership team for policies and plans. His research and academic interests include leadership and low-income community development, improving research and assessment of international education programs, and second language acquisition.

Lance M. Kenney is the Director of International Studies at Villanova University. He entered the field as an Assistant (Resident) Director for a program provider, living in Cheltenham, England for five years. While in the UK, he completed a Master's degree in International Relations at the University of Bristol, specializing in international political theory. Lance has been SECUSSA representative for Region VIII, and serves on a number of boards including those for the Pennsylvania Council on International Education and the Academic Council for the Institute for the International Education of Students.

Kim Kreutzer is the Associate Director for Study Abroad at the University of Colorado at Boulder. She is currently serving on the Forum Council and has also been very involved with NAFSA: Association of International Educators for the last 18 years. Kim holds a B.A. in Anthropology and Asian Studies and an M.A. in Anthropology. She worked as a research archeologist for 5 years before becoming an international educator.

Patricia C. Martin is the Associate Director of Study Abroad, Office of International Programs, University of Pennsylvania. She is a former national chair of NAFSA's section on study abroad, co-editor of NAFSA's Guide to Education Abroad (2005), Dean (and presenter) of NAFSA's Education Abroad national workshop on Health and Safety, Chair of the Interassociational Advisory Committee on Health and Safety, and a contributing editor to the Academy for Educational Development's *Handbook for Hosting: The AED Guide for Welcoming US Students to Your Campus* (2006). She was twice elected to the Forum on International Education's Advisory Council and serves on the Outcomes Assessment Committee.

Elaine Meyer-Lee is Director of the Center for Women's Intercultural Leadership at Saint Mary's College, and an Assistant Professor. Her doctorate in human development and psychology is from Harvard University, where she began studying college student development around issues of difference and the effects of intercultural education. She conducted major research projects at Boston College, Harvard/Facing History Project, Yale, Cambridge College, and now at Saint Mary's. She has given numerous invited talks and juried presentations, serves on the Outcomes Assessment committee of the Forum on Education Abroad, and wrote a chapter for *Internationalizing Undergraduate Education* (2005, University of Minnesota).

Ann Neville Miller (Ph.D., University of Georgia) is a Senior Lecturer in the Communication and Post-Graduate Departments of Daystar University in Nairobi, Kenya, where she served for six years as facilitator for orientation and debriefing of US and Kenyan students in a reciprocal exchange program. Dr. Miller has published peer-reviewed articles and book chapters on various intercultural communication topics. She obtained her own masters degree as an American student studying abroad in Africa.

William Nolting, a leading authority on work abroad and international careers, is the Study, Work, & Travel Abroad and Peace Corps Manager of the University of Michigan's International Center and International Educational Editor for *Transitions Abroad.*

Anthony Ogden studied at the School for International Training (SIT) where he earned his master's degree in International and Intercultural Management (MIIM). Anthony served as the Director for the Tokyo Center of the Institute for the International Education of Students (IES) where he also taught courses in ethnography and intercultural communication. He is an intercultural training consultant for Cartus and is also the current associate director for the Education Abroad (EA) office at The Pennsylvania State University. Anthony is currently working toward a doctorate in Educational Theory and Policy.

R. Michael Paige is Professor of International and Intercultural Education and Chair of the Educational Policy and Administration department at the University of Minnesota. He is the co-founder of the University's Comparative and International Development Education program, senior co-author of the *Maximizing Study Abroad Guides,* and co-principal investigator and consultant on three US Department of Education Title VI study abroad research projects: SAGE (Study Abroad for Global Engagement) and Maximizing Study Abroad at the University of Minnesota, and the Georgetown University language and culture learning outcomes project. Michael has written extensively on intercultural training and is the author of the chapter, "Instrumentation in Intercultural Training," that appeared in the 3rd edition of the *Handbook of Intercultural Training* (Landis, Bennett, Bennett, Eds., 2004, SAGE).

Chip Peterson is Assistant Director of the Learning Abroad Center, University of Minnesota, where he has served in various capacities in the field of education abroad since 1979. He is the founding director of the Higher Education Consortium for Urban Affairs' (HECUA) first Latin American program, and for four years served as the President of HECUA's Board of Directors. He chairs the Forum task force that has been working for the last two years to draft an education abroad glossary, an abridged form of which appears as Chapter 8.

Gary Rhodes is Director of the Center for Global Education at Loyola Marymount University. The Center serves as a national resource for the college and university study abroad field, while providing resources that are also available for students and parents. He received his Ph.D., M.A. and MS.Ed. from University of Southern California, and his B.A. from the University of California at Santa Barbara. He has taught courses on International Education at the graduate level USC and UCLA.

Donald L. Rubin is jointly appointed as Professor in the Departments of Speech Communication and Language and Literacy Education at the University of Georgia. He also serves on the Linguistics faculty and in the Center for Health and Risk Communication at Georgia. Rubin's articles have appeared in such journals as *International Journal of Intercultural Research, Research in Higher Education*, and *Journal of Language and Social Psychology*. In addition to on-going work assessing learning outcomes accruing from studying abroad, Rubin's current projects include a study of effects of rater biases on international students' oral proficiency test scores.

Mary E. Schmiedel, CPCM, has worked in Georgetown University's Office of Sponsored Programs (OSP) since 1991 and has been the Director since 1998. She has a B.A. in Political Science, completed a two year Certificate in Contracting and Procurement, and currently is a third year (evening) law student at Georgetown University Law Center.

Elizabeth Stallman has worked in international educational exchange since 1994, first as a JET Program participant in Shizuoka, Japan, and most recently as Assistant Director of International Services at Teachers College, Columbia University. Currently she is a Ph.D. student in Comparative and International Development Education at the University of Minnesota. At the UMN she has worked on two research projects which focus on education abroad: the Curriculum Integration initiative conducted by the Learning Abroad Center, and Beyond Immediate Impact: Study Abroad for Global Engagement conducted by R. Michael Paige and Gerald W. Fry (co-PIs). Her dissertation research will investigate ethnic identity and intercultural sensitivity.

Michael Steinberg is Executive V.P. for Academic Programs at IES and has oversight over IES's programs. He is a member of the Forum Council and Chair of the Forum Standards Committee. He is a frequent panelist at the NAFSA national conference and has given presentations related to study abroad at the Stetson Law Conference, the National Society for Experiential Education, CIEE, and the Modern Language Association. He earned his Ph.D. in history from the Johns Hopkins University.

Skye Stephenson is the author of *Understanding Spanish-speaking South Americans: Bridging Hemispheres* (Intercultural Press, 2003) and primary author of the "Overseas Program Direction" section of NAFSA's Guide to Education Abroad (3rd edition). She has conducted research and written about globally responsible study abroad, cross-cultural adjustment issues, study abroad impact on host communities and the role of international education in the global context. Skye was program director in Santiago, Chile for a decade and worked both at CIEE and SIT as Regional Director for Latin America and Caribbean programs.

Maia Stierankova is Technology Coordinator and Overseas Studies Advisor for Central Europe, Russia, Turkey, the Middle East, Northern Africa and IC-Status in the International Programs Office at Georgetown University. She holds an M.A. in History and Linguistics from Comenius University in Slovakia and an M.A. in Counseling with an emphasis on Student Development in Higher Education from Trinity University in Washington, DC. She is currently pursuing her third M.S. in Computational Linguistics at Georgetown University. She was the project coordinator of the Georgetown Consortium research project.

Lee Sternberger serves as Assistant Vice President of Academic Affairs and Executive Director of the Office of International Programs at James Madison University. She holds degrees in economics, psychology, and architectural history. Her research and teaching interests include the assessment of international learning, consortium management, and leadership in higher education.

Richard C. Sutton is Director of International Programs and Senior Advisor for Academic Affairs for the University System of Georgia Board of Regents. He held prior academic affairs positions with the Iowa Board of Regents and the University of Wisconsin System Administration. He also served as Director of International Education at the University of Wisconsin-La Crosse from 1984-1995. A Russian historian by training, he earned his Ph.D. from Indiana University and his A.B. from Duke University.

Michael J. Vande Berg is Vice President for Academic Affairs and Chief Academic Officer at CIEE. He has worked as an international educator for more than twenty years, holding teaching and administrative positions in Spain, France and the US. In addition to numerous articles focusing on international education and on literary movements and figures, he has published English-language translations of Spanish literature. He earned his Ph.D. in Comparative Literature from the University of Illinois, Urbana-Champaign, and is a founding member of the Forum on Education Abroad.

Brian J. Whalen is Associate Dean of the College, Executive Director of Global Education, and Associate Professor of International Studies at Dickinson College. He serves as the President and CEO of the Forum on Education Abroad, and he is the founding editor of *Frontiers: The Interdisciplinary Journal of Study Abroad*. He has worked in all areas of international education, including serving as a resident director in Italy for five years. Whalen holds a B.A., M.A., and Ph.D. in psychology.